MORE PRAISE FOR
CHAOS KINGS

"An extraordinary exploration of cutting-edge efforts to understand the manifold and interconnected risks slamming civilization at an alarming rate. It's a critical read for anyone with an interest in what's coming next and how to prepare for it."

—**Bradley Hope, *New York Times* bestselling co-author of *Billion Dollar Whale* and co-founder of Project Brazen**

"*Wall Street Journal* stalwart Patterson continues his explorations of high finance with a clutch of contrarian risk takers. . . . Deft, accessible analysis and guidance."

—***Kirkus Reviews* (starred review)**

"Combining risk theory, finance, and portraits of some of the most interesting billionaires of doom, Patterson takes us on a disturbing tour of what could come tumbling down. . . . You'll be left wondering whether these Chaos Kings are brilliant, opportunistic, visionary, or even loathsome."

—**Juliette Kayyem, former assistant secretary of the Department of Homeland Security and author of *The Devil Never Sleeps: Learning to Live in an Age of Disasters***

"An illuminating investigation. . . The author has a knack for translating complicated financial maneuvers into easily comprehensible terms. . . . Detailed yet accessible, this will appeal to fans of Michael Lewis's *The Big Short*."

—***Publishers Weekly***

"Fast paced like a thriller but, also, thought-provoking in its willingness to show us the range of possible catastrophes, *Chaos Kings* tracks the adventures of contrarian investors who, rather than hide from chaos and confusion, seek it out."

—Aaron Brown, former chief risk manager at AQR Capital Management, and author of *The Poker Face of Wall Street* and *Red-Blooded Risk*

"The world is an increasingly unstable place, threatening to go off the rails at any time. This chaos is devastating to many, but a boon to a few who are cashing in on it. Read this engaging book to learn about who they are and how they do it."

—Mark Zandi, chief economist of Moody's Analytics and author of *Financial Shock* and *Paying the Price*

"A richly reported work that features a fascinating ensemble of quirky characters. Important reading for anyone interested in risk-taking now—and in the future."

—Anita Raghavan, author of *The Billionaire's Apprentice*

"A captivating, important, and unsettling book. *Chaos Kings* takes a timely look at how to survive and prosper in an increasingly uncertain and unstable world of global warming, pandemics, and geopolitical danger."

—William Green, author of *Richer, Wiser, Happier: How the World's Greatest Investors Win in Markets and Life*

"A provocative look at those placing big bets . . . [The book] holds perceptive insights for anyone who lives—or invests—in our modern, uncertain world."

—Russell Gold, author of *Superpower* and *The Boom*

CHAOS KINGS

How Wall Street Traders Make Billions
in the New Age of Crisis

SCOTT PATTERSON

SCRIBNER

NEW YORK   LONDON   TORONTO   SYDNEY   NEW DELHI

Scribner
An Imprint of Simon & Schuster, LLC
1230 Avenue of the Americas
New York, NY 10020

Copyright © 2023 by Scott Patterson

First Scribner trade paperback edition July 2024

SCRIBNER and design are trademarks of Simon & Schuster, LLC

Simon & Schuster: Celebrating 100 Years of Publishing in 2024

For information about special discounts for bulk purchases,
please contact Simon & Schuster Special Sales at 1-866-506-1949 or
business@simonandschuster.com.

The Simon & Schuster Speakers Bureau can bring authors to your live event.
For more information or to book an event, contact the Simon & Schuster
Speakers Bureau at 1-866-248-3049 or visit our website at
www.simonspeakers.com.

Interior design by Erika R. Genova

Manufactured in the United States of America

10 9 8 7 6 5 4 3 2

Library of Congress Cataloging-in-Publication Data has been applied for.

ISBN 978-1-9821-7993-9
ISBN 978-1-9821-7994-6 (pbk)
ISBN 978-1-9821-7995-3 (ebook)

For Dad and Leo

CONTENTS

CHAOS KINGS

PROLOGUE

HELL IS COMING

I n the depths of a New York winter, Bill Ackman dreamt of disease. It was January 2020. A virus was spreading in China, replicating and infecting people at an astonishing pace. It was spreading *exponentially*—one sick person becomes two becomes four becomes sixteen becomes 256 becomes tens of thousands. The fatality rate was high. Two or three out of every one hundred people who got the disease died. He awoke from his nightmare in a cold sweat.

The billionaire hedge fund manager started obsessively following news about the disease. He became particularly concerned when he learned that five million people had fled Wuhan, where the virus originated, before the city went into lockdown. *It's not contained.* Many infected with the disease didn't know they had it. These asymptomatic carriers were spreading it to nearly everyone they encountered. *This could spread everywhere.* Most people didn't understand. They didn't grasp the frightening math of the exponential. The laws of probability were clear. It would move fast. Half the world could become infected. The steps taken by most governments weren't nearly enough to contain it. Ackman saw a black hole of doom menacing the future: a global depression, millions dead around the world, including the death of as many as one million Americans.

It was simple math.

On January 30, the World Health Organization declared that the outbreak of the deadly novel coronavirus constituted a global health emergency. Despite the mounting alarm, WHO urged countries to avoid travel restrictions. "This is the time for science, not rumors," WHO director general Tedros Adhanom Ghebreyesus said. Ackman was incredulous as people continued to travel blithely across borders. The final straw was Milan Fashion Week, which took place in February despite a severe outbreak of coronavirus in northern Italy. All those fucking fashionistas were going to jet back to their densely populated cities all around the world and spread the virus everywhere.

It's over, thought Ackman, founder and chief executive of the activist New York hedge fund Pershing Square Capital Management. The virus has escaped to the world.

He began to think hard about the billions of dollars' worth of investments his firm owned. Should he sell it all? Would the global economy crash? He was a big owner of Hilton stock. Hotels would go to zero if we didn't get a grip on this pandemic. He had another big position in Chipotle, the Mexican fast-food chain. Another time bomb. As he scanned his portfolio, he saw a powder keg of risk. It could blow up. It all seemed trivial compared to the mass death he saw coming. But it was his job.

Selling it all felt wrong. Pershing Square was a long-term investor, and he believed in the underlying strength of the companies he owned—in a normal world. But the world wasn't normal anymore. He started calling executives at some of the world's largest financial institutions to find out if they shared his concerns. None did. He emailed Warren Buffett, whom he considered a mentor in the realm of value investing, and told him he was going to have to cancel Berkshire Hathaway's much ballyhooed annual meeting, scheduled for early May, because of the coming plague. The all-seeing Oracle of Omaha reacted as if Ackman were smoking something (Buffett canceled the meeting mid-March).

One day in early February, Ackman was in a one-on-one meeting in a conference room in Pershing Square's Midtown Manhattan office explaining his concerns about the virus. The other person started coughing, and Ackman rushed from the room in a panic. He was getting scared about his personal risk and the risk that he could expose his elderly father to the disease. He also began to realize that he was putting his own employees at risk by continuing operations at Pershing Square. He decided to shut down the office and tell everyone to work from home. Rather than blame the virus, which he worried might spook employees who weren't aware of the threat they faced, he said it was going to be a short-term disaster-recovery test. Secretly, he feared the firm might not return to the office full-time for a year, if not more.

On Sunday, February 23, the silver-haired fifty-year-old investor began looking for a way to protect his firm—and his investors—from what he increasingly believed was a fast-moving worldwide disaster. He'd made similar moves before in times of chaos. In the Global Financial Crisis of 2008, Ackman had made a jackpot betting against companies exposed to the crumbling U.S. housing market such as U.S. lenders Fannie Mae and Freddie Mac. He thought the Covid-19 crisis could make 2008 look like a lazy stroll in the park. Scanning the market for a way out, he noticed bond markets weren't reflecting the same risk he saw—not remotely. The economy had been so steady for so long it seemed investors couldn't imagine its one-way fun house ascent could change course.

To Ackman, that meant an opportunity. He could bet against bundles of bonds grouped together in indexes, just like the Dow Jones Industrial Average is a bundle of thirty large companies. If the bond indexes fell just a little, he might lose it all. If they crashed, he'd make a fortune. It would be a giant bet on chaos.

Ackman quickly built up a massive position. He purchased insurance contracts known as credit default swaps on $42 billion in U.S. investment-grade debt, more than $20 billion in an index of European debt, and a $3 billion position in junk bonds. In all, he had insurance tied to $71 billion of corporate debt. It cost Ackman a mere $26 million to make the bet. Like fire insurance, it would pay off if those bond indexes got torched.

Soon after, bond markets began to quake as other investors slowly realized that the nightmare Ackman had foreseen in January was coming true. Entire industries—hotels, theme parks, restaurants, sports, airlines, entertainment—could go bankrupt if Covid-19 got out of control. Other investors suddenly wanted the same insurance Ackman had bought on the cheap. The prices started to rise. Then surge. At one point the prices skyrocketed so high that his position represented one-third of Pershing Square's assets under management.

On the afternoon of March 12, a Thursday, Ackman, working from his home office, scanned his positions. They'd been surging for days, but now they were going orbital. He made $780 million *that day*. It couldn't last. He'd heard chatter from the White House and the Federal Reserve about intervening in the markets to put a stop to the carnage.

Time to sell. Just weeks after he'd made his wager, he quickly began cashing in. He sold his exposure to $4.5 billion worth of the investment-grade bet, $4 billion of the European stuff, and $400 million of the junk bonds. By the time he was done, he'd amassed a $2.6 billion profit that helped offset the losses in the stocks he'd held on to. The stock market had dived a staggering 30 percent since the Covid-19 panic began.

Then, Ackman did something crazy. Something nuts. Taking literally Baron Rothschild's advice to buy when there's blood in the streets, he plowed his sudden windfall back into stocks. He bought Hilton, Berkshire Hathaway, Starbucks, Lowe's, and more. In March, even as the pandemic accelerated.

It was a gutsy move. Maybe even foolish. Most investors were running in terror from stocks. Ackman feared it would all be for nought if the U.S. didn't get a handle on the pandemic. With mounting horror, he watched news footage of teenagers partying on spring break in Fort Lauderdale. On the night of March 17, after hearing more disturbing news about the outbreak in Wuhan, he couldn't sleep. The next morning, he took to Twitter, addressing President Trump directly:

@BillAckman

> Mr. President, the only answer is to shut down the country for the next 30 days and close the borders. Tell all Americans that you are putting us on an extended Spring Break at home with family. Keep only essential services open. The government pays wages until we reopen.
>
> With exponential compounding, every day we postpone the shutdown costs thousands, and soon hundreds of thousands, and then millions of lives, and destroys the economy.

Scott Wapner, a host for the financial news network CNBC, saw the tweet and called Ackman. "This is serious," Wapner said, asking him if he'd talk on air. Ackman agreed.

"Hell is coming, okay," Ackman told Wapner—and the tens of thousands of viewers of the show, many of whom worked on Wall Street. "People are not used to thinking about exponential compounding on a daily basis. When I did the math, the laws of probability tell me this thing is going to be everywhere, 50 percent of the world is going to get infected."

Millions of Americans likely had the virus already, he said. "Why is this thing not going to spread to every corner of the world? Why won't everyone get it? The only way to deal with the virus would be to shut down the global economy."

He repeated his call for a national thirty-day lockdown. "America will end as we know it unless we take this option," he said. The canary in the coal mine, he told Wapner, was New York's Chinatown. People had already stopped going to restaurants there, and many were shutting down. It would work all the way up from the busboys to the waiters to the entrepreneurs who own the restaurants. That would happen to the entire U.S. economy if aggressive action wasn't taken immediately.

The notoriously cocky gun-slinging hedge fund manager sounded scared, even terrified. He was. "There's a tsunami coming, and you feel it in the air, the tide starts to roll out. And on the beach people are playing and having fun like there's nothing going on. And that is the feeling I've had for the last two months. And my colleagues at work thought I was a lunatic. A lunatic!"

Ackman's tirade alarmed viewers. He was among the best-known hedge fund managers in America—a Master among Masters of the Universe—making his career on high-profile investments in name brands such as Starbucks and Wendy's. When Ackman took a position in a stock, it was headline news. He was even better known for his bearish bets, such as a $1 billion short against Herbalife Nutrition, a health supplement company Ackman said was a pyramid scheme, a wager that pitted him against Carl Icahn—and that Ackman famously lost.

As Ackman spoke, the market—already sharply lower for the day—tanked. It fell so quickly, trading was halted. When the market reopened, the Dow industrials were down more than two thousand points. The *Guardian* called Ackman's performance "near-hysterical" and "doom-laden." *Forbes* said it was "frenzied" and that Ackman was a "hedge fund manager turned amateur health expert."

But it wasn't Ackman's diagnosis of the biological functions of the Covid-19 virus that alerted him to its threat in January—it was his understanding of the startling, out-of-control nature of *exponential spread*, the nonlinear math of *compounding*, when something small gets bigger and bigger like a snowball rolling down a hill. That understanding is key to managing risk—not only on Wall Street, where blowups happen all the time, but throughout the economy in a world that, by all appearances, is getting riskier all the time. He could sense the crisis unfolding before most people, even many professional epidemiologists who cautioned against extreme reactions until more information about the virus was available, because he was attuned to the explosive risk of the exponential. Ackman knew it was deadly.

So Ackman did what all good chaos kings do. He panicked early. Because if you wait, deer-in-the-headlights, to figure out what's going to happen as the crisis unfolds, trying to understand it better, get more information, more data, *it's already too late*. The house is flooded. The building's burned down. The plane has crashed.

Critics said he was talking his book, trying to drive down the market so he could make more on his big short. But Ackman had already unloaded a big chunk of it well before the call and started buying loads of stocks—he told Wapner as much—and a stock market collapse would have hurt him. His incentive was to keep the plane from crashing, the house from burning. And to protect himself and his investors. While Trump didn't heed his warning, it turned out his crazy wager on stocks in the midst of the madness worked out pretty well. Juiced by unprecedented Federal Reserve spending and trillions in aid handed out by Congress, the U.S. stock market roared back, enjoying an unprecedented rally following its shock crash in March. Ackman's investments ultimately netted another $1 billion, resulting in a total gain of $3.6 billion from his $26 million bet—a trade *Barron's* later said was one of the greatest of all time.

Ackman wasn't the only one who understood the nature of explosive exponential risk in early 2020—and the billions that could be made on it. Another trader, ensconced in the frozen woods of Northern Michigan that winter, had also made a giant bet on a crash. He was one of the original chaos kings.

PART I

SWANS & DRAGONS

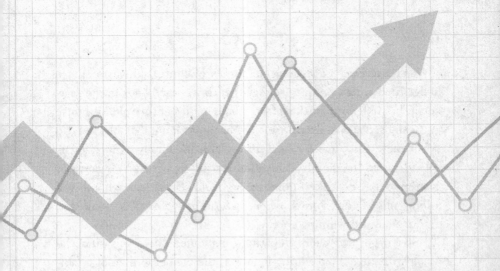

CHAPTER 1

BOOM!

Mark Spitznagel stared at his computer screen in astonishment. It was early Monday morning, March 16, 2020. He couldn't believe how dysfunctional markets around the world had become. Global markets had essentially died. Nothing was trading. Investors desperate to get out of their positions to avoid crushing losses couldn't as everything from stocks to commodities to bonds crashed into the void. Traders couldn't even sell *U.S. Treasury bonds*—T-bonds, the most liquid asset in the world. It was as if the value of American government debt had gone to zero.

As the Covid-19 pandemic spread in early 2020, financial markets across the globe wobbled, then collapsed. By early March, unheard-of daily free falls of more than two thousand points by the Dow industrials, followed by head-snapping two-thousand-point rebounds, seemed to have become routine. The market was going through an unprecedented seizure of volatility.

That was *good* for Spitznagel, founder of Universa Investments, a hedge fund with a unique strategy that thrived on chaos in the markets. The trader was working from home in his century-old log house in the densely wooded peninsula of Northport Point, Michigan. He'd flown there the previous week to be with his family as lockdowns spread across the country. Outside his window, across the waters of Northport Bay on Lake Michigan, he could see the snow-blanketed rolling hills of Idyll Farms, where he and his wife raised goats and produced award-winning cheese.

Spitznagel had been preparing for moments like this since he was a sixteen-year-old staring in awe at the pandemonium of a Chicago trading pit in the 1980s. The son of a Christian minister, he'd given up a promising career as a concert musician—with a spot at the Juilliard School—to pursue a career as a commodity trader. He'd climbed from the lowest ranks at the Chicago Board of Trade to senior positions at the banking houses of New York, ultimately opting to help launch a cutting-edge hedge fund in 1999 called Empirica Capital. Spitznagel was born to be a trader. As pandemonium broke out across world markets in March 2020, he was perfectly calm.

Communicating via intercom with his small team of traders back at Universa's headquarters on the twentieth floor of an ocean-side tower in Miami's Coconut Grove, he was monitoring the firm's finely calibrated positions in trades specifically designed to benefit from chaos. He watched the imploding markets with a sense of dread and fascination. Universa, which managed the risk of $4.3 billion for clients around the world, had been positioning itself for such a disaster for years.

Spitznagel, trim and tall with a shaved head and receding hairline, was the founder and chief architect of Universa, a trading machine with a strategy first designed in the late 1990s at Empirica alongside Spitznagel's longtime collaborator, Nassim Nicholas Taleb. A contrarian Lebanese-American trader and mathematician, Taleb would go on to become a world-famous author known for chart-topping bestsellers such as *The Black Swan* and *Antifragile*. When Empirica was launched, he was an obscure professor of quantitative finance at New York University with a background in trading complex financial instruments known as derivatives. He had grown convinced that financial markets and institutions had become far riskier than many realized. He'd made a killing on Black Monday in October 1987, when the Dow fell 22.6 percent in a single day. Like Spitznagel, he'd witnessed all the blowups of the nineties—the 1994 bankruptcy of Orange County, California; the Asian Contagion of 1997 triggered by currency devaluations; the 1998 collapse of the giant hedge fund Long-Term Capital Management after it made wildly misguided bets on Russian debt (among other things). Taleb had begun calling such crises Black Swans—extreme events no one could have predicted (like a sudden market crash). Once upon a time Europeans thought all swans were white . . . until they discovered black swans in Australia. A Black Swan is something totally off the grid, something that defies all previously known categories and assumptions.

In 1999, it was all theory. To test it, Taleb and Spitznagel launched Empirica, a hedge fund designed to reap enormous profits from crashes. They called themselves crisis hunters. It was the ultimate bear-market fund, the first of its kind. Unlike nearly all other trading outfits that made money in bull markets, Empirica *only* made a killing when the bear emerged growling from its cave. Every day, it purchased positions that produced extreme payoffs when stocks fell very sharply. Normally, the trades lost a small amount of money—the market didn't crash, the trades ended up worthless. But when the market *did* crash, Empirica's positions became wildly valuable.

Taleb and Spitznagel shut down Empirica in 2004 due in part to Taleb's aversion to the day-to-day slog of running a hedge fund and his desire to dedicate himself to writing after the success of his first book for laymen, *Fooled by Randomness* (in the 1990s he'd written a technical trading manual called *Dynamic Hedging*). Spitznagel, who only ever wanted to be a trader, rebooted the strategy in 2007 at Universa—and went on to perfect it. Taleb, who had the title of Senior Scientific Advisor at Universa, was never involved in its daily operations. Instead, the firm leveraged his fame as a world-renowned writer and thinker to channel attention from wealthy investors.

Universa had made a fortune during the 2008 Global Financial Crisis, as well as other turbulent periods such as the 2010 Flash Crash, the 2011 downgrade of U.S. debt, a freak implosion in 2015 that earned Universa $1 billion in less than a week, and other big spikes in volatility, like the so-called *Volmageddon* of 2018. Universa called the strategy the Black Swan Protection Protocol. The protocol's goal: to shield its investors from Black Swans.

What seemed to be lining up in March 2020 for markets and the global economy was the ultimate Black Swan—worse than anything the world had seen since the Great Depression of the 1930s. National economies ground to a halt as workers and families huddled in their homes. Millions of Americans suddenly found themselves out of work. By mid-March, the value of everything from stocks to bonds to commodities was in complete free fall.

As Spitznagel tracked the market's unraveling from Northport Point, Universa traders had stayed up through the night of March 16 managing the firm's positions as the turmoil rippled from Hong Kong to Europe to the U.S. Around 5:00 a.m. Monday morning, a few senior traders arrived at the firm's office. The calming chords of a Bach cantata played in the background. Others worked from home due to the firm's pandemic protocols. Universa's team of sixteen programmers and traders—Ph.D.s, computer nerds, mathematicians— were exhausted. But they had little time for rest. After working through the day's chaotic opening, Spitznagel hopped on a private plane and departed from a grass airstrip near his Michigan home. By the afternoon, he'd taken up his usual spot at a desk perched beside a floor-to-ceiling window with sweeping views of Miami and the emerald-green waters of Biscayne Bay beyond.

"Remember, we're pirates! Not the navy!" he'd exclaim from time to time to his elite team of derivatives traders, borrowing a line from Steve Jobs ("It's better to be a pirate than join the navy").

Covid-19 had sent shock waves through the global financial system. The Dow Industrial Average plunged 13 percent that Monday, its second biggest single-day fall ever, after 1987's Black Monday. Bond markets froze. Money market funds saw their biggest outflows on record. Mom-and-pop investors were getting annihilated. Wall Street veterans had never seen anything like it—not even in the Global Financial Crisis. "The 2008 financial crisis was a car crash in slow motion," Adam Lollos, head of short-term credit at Citigroup, told the *Wall Street Journal*. "This was like, 'Boom!'"

The following week, as the head-snapping volatility crushed the market, the small band of Universa traders would get little sleep, many napping just a few hours at a time on office couches or in their home offices before getting up, gulping down coffee, and quietly racking up a fortune.

Spitznagel and his team saw their investments go vertical, like a rocket. By the end of March, Universa's Black Swan Protection Protocol Fund had clocked an astonishing three-month gain of more than 4,144 percent. Spitznagel's bet of around $50 million yielded, in a flash, eye-watering gains of nearly $3 billion.

The returns were so astronomical some experts were skeptical. Some said the returns were *impossible*. Aaron Brown, a longtime risk manager on Wall Street—and longtime friend of Nassim Taleb's—wondered if Universa was speculating on a crash. That is, when Spitznagel sniffed chaos in the air, he juiced the firm's bets—made them bigger to get a better return. Spitznagel said Universa *never* speculated. It always kept the same crash protection in place for its clients, all the time, never turning the dial up or down no matter what was going on in the market.

Brown wasn't so sure.

"They deny it, but they have to have some kind of forecasting element to it that they don't disclose," Brown told me. "You can't make it work without that. Maybe they've discovered the secret of life, but it just doesn't add up. They do it so much better than anyone else."

Spitznagel would concede the last point.

> > < <

While Nassim Taleb had popularized the Black Swan concept, Universa was entirely Spitznagel's baby. After winding down Empirica, Taleb had become something of a celebrity thinker and philosophical gadfly as he extended his Black Swan concept far beyond trading and finance. His heart's desire was to become known as a scientist and philosopher, not a trader (though Taleb's involvement with Universa made him fabulously wealthy, the cash from the fund far outdistancing the substantial profits from his bestsellers).

One area he'd delved into was pandemics, a particularly deadly Black Swan. In 2010, he predicted in the *Economist* that the world would face "severe biological and electronic pandemics, another gift from globalization." In *Antifragile*, his 2012 follow-up to *The Black Swan*, he wrote that globalization would increase the risk of planetary pathogens "as if the entire world became a huge room with narrow exits and people rushing to the same doors." In a 2014 paper titled "The Precautionary Principle," he and several coauthors wrote that "the tightly connected global system implies a single deviation will eventually dominate the sum of their effects. Examples include pandemics, invasive species, financial crises."

In other words, in today's highly mobile super-networked world, the risk of extreme events such as pandemics is greater than ever. In January 2020, Taleb had seen it coming and raised the alarm. His warning was all but ignored.

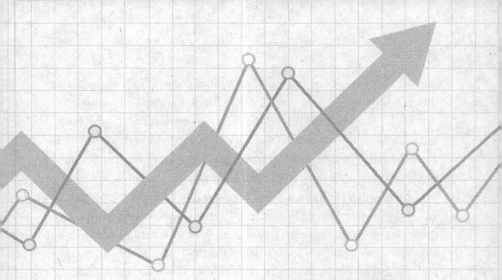

CHAPTER 2

RUIN PROBLEMS

Nassim Taleb squinted at a chart on the screen of his Apple MacBook. It was January 2020, and he was working from Universa's Miami office. He'd learned of a disturbing feature of the novel coronavirus that was sweeping through Wuhan, China. At the time, Covid-19 had killed a few hundred people. Thousands more had become severely ill. Beijing had implemented a sweeping lockdown on the region. It all seemed so very far away.

Few believed serious measures were required outside China. U.S. President Donald Trump and UK Prime Minister Boris Johnson dismissed the virus as another seasonal flu that would fade away with the spring. Stock markets hit records in America, Europe, Asia. Good times lay ahead.

Taleb, whose once coal-black beard had lately turned snow-white, learned that some epidemiologists estimated Covid-19 had an R0—called an "R naught" or "R zero"—of three or four, maybe higher. That meant one person who had the disease typically infected three or four people—higher than the R0 of standard influenza.

Such a high rate of contagion was alarming. Crunching the numbers on a computer program called Wolfram Mathematica, Taleb grew increasingly unnerved. If the disease got out of control, it could be devastating. Millions could die. Videos emerging from Wuhan of overrun hospitals and doctors in space-age protective suits frightened Taleb. He called Yaneer Bar-Yam, a friend and expert in complexity theory—the broad, interdisciplinary study of interactions within and among systems ranging from cells to forests to the global climate— and the disturbing dynamics of pandemics in the modern world.

"You've got to pay attention to what's going on in Wuhan," Taleb told him.

Bar-Yam agreed.

Founder of an elite research center called the New England Complex Systems Institute, or NECSI, Bar-Yam had for years been growing progressively worried about the outbreak of a global pandemic. He'd worked with the United Nations on the Ebola virus and saw how it had nearly jumped well beyond Africa's borders. In 2016, he'd written a report called *Transition to Extinction: Pandemics in a Connected World*. Highly fatal pathogens tend to spread quickly at first, then burn out as they kill all their hosts. That's why the most vicious bugs are less likely to spread to a broad population. Not anymore, Bar-Yam warned. With the ubiquity of long-range transportation, "there is a critical point at which pathogens become so aggressive that the entire host population dies. . . . We call this the phase transition to extinction. With increasing levels of global transportation, human civilization may be approaching such a critical threshold."

Taleb wondered if the Trump administration was formulating plans to address the looming crisis. To find out, he called an acquaintance who served on the National Security Council in the White House. "Are you seeing what's going on in Wuhan?" Taleb asked him. "Are you taking it seriously?"

"We're seeing it," the official replied. But he wasn't sure about the second question. Trump didn't seem to be taking Covid-19 seriously at all. Nor were his top advisers. He asked Taleb if he could write a memo to the White House outlining his concerns.

Taleb called Bar-Yam. "We should write something," he said. It was January 24.

Taleb, like Bar-Yam, had been studying the jarring mathematics of pandemics for years. Decades before, he'd learned about characteristics of financial markets that acted in ways similar to pandemics. Sudden crashes were extreme, often unpredictable events—like plagues and pandemics. He knew that highly contagious viruses can spread exponentially, resulting in mass death. In *The Black Swan*, he wrote: "As we travel more on this planet, epidemics will be more acute. . . . I see the risk of a very strange acute virus spreading throughout the planet."

Like Pershing Square's Bill Ackman, Taleb also knew that most people didn't grasp the frightening portent of the exponential. IBM executive John E. Kelly gave *New York Times* columnist Thomas Friedman an apt description of our all-too-human relationship with the exponential, a conversation Friedman relates in his 2016 book *Thank You for Being Late*. "We live as human beings in a linear world—where distance, time, and velocity are linear," Kelly told Friedman. But technology is growing on "an exponential curve. The only exponential we ever experience is when something is accelerating, like a car, or decelerating really sudden with a hard braking. And when that happens you feel very uncertain and uncomfortable. . . . The feeling being engendered now among a lot of people is that of always being in this state of acceleration."

New, ever-evolving technologies dominate modern life. Mark Zuckerberg founded Facebook in 2004. The iPhone didn't exist until 2007. Tesla produced its first all-electric Roadster in 2008. The MRNA vaccines that protect against Covid-19 are a marvel of modern techno-science few understand. We increasingly live in an exponential world—but our brains are hardwired for the linear.

The study of the exponential was Taleb's bread and butter—the mathematical keystone of his Black Swan worldview. Pandemics, of course, aren't new. They're as old as civilization. But new viruses can have Black Swan qualities—unknown unknowns. When they first burst upon the world, no one knows what they do to the human body, how to cure them, how contagious they are, if people can spread the deadly bug without knowing they're infected, or how leaders will respond to the outbreak. Taleb feared this new coronavirus might have several such unknown properties.

Taleb, Bar-Yam, and another researcher at NECSI, Joe Norman, quickly drafted a memo outlining the existential risks of the virus and the steps needed to address them. Then Taleb sent it to the White House. Days later, January 26, a time when most Americans were barely aware of the coming plague, they made it public.

"Systemic Risk of Pandemic via Novel Pathogens—Coronavirus: A Note" was a single-page, screeching alarm bell that urged swift, sweeping action to halt the disease in its tracks. Social distancing. Quarantines. Border shutdowns. The spread of the virus was likely happening much more quickly than most realized, the paper said.

"Clearly, we are dealing with an extreme fat-tailed process owing to an increased connectivity, which increases the spreading in a nonlinear way," the memo said. "Fat-tailed processes have special attributes, making conventional risk-management approaches inadequate."

"Tails" refer to the outer edges of a bell curve that measures the probability of some kind of event, like the average daily ups and downs of the stock market in the past fifty years or the daily temperature of New York over a century. A standard distribution curve looks like a bell, with most of the samples coming in the middle—gains or losses between say 0.1 and 5 percent—with other, less likely events captured in the tails of the curve. A "fat" tail is when you have a lot more—or much larger—edge cases happening than you'd expect with a normal distribution, for example in 1987's Black Monday.

Standard Bell Curve

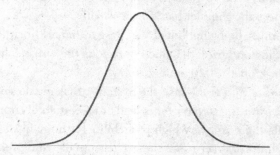

Pandemics are extremely fat-tailed.

That's because a pandemic is *nonlinear*. In statistics, something is nonlinear if its output is disproportionate to its input. As opposed to a phenomenon that's linear—1, 2, 3, 4, 5, 6—nonlinear output can be exponential—1, 2, 4, 16, 256, 65536, etc. In other words, nonlinear events tend to get very big, very fast. One infected person, possibly asymptomatic, spreads the virus to 2 people, those 2 spread it to 4, 4 to 16, 16 to 256 . . . and on and on to the millions. Exactly the dynamic that freaked out Bill Ackman in January 2020. Now, due to the modern world's hyper-networked, jet-fueled, megacity inter-mixing, the spread—the R0—could be even *more* nonlinear, *more* exponential.

"Global connectivity is at an all-time high, with China one of the most globally connected societies," the "Systemic Risk" memo explained. "Fundamentally, viral contagion events depend on the interaction of agents in physical space."

The solution: Break the chain. *Panic now—panic early*, a phrase Taleb and his memo coauthors would go on to use throughout the Covid-19 crisis and that became a hallmark of the chaos king play-book.

Failure wasn't an option. The risk to humanity was what's known in statistics—and sophisticated corners of gambling—as a ruin prob-lem. That is, *the destruction of the human race*. Think of a gambler with $1,000 doubling down every time he or she loses a bet. Lose $5, bet $10. Lose $10, bet $20. Such a strategy, known as a martingale, will inevitably lead to *gambler's ruin*—a guaranteed strategy to go broke (unless the gambler has *infinite* wealth).

Pandemics, being nonlinear, can pose a similar threat to humanity depending on how lethal and contagious the virus is, how fast it spreads. In January 2020, no one knew.

"These are ruin problems," the Systemic Risk memo said, "where over time, exposure to tail events leads to a certain eventual extinction. While there is a very high probability for humanity surviving a single such event, over time, there is eventually zero probability of surviving repeated exposures to such events. While repeated risks can be taken by individuals with a limited life expectancy, ruin exposures must never be taken at the systemic and collective level."

Historic pandemics—the bubonic plague, the 1918 virus, etc.—occurred in a different world, a world without widespread international air travel, without United Airlines and Lufthansa, without multiple highly congested urban centers of tens of millions. Today's über-networked global society makes the extreme risk of the ruin problem more of a threat than ever.

All hope is not lost, if humanity learns the lesson of the coronavirus pandemic, according to Taleb and his coauthors. In future outbreaks, the response needs to match the threat. The world needs to act as if everything is on the line. That means applying the "precautionary principle," which, according to the memo, "delineates conditions where actions must be taken to reduce the risk of ruin, and traditional cost-benefit analyses must not be used."

"Outbreaks are inevitable," it said, "but an appropriately precautionary response can mitigate systemic risk to the globe at large."

Taking a highly precautionary response in early 2020 was a view few people heard from health experts or politicians, many of whom were more concerned about the impact on the economy from an aggressive approach than the potential mass death the outbreak could cause. "It says something not good at all about the state of medicine, public health, and the leadership of Western societies generally that it's Taleb who has been speaking relentlessly, and largely alone, about the importance of the precautionary principle," Susan Webber, who writes under the pen name of Yves Smith, opined at the time on her popular financial website, Naked Capitalism.

It's unclear whether the White House did anything in response to Taleb's warning. He thought it might have factored into the decision to shut down the U.S. border to China, which happened several days after he sent it to his friend on the National Security Council. Regardless, it wasn't long before Trump was predicting the virus would disappear "like a miracle." Others in the White House were also giving voice to an entirely different approach than the memo recommended. In this group's view, because the nature of the disease—its degree of contagiousness and lethality—was so uncertain, it was best to gather more data to understand the risk before taking drastic measures that could upset the economy—and Trump's reelection hopes. We simply don't know enough yet, they reasoned. We need more information. The cure can't be worse than the disease. Such people had the ear of the president of the United States. Other countries, including Great Britain, were also taking the wait-and-see approach.

Taleb would later say the wait-and-see camp have it backward when it comes to Black Swans and global systemic risk—and pandemics. "Absence of knowledge should give you *more* certainty regarding what to do," he told me. "If you're uncertain about the pilot's skills, don't get on the plane."

> > < <

As word leaked about Universa's 4,000-percent-plus windfall, rival traders across Wall Street marveled with envy—and, like Aaron Brown, disbelief. The average stock-focused hedge fund had lost 14 percent through mid-March, according to Goldman Sachs. Other risk-mitigation strategies also suffered. Stocks and bonds fell simultaneously—usually they move in opposite directions, providing investors with a measure of protection during crashes—crushing the classic "60/40" mix of stocks and bonds many Americans rely on for retirement.

Maybe Universa was just lucky. Maybe Spitznagel, panicking about Covid-19 like Bill Ackman, had made a big bet that the market would crash.

Not exactly. Universa was *perpetually positioned* to make explosive returns in a crash. Because the market could crash anytime, without warning. No one could predict when the crash would happen. And that meant the hedge fund's investors didn't have to worry about the crash. They could sleep at night. In a post-crash letter to Universa investors, Spitznagel wrote that "going forward, there is every good reason to expect that protecting against large drawdowns with Universa should remain the superior risk mitigation strategy, saving you the needless costs and risks associated with most financial engineering and Modern Finance solutions, while providing superior 'crash-bang-for-the-buck' should the crash continue."

Universa's 2020 bonanza had been decades in the making. By the late 2000s, it was managing positions to protect billions of dollars against outsize losses, making Spitznagel extremely rich indeed. (He used some of his winnings in 2009 to buy a Bel Air mansion from Jennifer Lopez for $7.5 million.) Universa's success sparked a wave of copycats at both hedge funds and massive asset managers such as California's Pimco. Wall Street even cooked up Black Swan–branded exchange-traded funds, such as the Amplify BlackSwan Growth & Treasury ETF.

The headline-grabbing 2020 performance cemented the strategy's place on Wall Street. "Markets were once dominated by bulls who thought stocks would go up and bears who thought they would go down," the *Wall Street Journal* noted in June 2020. "These days, another animal is on the rise. . . . These investors are focused on volatility, the amount of movement in prices over time. In recent years, volatility has gone from a specialty of derivatives traders to a vehicle for trading in its own right."

Spitznagel and Taleb weren't flattered by the imitators. They thought most of the copycats didn't know what they were doing and were giving their strategy a bad name.

The guiding philosophy behind Spitznagel and Taleb's trading strategy is threefold. One, the future, dominated by big, impactful events, is very hard if not impossible to predict. Anything can happen (Black Swans). Two, extreme events are more devastating than many assume, because standard risk metrics like the bell curve don't capture them. That means, in financial markets, extreme events are usually underpriced: a moneymaking opportunity. It also means most other investors are taking on more risk than they realize. It's a common human frailty to assume the world tomorrow will be the same as today, despite all the signs of change around us. People focus on the mundane bulges in the center of the bell curve, rather than the wild explosions in the tails of the curve.

Three, drawdowns matter more than wins. Spitznagel years ago realized an essential truth for anyone betting on a future outcome: A single large drawdown matters far more than a long series of small wins. Say you invest $1,000 in a stock. If for some reason there's a bad earnings report or executive scandal—or people stop buying the widgets the company makes—that stock falls 50 percent. You now have $500.

Here's the catch: To make back your money, just to get back to even, the stock needs to rise *100 percent*—not the 50 percent you lost.

The lesson: Avoiding big losses is crucial. Universa achieved this by purchasing options that have mammoth payoffs in crashes, and only in crashes. Options are contracts that give their owner the right to buy or sell a stock for a certain price within a specified time frame.

Every day, Universa buys so-called *put* options that make money in a crash. Usually the bets don't pay off and Universa takes a small loss (a process they call bleeding). But the payoffs, when they come, are much bigger than the incremental losses. Spitznagel calls the effect *explosive downside protection*. Think of it like fire insurance that pays off triple the value of your mortgage (or more) if your home burns to the ground.

This happens to be the polar opposite approach to investing

practiced by most professionals on Wall Street. There, traders invest expecting to make a small, incremental gain every day, on average, with an eye on the wallet-fattening year-end annual bonus. By doing so, they also take the risk of losing a large amount on those infrequent days when the market collapses. Universa, by contrast, can *never* lose a large amount in a day or week—but it can and does usually lose a small amount nearly every day. It's a strategy that thrives on avalanches, earthquakes, hurricanes. (As Taleb once told me, "I don't want rain, I want droughts or floods.")

As of the early 2020s, it had been a strikingly successful strategy. Ernst & Young audited Universa's Black Swan strategy from its launch in 2008 through December 2019 and found that its average annual return on invested capital, a common metric for measuring hedge funds' success (or failure), was an eye-watering 105 percent. That is, on average Universa returned 105 percent *per year*, a track record putting it on par with or better than the best hedge funds in the world. And that didn't even include the 4,000-plus percent bonanza of early 2020.

The gains came entirely without anyone at Universa making a single prediction about the direction of the market, up, down, or sideways. But while Spitznagel would never attempt to predict *when* the market might crash, he does absolutely, deep-in-his-soul, believe that the American stock market—and bond market—fueled by central bank interventions, has long been trapped in an unsustainable super bubble that will ultimately explode like a barrel full of TNT. A core tenet of Spitznagel's worldview is that the U.S. Federal Reserve has been addicted to blowing bubbles for decades, creating dry tinder for crash after crash. Neither Spitznagel nor Taleb claim to know when the crashes will happen. As Spitznagel wrote in a 2020 letter to investors, "There are no crystal balls!"

Not everyone agrees that it is impossible to predict market crashes, however. A growing breed of mathematicians, many of whom are steeped in a fiendishly arcane branch of science called complexity theory, practiced by brainiacs such as Taleb's friend Yaneer Bar-Yam, have claimed they can detect certain signals in the market's noise that auger collapse. Experts in the theory, such as French physicist Didier Sornette, have devised experiments to demonstrate the reliability of their predictive systems, with some surprising successes.

As for Taleb, he isn't entirely opposed to the notion that some market hiccups can be predicted. He calls these events Gray Swans, a category he says included the Global Financial Crisis of 2008. His contention, however, has been that it is wickedly hard to predict the timing of these catastrophic events and that the forecasting tools deployed by market wizards such as Sornette are entirely incapable of managing risk. (The debate is a central theme of Chapter 12.)

While eschewing specific market forecasts, Taleb and Spitznagel do predict that the world will change, repeatedly, with head-spinning ferocity—and so will the stock market. Those who aren't prepared are doomed to suffer.

In March 2020, it seemed as if the suffering for investors had just begun. Then something uncanny happened. Stock markets around the world began to rise—then surge. Even while the U.S. began undergoing an epic economic collapse that saw millions lose their jobs as Covid-19 ravaged the nation, stock indexes began an inexorable march higher, eventually hitting records time and again.

There were a few reasons for the seemingly irrational exuberance. Spitznagel's bugaboo, the Federal Reserve, was pumping unprecedented amounts of liquidity into the financial system by purchasing billions of dollars of corporate bonds. It even bought junk bonds. The U.S. Congress rolled out trillions of dollars in financial aid for struggling companies and families. The combined force of the Fed and Congress, in addition to other bailout packages in Europe and elsewhere, triggered a historic amount of risk-taking. With interest rates at all-time lows, bonds provided little return at all, forcing investors who were eager for any kind of yield they could get into the only place they could get it—the stock market. Stocks were so frothy that the markets began to pull in a new wave of day traders at a rate not seen since the dot-com bubble of the late 1990s.

To Spitznagel, it was simply more TNT—and more bang-crash profits for Universa when the whole thing came tumbling down.

Indeed, as the 2020s lurched forward with the seemingly endless Covid-19 pandemic and its never-ending variants, its horrific climate catastrophes, and a deadly land war in Europe that raised the specter of nuclear annihilation, it seemed as if globe-shaking risks were mounting at an unprecedented pace.

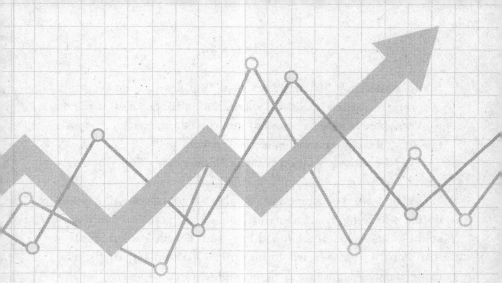

CHAPTER 3

WORSE LIES AHEAD

A cold rain fell from the sky on the highest point of a massive glacier in the arctic interior of Greenland, two miles above sea level. It was August 2021, the first time on record that rain had fallen on one of the planet's most reliably frozen regions. The rain shower was an "unprecedented shock to the system," John Walsh, a scientist with the International Arctic Research Center, told the Sierra Club. "This has never happened before. Something is going on in the atmosphere that's taking us into uncharted territory."

Unprecedented and *never happened before* and *uncharted territory* were watchwords of the new decade. In a September 2020 article titled "The Turbulent Twenties," sociologist Jack Goldstone and scientist Peter Turchin predicted that a confluence of structural factors in America would lead to more and greater societal instability and "the highest level of vulnerability to political crisis seen in this country in over a hundred years." Disruptions such as the Black Lives

Matter protests of 2020 and the Covid-19 pandemic "are occurring at a time of extreme political polarization, after decades of falling worker's share in national income, and with entrenched elite opposition to increased spending on public services."

"We are already well on our way," they wrote. "But worse lies ahead."

What made Goldstone and Turchin's forecast intriguing—and deeply disturbing: It wasn't new. Using a computational model created by Goldstone, Turchin had forecast a decade earlier, in 2010, that global turbulence would hit critical mass in the 2020s. The model analyzed structural demographic forces—poverty, wealth gaps, and competition among elites for power—all of which can tilt a society toward instability. It projected a coming Age of Discord highlighted by civil conflict, violence, and the decline of democracy. In the 2020 article, they even predicted the jarring events following the upcoming presidential election. "If Trump loses, he is likely to contest the outcome as a 'rigged' election. . . . Trump may call on his many armed civilian supporters to defend their 'all time favorite president' (as he put it) against the so-called 'liberal tyranny.'"

Forecasts of a coming age of chaos were rampant as the new decade unfolded. Cassandras were on every street corner. In a March 2021 report called *Global Trends 2040: A More Contested World*, the U.S. National Intelligence Council predicted that highly disruptive events "are likely to manifest more frequently and intensely in almost every region and country. These challenges—which often lack a direct human agent or perpetrator—will produce wide-spread strains on states and societies as well as shocks that could be catastrophic."

Driving the chaos: a highly connected global order. "During the past year, the Covid-19 pandemic has reminded the world of its fragility and demonstrated the inherent risks of high levels of interdependence," the report said. "In coming years and decades, the world will face more intense and cascading global challenges ranging from disease to climate change to the disruptions from new technologies and financial crises."

While globalization had brought numerous benefits to humanity—life expectancy globally expanded more than two decades since 1960 as famines and infant mortality declined sharply—it also brought new risks through the complex technologies, networks, and control mechanisms it was founded upon. Some feared those risks threatened ruin.

"There is a specter haunting globalization and modern life: the potential for widespread civilizational collapse," members of Princeton University's Global Systemic Risk project wrote in a July 2022 paper. "Our world is existentially anxious because we sense that our trajectory is not sustainable. . . . Global systemic shocks like 9/11, the Global Financial Crisis of 2008, and Covid-19 have heightened the awareness of the fragility of our increasingly globalized and interdependent way of living."

Market crashes. Pandemics. Terrorist attacks. Riots. Megafires. Superstorms. Extreme, destructive, often deadly events seem to be happening across the planet with greater frequency—and greater harm. They happen suddenly and strike widely. The smallest event can cause them, the proverbial flapping of a butterfly's wings whipping up tornadoes across continents. A chillingly perverse result of their increasing frequency is that such events are becoming more predictable in certain ways. They are not Black Swans that sweep in out of the blue. They are Taleb's Gray Swans—devastating events that are all-too-foreseeable. The coast-smashing hurricanes that occur with numbing regularity. The West Coast wildfires that appear on cable news in the summers like a reliable seasonal affect—akin in their cyclical nature to autumnal foliage or winter snowstorms. (Sornette called these predictable catastrophes Dragon Kings.)

Taleb has argued that our increasingly unstable world is the paradoxical result of humankind's efforts to control it with technology, quantitative models, and ubiquitous just-in-time optimization, resulting in an ever-more-complex, human-built, fragile society susceptible to shocks. Extreme events "are necessarily increasing as a result of complexity, interdependences between parts, globalization and the beastly thing called 'efficiency' that makes people now sail too close to the wind," he wrote in *Antifragile*.

In 2020, the infection of a single person in Wuhan by a microscopic virus killed millions and pushed the global economy into free fall. The murder of an African-American man by a police officer in Minneapolis, recorded on a cellphone, ignited waves of protests not only across the United States, but around the world. The intransigence of a single man—Donald Trump—radicalized tens of millions of Americans, pushing U.S. democracy to the brink. And in 2022 the intransigence of another man, Vladimir Putin, would bring the world to the edge of World War III.

As globalization expands, connectivity accelerates. Complexity breeds complexity, and speed breeds speed. Social networks spread news—and conspiracy theories—like a virus. Rapid air travel can cause infections that might have died out in a small village to explode across borders.

The ever-more dire effects of global warming—a direct outcome of population growth, cultural complexity, and society's dependence on fossil fuels—are spreading, eroding coastlines, unleashing powerful hurricanes, and sparking megafires that have ravaged some of the most expensive property in America. In the western U.S., climate scientists fear a megadrought could plunge tens of millions of people into a widening crisis of water scarcity and creeping desertification. While there is little evidence that global warming is increasing the *frequency* of hurricanes and typhoons—the most destructive and costly of all natural weather disasters—there is widespread evidence that they're becoming stronger and more dangerous, powered by energy from warmer seas and hotter air that can hold more water, as seen in the deadly California floods of January 2023 caused by relentless waves of atmospheric rivers.

Jeffrey Bohn, chief strategy officer at One Concern, a San Francisco outfit that uses artificial intelligence to predict extreme weather events, is building models that can help businesses prepare for unforeseen disruptions from natural disasters. The problem:

Storms are getting a lot harder to predict as climate chaos scrambles the models. "It may be the case that you have fewer hurricanes and typhoons making landfall, but the ones that do are much more destructive," Bohn told me. That's why he's "building more extreme events into the system—more rainy seasons, hotter summers, worse winters, more droughts. The climate guys talk about global warming. They picked the wrong term. It's *extreme* climate change."

One industry—insurance—is seeing mounting risks and societal damage amid a surge in payments to cover increasing claims. In 2021, life insurance payments rose 15 percent from the previous year due to the Covid-19 pandemic, and cyber-insurance payments rose 74 percent from the year prior, to more than $4.8 billion, as a result of skyrocketing cyberattacks. Some upticks have been even starker. Over the past quarter century, insurance checks written to farmers for crops lost to drought and flood have increased 300 percent.

Political extremism is on the rise across the planet, a dark and ironic symptom of the world's expanding interconnectedness and addiction to online social networks. In the U.S., polls show Americans since the early 2000s have been pushed farther to the right and to the left with an increasingly hollowed-out middle ground (in the U.S. and Europe, extremism is far more prevalent on the far right, as any Google search for the term will demonstrate). The impact of social media, from YouTube to 4chan to Facebook to Reddit, has radicalized youth populations via toxic artificial-intelligence algorithms that feed addicted viewers increasingly fanatical content. A November 2021 study that examined demonstrations between 2006 and 2020 found that protest movements around the world had tripled over that time period, with increases in every region.

In American politics, the pendulum has swung from one extreme to the other, from Barack Obama, a left-leaning African American and former community activist, to Donald Trump, a far-right president so extreme in his views and behavior that he defied all precedent, to Joe Biden, who is, by disposition and values, Trump's complete opposite. QAnon, a toxic conspiracy theory embraced by a significant percentage of Trump supporters, is just one example of snowballing swings to the political extreme. Heading into the 2020 election, the *Atlantic* described the environment as "one of the worst climates of partisan polarization and distrust in American history." A Reuters/Ipsos poll in September 2022 found that one in five Americans thought political violence against those they disagreed with was acceptable. A study by the University of Chicago's Project on Security and Threats taken the same month estimated that 15 million Americans believe force would be a justified response if Trump is prosecuted in one of the many investigations into his attempt to overturn the 2020 presidential election.

A December 2021 study of political polarization in the U.S. suggested it was reaching a critical phase akin to a bomb exploding. The study, called "The Nonlinear Feedback Dynamics of Asymmetric Political Polarization" found there are "critical thresholds or moments when processes become difficult if not impossible to reverse. Our model suggests that this threshold has been crossed by Republicans in Congress and may very soon be breached by Democrats." In response to a query by *New York Times* columnist Thomas Edsall, the authors of the report wrote: "Political processes, like any other natural dynamical process, in nature, technology, or society have the capacity to feed themselves and enter an unstable positive, or self-reinforcing, feedback loop. A classic example is an explosion: When thermal energy is provided to burn a few molecules of a combustible substance, they in turn produce more energy, which burns more molecules, producing more energy in a never-ending loop."

"Polarization has become a force that feeds on itself," Edsall later wrote.

Financial markets, and the economies that depend on them, have become increasingly complex, unstable, and prone to crashes. In the early 2000s, economists such as Ben Bernanke, who would later become chairman of the Federal Reserve, claimed that the global economy had entered a so-called Great Moderation. The steady hand of economic technicians, the spread of derivatives and other products of Wall Street's financial engineers (the quants), and low inflation meant the world was set to enjoy untold prosperity, the gift of not-too-hot-not-too-cold, centrally managed perpetual growth. Then came 2008, when the collapse of the U.S. subprime mortgage market ignited a global economic panic attack. The loss of a few hundred billion dollars in mortgages spread like a contagion through derivatives markets, leading to trillions in losses.

Such extreme swings can self-perpetuate and trigger machine-like feedback loops that push extremes to even further extremes, ending in crashes and chaos. Financial and economic collapses can lead to surprising outcomes in the political and social spheres—the election of Barack Obama, the rise of the ultra-conservative Tea Party in 2010, and the 2016 election of Donald Trump are arguably traceable to the Global Financial Crisis of 2008, which itself was (arguably) caused by unprecedented monetary stimulus from Alan Greenspan's Federal Reserve in response to the September 11, 2001, terrorist attack in America.

British historian and economist Adam Tooze coined a term for the converging, expanding risks the world faces—the *polycrisis*. It's a world in which pandemics, inflation, recession, the climate crisis, nuclear escalation, and other risks combine to magnify harm via a series of vicious feedback loops. A pandemic triggers supply chain snags, causing prices to rise, tipping economies into recession, resulting in a global hunger crisis that affects poor people in low-income countries, leading to destabilizing mass migration that triggers political unrest and topples governments. "A polycrisis is not just a situation where you face multiple crises," Tooze wrote. "It is a situation . . . where the whole is even more dangerous than the sum of the parts." It's what world national security expert and former Homeland Security official Juliette Kayyem calls "the age of disasters."

Feedback loops are a key factor driving climate crisis. One example: The warming planet is melting permafrost in Siberia, releasing into the atmosphere billions of tons of methane—a greenhouse gas with eighty times the heat-trapping effect of carbon dioxide. More methane, more warming, more methane, etc.

"Roughly 65 percent of Russia's territory is covered in permafrost," the *Moscow Times* observed in November 2021 as wildfires spread across the frozen tundra. "As air temperatures have risen in recent decades, this soil that has been frozen for millennia has begun to thaw. . . . And as permafrost melts, it releases long-stored greenhouse gases like methane, triggering an accelerating feedback loop of warming."

Extreme events are often fearful and intimidating in part because they're unpredictable. Here's the multitrillion-dollar question: Can preparing for Black Swans looming on the horizon, even if we can't see them coming, protect us from their most harmful effects?

Perhaps, but it's a tricky problem indeed. The lack of a rich history of data to inform predictive models makes extreme events very slippery phenomena. But we know they're coming—and they're getting worse. The trouble is the exact path the future takes is always extremely uncertain, even if we know major upheavals are heading toward us like the planet-killing comet in Adam McKay's 2021 hit film *Don't Look Up* (in which the President's response to the threat was "sit tight and assess"). And as with the disastrous response to Covid-19 in much of the world, uncertainty often leads to complacency, confusion, inaction—sitting tight and assessing—resulting in certain disaster.

As the world entered the third decade of the Third Millennium, it was as if many homeowners, uncertain about the prospect of a fire or flood, had decided against buying insurance at all. Even worse, they didn't have other homes to move into. In other words, it was a ruin problem.

It was just such problems that prompted Taleb, Bar-Yam, Norman, and another collaborator, the English philosopher and climate activist Rupert Read, in 2014, to write "The Precautionary Principle," a preview of the January 2020 note that recommended dramatic, immediate action to stop the spread of Covid-19 despite overwhelming uncertainty about its properties.

The precautionary principle itself is designed to guide actions and policies in the realms of uncertainty and risk "in cases where the absence of evidence and the incompleteness of scientific knowledge carries profound implications and in the presence of risks of 'Black Swans,' unforeseen and unforeseeable events of extreme consequence," Taleb and his coauthors wrote in the 2014 paper. If the risk of an action (or inaction) is global, uncertainty demands a strong precautionary response.

Critics of the precautionary principle complain it's too vague, subjective, paranoid, and contradictory, the enemy of progress and the ever-churning creation and destruction at the heart of capitalism. A permanent state of panic is not a comforting future to contemplate. It seems almost a return to the more fraught mindset of our premodern ancestors, always on alert for the next invader, the next wild predator lurking in the bushes. And there's the risk of debilitating paranoia, the proliferation of conspiracy theories and end-of-world doomism that breeds a paralyzing complacency.

It doesn't need to be that way, according to Taleb and his coauthors, because the principle as formulated in the 2014 paper only applies to worldwide threats—systemic Black Swans. "We believe that the PP should be evoked only in extreme situations: when the potential harm is systemic (rather than localized) and the consequences can involve total irreversible ruin, such as the extinction of human beings or all life on the planet," they wrote.

"The precautionary principle lets you relax about local problems," Taleb told me. That doesn't mean local problems should be ignored; it just means they don't require the extreme measures prescribed by the precautionary principle.

This view of safeguards ties directly to Taleb's experience as a trader and his approach to the risk of blowing up. Financial markets can pose a systemic risk known as *contagion*—a problem in one part of the market can spread to other parts, like a virus, leading to an explosive chain reaction and total chaos. Financial blowups are like pandemics—fast, exponential, destructive. The solution for Taleb: *Don't play in the systemic-risk casino*. Avoid those dice. Don't get on the plane if you have doubts about the pilot. Panic early. Apply the precautionary principle. In practical terms, don't use borrowed money (or leverage) and protect yourself from major crashes.

That was precisely what he'd done alongside Mark Spitznagel at Empirica. They crafted a trading machine that could never blow up. On the contrary, it thrived in blowups—it was, as Taleb later said, *antifragile*. Universa perfected the strategy.

Are there lessons to be learned from these chaos kings about how to adapt to our world of mounting uncertainty and rising risks, some existential? Even better, how to *protect* the world from those extreme risks? While Taleb and Spitznagel's sensitivity to extreme events was born in the sharp-elbowed world of trading—far away from the darker realms of global warming, pandemics, and other systemic threats— there are meaningful harmonies across these domains.

The birth of their strategy, for both Taleb and Spitznagel, occurred in the 1980s. For Taleb, it started with one of the biggest market blowups of modern times—Black Monday. For Spitznagel, it came from the wise advice of a veteran corn trader in the hard-charging trading pits of Chicago.

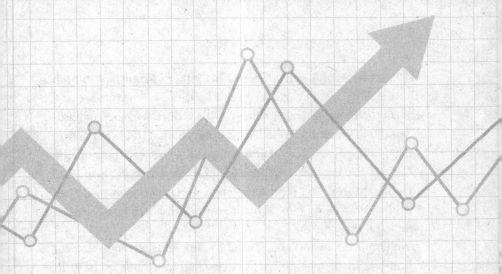

CHAPTER 4

THE SIZZLER

A riot of noise greeted Mark Spitznagel as he stepped into the visitors' gallery of the Chicago Board of Trade's cavernous Grain Room. It was the summer of 1987. The market was on a roll, and so was America. The Dow industrials closed above two thousand points for the first time. In Berlin, Ronald Reagan exhorted Mikhail Gorbachev to *tear down this wall*. Michael Jackson released *Bad*. Prozac was approved by the FDA. Inside the Board of Trade, the adrenaline-soaked machinery of naked capitalism was hard at work. Spitznagel's teenage eyes widened at the sights before him.

Shouting hordes of traders—sardined into the open-outcry floor, many outfitted in brightly colored jackets—made wild indecipherable gestures. Discarded tickets lay scattered like confetti across the black linoleum. Spitznagel could feel the vibrations humming in the air as buy and sell orders flew across the pits in the cavernous high-ceilinged space. Utter chaos. Yet somehow, *organized* chaos.

He was sixteen. A parishioner of his father's Protestant church on the outskirts of Chicago, Everett Klipp, was a corn trader and veteran of the Board of Trade, known as the CBOT, a bastion of hard-core bond and commodity markets dating back to 1848. Spitznagel was tagging along with his dad as he paid a visit to Klipp on the CBOT floor. Having had no experience of trading or markets, he had no idea what to expect. He'd envisioned something akin to a posh casino in a James Bond film. What he saw was something altogether different and thrilling.

The Grain Room was the central trading floor of the exchange. The building itself was an Art Deco masterpiece built in 1930 in the heart of the Windy City's business district at 141 West Jackson Boulevard. It was where the old established rich guys traded corn, wheat, oats, and soybeans. The size of a football field, it was engulfed by giant price boards where row upon row of red, green, and yellow numbers flickered and danced in response to supply and demand signals for commodities across the globe.

Mark loved it.

He wasn't a nerdy kid drawn to the numbers and the arcane culture of the market. Growing up in the rural enclave of Northport, Michigan, he'd gotten into sports—baseball, soccer. He loved racing sailboats on nearby Lake Michigan. But he wasn't what you'd call *normal*. He was fanatical about playing the French horn, practicing three, four hours a day. Walking around his house, he'd mutter *self-discipline, self-discipline, self-discipline*, alarming his parents. In addition to being a Protestant minister in Northport, his father, Lynn Edward Spitz-Nagel (Mark would later discard the hyphen), was a civil rights activist. Cat Stevens was the family's daily soundtrack. One day, Mark walked into his bedroom to find a stack of Gandhi books his father had left in an unsuccessful effort to get him to register for the military draft as a conscientious objector. Mark was more receptive to his father's lessons on meditation, which he later came to believe gave him an edge as a trader.

The elder Spitz-Nagel had given up a profitable career heading a state hospital in Upstate New York for his life as a poorly paid minister, a move reflected in the smaller, draftier homes the family lived in. The lesson was supposed to be that money didn't matter. Mark learned the opposite. He hated being poor and never wanted to be in such a position as an adult. Later in life, he'd look back at his belt-tightening origins with a sense of pride. Unlike nearly everyone he'd eventually meet in the heady upper echelons of global finance, he'd started out with almost nothing.

When Mark was in sixth grade, his family moved to the Chicago suburb of Matteson, where his father became minister of a larger congregation. Mark wasn't a fan of the cookie-cutter suburbs and missed the sprawling free-ranging woodlands of northern Michigan. But there was one significant benefit. The move put his family in close proximity to the commodity trading hub of the CBOT and its veteran corn trader, Everett Klipp.

> > < <

In his interests, Mark exhibited an obsessiveness that made him the neighborhood trendsetter. "When he decided something needed to happen, we all followed suit," his left-leaning brother, Eric Spitznagel, a writer for publications such as *Rolling Stone* and *Vanity Fair,* told me. "He decided to get a ventriloquist dummy. We were all like, 'That's the thing we're doing now.' Suddenly, all the kids in the neighborhood had a ventriloquist dummy." Mark made dozens of home movies on an eight-millimeter camera—a medley of knockoffs inspired by such disparate source material as *Star Wars*, Westerns, and *The Incredible Hulk*. Occasionally, he let his brother or friends direct. The resulting product usually fell under withering scorn—from Mark.

Rebelling against his parents' hippie-style liberalism, he immersed himself in the writings of arch conservatives such as William Buckley. Like his idol Warren Buffett, he began delivering newspapers and eventually monopolized local routes, hiring classmates to take up routes for a fixed wage. Friends began asking for loans—showing him the value of having lots of cash on hand. He identified with the right-leaning teenager Alex Keaton, played by Michael J. Fox in the hit eighties sitcom *Family Ties*. He religiously watched the CNN political debate show *Crossfire* and always took the side of the Republican host, Patrick Buchanan. He subscribed to Buckley's conservative magazine *National Review* and became smitten by the libertarian worldview of Texas Congressman Ron Paul. He was a natural at math. He turned himself into one of the country's best French horn students and was accepted into the Juilliard School in New York.

His visit to the CBOT changed all that. He scrapped his plans for Juilliard, realizing a music career would never make him rich. "Did I have a little greed in me?" Spitznagel says today. "Of course, it was the eighties." He stopped caring so much about politics and gave up any serious plans for soccer or baseball. He borrowed *The Grain Traders: The Story of the Chicago Board of Trade* by William Ferris from the library and never returned it.

Klipp took him under his wing and gave him work. At first he was a *runner*—a job that involved taking cards around the floor to other traders to confirm orders. "Is this trade good?" Then he might fetch lunch for the traders. All the time, he was soaking it in, learning the ropes—how trading worked, the weird hand signals, who was in control, who wasn't.

More important, he learned from Klipp. Known as the Babe Ruth of the CBOT, Klipp had grown up without electricity and survived both the Depression and the Pacific Theater in World War II. After the war, he moved to Chicago and in 1946 began working as a runner at the CBOT for a firm that later became Merrill Lynch. Klipp purchased a seat in the wheat pit in 1953, gaining the right to trade with his own money. In 1978, he launched his own firm, Alpha Futures.

Klipp's trading philosophy was simple, and mind-bending: Successful traders *love to lose* and *hate to win*. "You have to love to lose money," he told the young Spitznagel in his deep, gravelly voice soon after he started working for Alpha. "And hate to make money. It's against human nature, and that's what you have to overcome."

That meant that if a position started to lose money—*sell*

immediately. Doesn't matter if you think it's going to bounce back. Doesn't matter if you think the market's wrong. Doesn't matter what you read in the *Wall Street Journal* that morning or what that fancy chart says. Sell, lose. *Love to lose*. And move on. "You need to look like an ass and feel like an ass," Klipp told Mark.

The strategy worked by limiting traders' downside risk. You might lose a little bit, but you could never lose it all . . . you could never "blow up," as traders say, unless you were incredibly unlucky. It's what kept Klipp in the game all those years, what made him known as the Babe Ruth of the CBOT. And it was a lesson that would guide Spitznagel's approach to trading for the rest of his life.

Klipp was effectively teaching Spitznagel that key chaos king trait: Panic early. Cut your losses immediately, because if your position keeps falling, you can be wiped out. By making it into an iron law, he turned the strategy into a natural reflex—for those who could stomach it.

Klipp's approach to trading wasn't entirely unique. From their first days on the floor, cub traders are repeatedly told "cut your losses, let your profits ride." What set Klipp's approach apart was how fanatical he was about enforcing the rule—and how convinced he was *that nothing else mattered*.

"There was something about Klipp, the way he presented it," Spitznagel recalls. "To him it wasn't about the mechanics of the market, like this is where supply meets demand and price discovery, none of that bullshit. To him it was about the discipline of it. That was my introduction to trading. The discipline. Trading was about discipline; the rest was just detail. You have to do the opposite of what feels good. You have to put yourself in discomfort. Overcoming that means you'd be successful. And it would also mean you'd be wildly rich."

Another challenge to the Klipp approach: It was incredibly hard to keep it up, and few could do so consistently. It was, as he'd say, *against human nature*. One slip could lead to ruin. It took a while for Spitznagel to get it. He thought if he studied the market enough, he'd be able to predict its direction. He had charts of corn and soybean prices pinned to the walls of his bedroom. He constructed a potted corn and soybean plant laboratory to track crop growth stages and rainfall. He studied long-term weather forecasts for the summer and pored over U.S. Department of Agriculture data. He'd go up north to wade through cornfields and examine the development of the ears, trying to figure out what it meant for yields. Then he'd bring his new-found insights to Klipp at the CBOT or his dad's church.

"Can I show you this weather map with the degree days for the coming corn crop? Why aren't prices higher?" Mark asked him.

"It's crap," Klipp snorted. "You're wasting your time. No one can predict the prices."

> > < <

If college was ever wasted on anyone, it was wasted on Mark Spitznagel. He studied political science and math at Kalamazoo College in Michigan under the premise that it would have the least influence on his trading (at the time he didn't think math had anything to do with trading). During summers he'd work as a clerk for Klipp's traders, always lugging around that page-turner, *The Treasury Bond Basis*, to read during lunch breaks. He took a semester off to clerk under CBOT legend Charlie DiFrancesca, known as Charlie D., the Board's biggest individual trader at the time.

Spitznagel graduated when he was twenty-one and immediately went back home—to the CBOT. He found time to design a trading program for a handheld Hewlett-Packard computer that calculated a trader's position and profit and loss in real time, giving him the ability to react more quickly to changing prices. He originally made it for himself, then started selling it to clerks on the floor. "I made a ton of money on it; that's how I started trading so young," he recalls.

Within months, backed by Klipp, earnings from his trading program, and some cash from his grandmother, Spitznagel leased a membership on the Board of Trade. Clad in an aqua-green Alpha Futures trading jacket and a necktie featuring the profile of the free-market economist Adam Smith, Spitznagel was a so-called *local*, which meant he was trading his own money (the other traders in the pit, brokers, bought and sold for institutions such as banks or investment firms . . . in other words, with other people's money).

Locals were essentially market makers, the liquidity providers—they made markets work by greasing the wheels of the exchange through buying and selling no matter what direction the market was heading. Brokers reacted to the wishes of their clients, perhaps a big agriculture company looking to hedge its winter wheat harvest or an insurance company that wanted to protect itself against a drop in Treasury-bond prices. Locals, by contrast, were pure traders betting on short-term swings in prices.

With full membership, the twenty-two-year-old Spitznagel was the youngest local in the Treasury-bond futures pit. And the T-bond pit was where the action was. "The world's most active futures-trading pit," according to a 1991 *Wall Street Journal* article. At the time, two out of every three contracts traded on the CBOT were T-bond futures.

The CBOT was the birthplace of futures—agreements to buy a specific amount of a commodity for a specific price at a specific time. Back in the 1800s, Midwest crop merchants would meet in Chicago and sell their products for whatever price buyers were offering at the time. Eventually, futures contracts were developed that allowed them to sell their produce for a fixed price *in the future*. Say you owned a biscuit business. You could buy a futures contract for one thousand bushels of wheat on August 1 for $20 a bushel. That would allow you to lock in the price ahead of time and protect yourself from a spike in prices. The middleman who sold you the contract—the local—could benefit if prices fell below that twenty-buck bushel. He could also benefit just by trading around moving prices, trying to buy low and sell high.

T-bond futures were essentially the same thing, for bonds. Trading in the contracts had surged in the 1980s as the Reagan administration funded an economic boom by issuing billions in Treasurys. Futures contracts helped big institutions buying the bonds to protect themselves against losses—a trade known as a "hedge."

In the exchange's legendary pits, memorialized in the 1903 Frank

Norris novel *The Pit*, Spitznagel suddenly found himself working side by side with some of the biggest traders in Chicago. The pits were organized as a hierarchy, literally. Steps of the octagonal structure ascended from the floor to the top of the pit like an inverted tiered wedding cake. Small fries such as Spitznagel lurked around the low inner steps of the pits, trying to get a cut of the action with tiny trades of a few thousand bucks. On the top outer steps loomed the Big Dogs—super-wealthy traders who could throw millions at a position and not blink. They were the *top-step* traders.

The secret of the tiers: *sight lines*. The higher you were, the better your view of the pit, vastly increasing your ability to know what was going on and bringing you closer to the massive orders flashed from the outside. Down on the lower steps, inside the pit—called "down in the hole"—your sight lines were terrible, and there were fewer brokers to trade with. It was kind of like a Monopoly board. Traders at the top owned Park Place and Boardwalk. Traders in between owned the yellows and reds like Atlantic Avenue. Spitznagel held a lowly purple—dirt cheap Baltic Avenue.

It was the high crest of the CBOT's hotshot pit traders. Within a decade, the electronic bots, the high-frequency speed demons, would take over futures markets. But in the early 1990s, no one saw it coming. The T-bond futures pit was the top of the top at the CBOT, where legendary Big Dogs like Thomas Baldwin made vast fortunes. Baldwin was the most active trader in T-bond futures. A local trading his own money like Spitznagel—but far, far more—Baldwin was "one of the few individuals able to move prices in the multibillion-dollar market," the *Wall Street Journal* proclaimed in a February 1991 feature about the trader.

"Baldwin would throw spitballs at me all day," Spitznagel recalls. "It was like a hazing. He made my life miserable. I was flattered. The greatest pit trader of all time was bothering to pick on me."

Spitznagel made it a point to get as close to Baldwin as possible so he could study his moves. Baldwin was "a man possessed," he later wrote, "but what was so astounding about him was his disciplined control in alternating between tremendous patience and over-whelming aggression." Known for his wild gestures to attract other traders' attention—his manic jumps in the air dubbed the *Baldwin leap*—Baldwin was the polar opposite of loss-loving Klipp. Instead of cutting his losses, he'd plow more cash into losing positions hoping to turn the market in his favor. That could lead to some big losses indeed. In 1983, he coughed up more than $300,000 on a single trade, and in 1989, he once lost $5 million in a single day. But more often than not he was able to muscle bonds in his direction, an aston-ishing feat in what at the time was a half-trillion-dollar market.

In his aqua-green jacket emblazoned with a SIZ trading badge (three-letter shorthand for Spitz) that earned him, courtesy of Bald-win, the nickname "the Sizzler," Spitznagel slowly, steadily began to climb the stairs. Taking small losses every day, at times book-ing respectable wins, he learned to sense in his bones the lurching, gut-wrenching swings of the market. They resembled a flock of birds always shifting in flight through the air. He'd try out other markets, like soybeans and corn, from time to time. But his favorite pit always remained T-bonds. Still coached by Klipp, who'd roam the pits mut-tering *love to lose, hate to win* like a Buddhist mantra, he steadily built up the daily discipline of stomaching those daily losses—like a major-league batter taking balls and strikes until he spotted a pitch he could belt out of the park.

Spitznagel was unnerved at times by the intensity of it all. Trades could be executed with another trader across the room just by a wink or a nod. At the end of the day, a trader might approach him and say, "I did this trade with you." Spitznagel had no idea what the hell the guy was talking about. Other locals in the pit would elbow him, poke him in the ribs, spit on him, shove him off the steps. Locals com-peted against one another for orders, and there were only so many to go around. The more locals, the smaller each piece of the pie. Fights broke out constantly, though the traders usually had the courtesy to exit the floor onto the street before swinging fists.

Spitznagel got his first taste of a severe market crisis as an active trader in 1994. The economy had been expanding for three years. The bond market was on fire. And a new factor, the rise of the quants—traders or risk managers who use advanced mathematics and computers to predict the market or build complex financial products such as derivatives—was making things ever more complicated. The bond market wasn't just bigger, it was becoming more opaque as Wall Street's financial wizards learned to hide risk in these secretive mathematized fun-house machines. Derivatives also had the habit of magnifying volatility as the risk ramified from the underlying asset— interest rates, commodities, bonds—into the derivatives like a fuse setting off a bomb. Derivatives had another trait that made the quants giddy: Their growth was theoretically infinite. A company could only issue so many bonds, but a bank could sell a limitless number of derivative contracts linked to a single basket of bonds or commodity.

As the economy gained strength, Federal Reserve chairman Alan Greenspan began to fret about inflation. Slowly at first, he started cranking up short-term rates to stifle growth, dealing incremental pain to bond investors (as interest rates rise, the value of bonds declines). By August, the Fed had boosted rates nearly two percentage points. Then, in November, Greenspan swung for the fences: a staggering three-quarters of a percentage point increase, bringing the federal funds rate to 5½ percent.

The surprise move sparked a global bond-market panic. Traders all around Spitznagel blew up, including his idol, Tom Baldwin, who fought a losing battle against the unstoppable force of the crash. They'd grown complacent. Stanley Druckenmiller, one of the world's biggest hedge fund managers, lost $650 million *in two days*. Famously, the rate hikes bankrupted Orange County, California, which had made ludicrous bets on interest-rate derivatives. At the time, it was America's biggest municipal bankruptcy.

For Spitznagel, the great bond massacre of 1994 was when Klipp's lessons truly paid off. He never held on to a position after it took a small loss, which meant he was never at risk of losing everything. He even managed to eke out a healthy profit. The calm markets of the previous few years, he realized, had been an illusion—one that deceived some of the most sophisticated traders on the floor. It was an important lesson.

He'd survived his first test. After a few years, Spitznagel rose to the second highest stair in the pit, a hair's breadth from the Big Dogs like Baldwin. But he wasn't a Big Dog himself. Not yet.

> > < <

Spitznagel looked at the numbers and scratched his head. A quiet, eerie panic had broken out all around him. It was late October 1997. Figures flickered across his Bloomberg Terminal. Stocks worldwide were in free fall. Hong Kong's Hang Seng Index was down 10 percent, bringing a four-day decline to a total of 23 percent. Shock waves from the fall rippled across global markets, sending indexes in China, Japan, Germany, France, UK, and the U.S. down sharply. "There's global shock," a Morgan Stanley strategist said.

Markets had been wobbling up and down for months amid widespread currency turmoil in Asia. Currencies in Thailand, Malaysia, South Korea, Hong Kong, and elsewhere were cratering as the countries' economies buckled under the weight of the truckloads of debt they'd incurred during a red-hot expansion in the 1990s. The financial tailspin was later dubbed "the Asian flu."

Spitznagel was sitting amid rows of seasoned traders in the Manhattan office of Eastbridge Capital, a major dealer in U.S. Treasury bonds. He glanced at the trader next to him, a white-haired guy in his mid-forties who, on a daily basis, traded hundreds of millions in bonds. All across his screen: red numbers. His positions were getting crushed. He was losing millions. And yet, Spitznagel marveled, you couldn't tell if he was winning or losing. His face was a cipher.

Spitznagel had moved to New York City earlier that year. He'd given up his dream of being a pit trader, sensing that the rise of computer trading would have a profound impact on open-outcry trading. (It did.) He also sensed bigger fish at the money-center banks in New York—the ones that sent to the CBOT Big Dogs the massive orders that swept through the pits like a tornado. He'd branched out into other markets, such as options and Eurodollars, which were U.S. dollars in the accounts of the overseas branches of American banks, usually European branches. Since they sat outside the U.S., they weren't subject to the oversight of the Federal Reserve. That made them easier to trade.

As a proprietary or "prop" trader, Spitznagel was buying cheap options that would pay off in a market crash as investors piled into safe-haven assets such as Eurodollars. He'd come a long way from scalping corn futures on the floor of the CBOT. But it was still, at bottom, the Klipp trade, with small losses and the chance of a big gain, only now made through more exotic options.

It was a complex trade, fiendishly hard to manage, requiring constant attention. He'd gotten married that September. On his honeymoon in Santorini, Greece, he was constantly trading from his portable Bloomberg machine as global markets throbbed with the worsening turmoil of the Asian flu. Spitznagel's new wife, Amy, gave him endless grief about it.

Spitznagel made a mint on his market-crash bet when stocks collapsed in October. While the other traders around him at Eastbridge blew up, one by one, his positions surged as the crisis worsened and investors fled to safety. It wasn't enough to save the firm—Eastbridge shut down a year later—but it was enough to satisfy Spitznagel that his strategy had worked. His "trial and error" experiments, as he liked to call them, were proving themselves with the certainty provided by cold hard cash. His next experiment, the following year, made even more money when the giant quant-packed hedge fund Long-Term Capital Management blew up, triggering more panic.

That gave him the financial cushion to quit trading for a while and—hoping to add some scientific rigor to his pit-trader experiments—take what he called a "learning sabbatical." He enrolled in New York University's elite Courant Institute of Mathematical Sciences, one of the world's top applied mathematics schools and home to some of the brightest quantitative minds on Wall Street—including a freshly minted professor of finance, Nassim Nicholas Taleb.

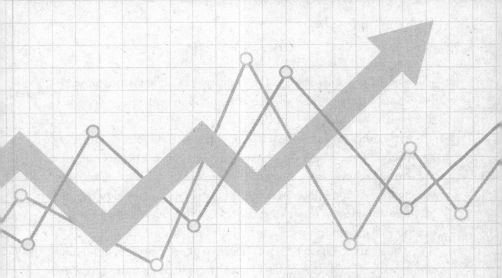

CHAPTER 5

THE WORLD ACCORDING TO NASSIM TALEB

Nassim Nicholas Taleb sat perched on the edge of his chair at a row of desks, eyes red and wide. He was on the trading floor of the giant investment bank First Boston at Park Avenue Plaza, a stone's throw from St. Patrick's Cathedral in midtown Manhattan. Pandemonium had broken out all around him. Digits were moving rapidly on his computer screen in ways he'd never seen before. It was October 19, 1987. Black Monday.

The stock market was crashing.

He had no idea why. No one did. Markets were going wild around the world *for no reason*. The twenty-seven-year-old trader stayed focused on his positions. They weren't in stocks. They were in Eurodollars. Rather, they were options on Eurodollars. For months he'd been building up a huge position in bargain-basement Eurodollar options that would, in theory, benefit from a big swing in volatility. Stocks had been ripping higher for years. Despite a few ominous wobbles in previous weeks, the bull market seemed unstoppable. Few expected that would change anytime soon—making Taleb's bets dirt cheap. No one else wanted them.

In the middle of the day, a trader, pale white and clearly suffering, approached him. "Don't they know that six sigma events only happen once in a lifetime?" he said in an eerily quiet voice. (A six sigma event is roughly two in a billion in a normal distribution; in reality they are far more common in the financial world, which doesn't obey the laws of a normal distribution—it has fat tails and Black Swans.)

"The market doesn't know," Taleb replied. Some people stood shell-shocked in the middle of the trading room quietly crying. Jimmy Powers, Taleb's boss, kept begging the prices on his screen to *stop moving*.

At the end of trading, Taleb left the office and began to walk, dazed, to his Upper East Side apartment. On the way he ran into a colleague and began chatting about the day's insane events. A woman walked up to them looking terrified. "Do the two of you know what's going on?" she asked, unnerving Taleb. Her eyes spoke of pure panic.

Back in his apartment, he started phoning colleagues to see how they were doing. A cousin called and said the police were outside his building at 72nd Street and First Avenue. Someone had jumped to their death from their upper-floor apartment. "It hit close to home," Taleb said later.

While other traders had suffered enormous pain that day, Taleb's portfolio had fared relatively well. But it wasn't career-making. That changed the following day, when Alan Greenspan at the Federal Reserve injected vast amounts of cash into the financial system. Taleb's positions in Eurodollars shot to the moon. Contracts he'd bought for $2 or $3 were selling for $300, $400, $500.

At the desk, he felt he was losing his mind as he watched his positions rip higher. He knew what was happening should *not* be happening. "Sell for three-fifty!" he screamed over the phone to his floor broker in the pit. A minute later, the broker called back. "Sold for four-fifty!" "Sell for five hundred!" "Sold for five-fifty!"

Statistically, the move was virtually unquantifiable, one that shouldn't have occurred in the history of the universe, or ten universes—in a normal world. As Taleb was learning, in finance things were often far from normal, and those who assumed they were normal would get them wrong again and again.

It was a lesson Taleb would never forget. He felt vindicated. His strategy of wagering on rare events, derided by other traders who racked up gains day after day, had worked like a miracle. At the time, it wasn't so much the result that mattered as the revelation that the methods and models those traders used were deeply flawed. It was mostly gut instinct and Taleb's deeply ingrained contrarian nature. But his experience planted the idea. If all these guys are so smart, why'd they blow up?

And why didn't I?

> > < <

Bombs rattled the basement ceiling. Clouds of dust feathered to the floor. Taleb swiped the dust from the pages of his book as the lights flickered. A teenager, Taleb was oblivious to the bombs. He'd grown used to them. Instead, he was entranced by *Our Man in Havana*, the Graham Greene novel about bumbling British spies in Cuba. School was closed. Life was boring (if you call boring living a short walking distance from the hot zone of a brutal civil war). Life, for Taleb, was books.

It was 1975. Beirut had erupted in a violent struggle between Christians and Muslims, a war that eventually left more than 90,000 dead (including 241 American military-service members who died in an October 1983 bombing of a Marines Corps barracks). Daily life ground to a halt. To occupy his time, huddling in his parents' basement, Taleb immersed himself in books: philosophy—Hegel, Marx, Toynbee, Fichte—as well as fiction by writers such as Graham Greene. Among the books he most loved was *Berlin Diary: The Journal of a Foreign Correspondent, 1934–1941* by the American journalist William Shirer (author of one of the first definitive histories of the

Nazis, *The Rise and Fall of the Third Reich*). What fascinated Taleb about *Berlin Diary* was its on-the-scene reportage of events leading up to World War II and how Shirer, among the most informed observers of Adolf Hitler's devious machinations, had no premonition of the world-shaking events to come. Taleb was experiencing a similar sense of distortion in his daily life. No one had seen the Lebanese Civil War coming. Even as it raged, most thought it would end any day. (It lasted fifteen years.) The lesson for Taleb, the burgeoning young skeptic: People have no clue about what's going to happen in the future. Only in retrospect do they look back and say they knew it all along.

Taleb's early life provides few clues to his unlikely future as a Wall Street derivatives trader, bestselling author, and cosmopolitan jet-setter. Born in 1960 in Amioun, Lebanon, a small, remote, predominantly Greek Orthodox town north of Beirut, he was rebellious in his youth, fiercely opposed to the ostentatious pursuit of luxury and wealth he saw all around him. At fifteen, he was jailed for allegedly attacking a policeman with a chunk of concrete during a student riot. A fellow student was shot dead in the mayhem.

That same year, 1975, the civil war broke out. Much of his family's large land holdings were destroyed in the fighting, including the family home. His mother's father, Fouad Nicholas Ghosn, a former deputy prime minister of Lebanon, fled the country and landed in a run-down apartment in Athens. A friend killed himself playing Russian roulette, an early lesson in the grim hazards of chance.

To escape the violence, Taleb fled Lebanon for the University of Paris, where he studied math and economics. He then moved to the U.S., earning a master's of business administration degree from the University of Pennsylvania's Wharton School, among the world's elite business schools—and a world away from the deadly streets of Beirut. Exposed to a conveyor belt of CEOs from some of the world's biggest companies, Taleb was struck by their superficiality, their stuffed shirts. He had a sneaking suspicion that they didn't have a clue about what was *really* going on at their companies.

In Wharton's cafeteria, foreign students congregated at a single lunch table. One of those students was a Sri Lankan with a strong British accent, Raj Rajaratnam. He struck Taleb as a person who'd be good at computers but would never be rich. Rajaratnam went on to found the Galleon Group hedge fund in New York, becoming very wealthy indeed—until he was arrested by the FBI for insider trading in 2009.

Taleb first learned about options at Wharton, and he fell irreversibly in love with them. He realized options had a curious trait—they were *nonlinear*. Profits that could be made on certain trades seemed far out of whack from the risk taken, the one or two bucks you paid for the contract. The risk was all held by the *seller* of the option. The buyer only risked losing his one or two bucks. What looked especially interesting, thought Taleb, were options for highly unlikely events—the big crashes that rattled markets or bankrupted companies. Such options were very cheap indeed. Their sellers were acting like tomorrow would be just like today. Taleb knew that was a foolish bet.

His first job out of Wharton was at Bankers Trust, a firm that was gaining a reputation on Wall Street as a gun-slinging risk taker rife with derivatives-crazed mad scientists (i.e., quants). He then moved onto French bank Indosuez to trade currency options, which give the holder the right to buy or sell a currency at a fixed exchange rate. That's when he had his first stroke of good luck. On September 22, 1985, the so-called G-5 nations—U.S., UK, France, Germany, and Japan—signed the Plaza Accord, an agreement to push down the dollar relative to the Japanese yen and German deutsche mark to help reduce the U.S. trade deficit. Taleb had been gorging on cheap currency options, which suddenly surged in value. By pure luck, he'd made a fantastic trade.

Taleb's boss started calling him "the Bobby Fischer of options," alluding to the Brooklyn chess prodigy who, at age twenty-nine, had become a media sensation by winning the world championship, on the way winning twenty straight matches against the top grandmasters in the world. Taleb's trade was so wildly profitable—think a $500 position that turns into $2 million—that the firm's computers couldn't calculate the gain. Indosuez's higher-ups back in France, suspicious, flew in a team of inspectors to go over the books. Every time they were scheduled to come onto the trading floor, Taleb's boss told him to get lost so he wouldn't be quizzed by the inspectors.

At age twenty-six, he joined the powerful investment bank First Boston. Based on the firm's trading floor at Park Avenue Plaza in New York, he worked under a New York Irishman from Brooklyn named Jimmy Powers (the same trader who later, on Black Monday, would beg the numbers on his computer screen to *stop moving*). Powers was a street-smart gut trader who Taleb thought might have a side job as a minor gangster. He'd describe trades to executives in the way Sonny Corleone might have explained a hit job in *The Godfather*. "We did this and then we did that, badaboom, badabing, and then it was all groovy," he'd boast.

As at Indosuez, Taleb started accumulating a large position in dirt-cheap out-of-the-money call options on Eurodollars ("out of the money" meant Taleb couldn't cash in on the options at the time because the Eurodollar contract was set at a price above where the currency was priced). It was a strange trade that didn't provide the steady profits the firm was looking for. One day Powers brought him into his office and handed him a breakdown of his strategy, showing far more down days than up days. Stone-faced, Taleb held the paper in front of Powers, slowly ripped it down the middle, and walked out of the office. He wasn't fired, and Powers left him alone after that. Lucky for them—he kept buying Eurodollars, positions that hit the jackpot in the crash of October 1987. The winnings gave Taleb what he liked to call *fuck you money*. In other words, freedom.

In 1991, after working for a few years at a Swiss bank, Taleb took up trading on the floor of the Chicago Mercantile Exchange. He wanted to learn the arcane art of open-outcry pit trading.

> > < <

As Nassim Taleb gazed out at the hectic scene before him, a mad cacophony of pit traders making crazed gestures, swinging their arms, screaming, shouting, he began to wonder what the strange sensation constricting his throat could be.

It took a nanosecond to figure it out.

Four security guards sprinted toward him as he struggled to peel the hands of another pit trader from around his throat. He'd made the fatal mistake of wandering onto the prized spot of a competitor—an unforgivable faux pas in the cut-throat world of the pit. As the security guards dragged his foe away, Taleb, shaking off the shock, thought, *I hate this fucking place.*

But he also loved it. It was nothing like the sedate desks of derivatives traders parked in front of blinking screens at First Boston. *These guys are animals. They can sense fear in the twitch of an eye. They detect things.* Many had known one another for decades. They'd visit over weekends for backyard picnics, wives hugging, kids playing. Monday morning, they were back at each other's throat—sometimes literally—viciously competing for trades.

When he joined the Merc, as traders called it, Taleb had to wear a humiliating badge that read "New Member." The first day he stepped onto the floor, a trader took him aside.

"Come over here, kiddo. See the guy over there?"

"Yes."

"His name is Ed. He made seven million dollars in seven years."

"Yes."

"He lost it all in seven seconds. Now you can go."

Taleb had come to the Merc because he wanted to know more about how the blinking prices he'd watched on his computer screen in New York formed on the floor. It took him about six months to learn how to read prices in the pit. He saw that locals—renegade independent traders like Spitznagel—scanned the floor for information, looking for the weak hand. Then, in a pack, they'd abruptly switch the price action, in a flash bidding much higher or lower to squeeze other traders to sell or buy. Action went from squeeze to squeeze and had virtually nothing to do with market fundamentals. Taleb learned more about market dynamics in those first six months than in all his years sitting at a desk.

He left the floor in 1993 and over the next few years grew restless, bouncing from CIBC Wood Gundy to BNP Paribas. But something was nagging him. Trading at the Merc required *a lot* of shouting—as well as occasionally wrestling with an enraged pit trader clamping his meaty fists around his neck. As a result, or so he thought, he'd developed a stubborn catch in his throat. After moving back to New York, he decided to have it checked out by a doctor on the Upper East Side. Setting down the pathology report, his doctor gave him the news.

"It's not as bad as it sounds. . . ."

It was throat cancer. Taleb stumbled from the building into slanting rain. Just as on the night of Black Monday, he began slow-walking the streets of New York in a trance. He soon found himself standing before a medical library. Reading about his affliction confused him more. Throat cancer was usually caused by smoking. Taleb didn't smoke. It usually hit older people. Taleb was in his thirties. It didn't make sense. It didn't fit the model. He was an outlier. He was a . . . Black Swan?

> > < <

In 1996, Taleb met Victor Niederhoffer, one of the most successful hedge fund managers in America, who spent his spare time playing tennis with George Soros. He'd made his name in the 1980s as the manager of Soros's massive fixed-income and foreign-exchange operations. Soros was so impressed by Niederhoffer's trading acumen that he had his own son work alongside him. In 1996, the Brooklyn-born trader was crushing it, eventually racking up a gain of 35 percent for the year. *MARHedge*, a newsletter that tracked the hedge fund industry, named him the world's number one hedge fund manager.

"Here was a guy living in a mansion with a thousand books, and that was my dream as a child," Taleb told Malcolm Gladwell for a 2002 *New Yorker* profile, in which Gladwell dubbed Taleb "Wall Street's principal dissident."

Despite his respect for millionaire traders such as Niederhoffer, with their big-brain libraries and sprawling mansions, Taleb suspected that, at bottom, their success was the result of a lot more luck than skill—random flips of the coin that came up ten tails in a row. That meant disaster—ten heads—was equally possible. They were fools of randomness. Confirming Taleb's doubts, Niederhoffer lost everything just a year later when the Dow plunged 554 points in a single day—losses that forced him to mortgage his house and sell his antique silver collection.

Taleb's skepticism of Wall Street and its mounting legions of quants was growing day by day. Complex derivatives and the mind-bending strategies that deployed them were ubiquitous. He had serious doubts about the models the strategies were based on, and he was increasingly outspoken about his concerns. One day in the mid-1990s, he decided to complete a project he'd been working on for years hashing out in precise detail what he believed was wrong with the models, which involved complicated trades to offset risk of losses in portfolios of stocks, bonds, and options. Walking down Park Avenue, at the corner of Forty-Fifth Street, he tossed his necktie into a garbage can and proceeded to seclude himself in his attic at home. Over the course of the next few years, he hammered out the dense 528-page tome, *Dynamic Hedging: Managing Vanilla and Exotic Options*. Published in 1996, it was the culmination of more than a decade of research and hard-won experience on the trading floor.

In an interview that year for the trade journal *Derivatives Strategy* titled "The World According to Nassim Taleb," he attacked the heavy reliance on math in the chaotic world of Wall Street, which had come to be known as *financial engineering* to give it a patina of a hard science.

"What problems do you have with financial engineering?" the interviewer asked.

"Some folks looked at the literature and saw differential equations and said, 'Gee it's like engineering,'" Taleb said. "Engineering relies on models because you can capture the relationships in the physical world very well. Models in the social sciences serve a different purpose. They make strong assumptions. Economists have known for a long time that math in their profession has a different meaning. It's just a tool, a way to express yourself."

"So real engineering could lead to a bridge that you could reliably drive cars across," the interviewer summarized. "But modeling in financial engineering isn't certain enough to run a portfolio."

"Exactly. In finance, you are not as confident about the parameters. The more you expand your model by adding parameters, the more you become trapped in an inextricable apparatus of relationships. It is called overfitting."

Taleb earned a Ph.D. in mathematics in 1998 from the University of Paris–Dauphine. Then he hit the jackpot again when Russia defaulted on its debt (a move that devastated Long-Term Capital Management). Prior to the default, Taleb had purchased a bunch of put options on Russian banks, positions that would pay off if the banks plunged. They did, handsomely.

> > < <

In a small classroom in Greenwich Village ripe with the scent of car exhaust and Chinese takeout, Taleb stood before a whiteboard scribbling equations. *Let $x1$, $x2 = n1$.* He was teaching a graduate course in finance at New York University's elite Courant Institute of Mathematical Sciences. Neil Chriss, a cerebral former Goldman Sachs quant, had started a program at NYU in applied mathematical finance, among the first of its kind. Chriss admired Taleb's trading tome, *Dynamic Hedging*, and hired him as an adjunct professor. The name of Taleb's course was Model Failure in Quantitative Finance.

One of his biggest complaints, he told his students, was with a widely used metric at banks called VaR—value at risk. It was a broad measurement of the risk of a bank's portfolio, of its exposure to extreme losses. Created by a group of math whizzes at J.P. Morgan and elsewhere on Wall Street in the late 1980s and early 1990s, the metric measured how much the assets in a portfolio had moved up or down historically, with various tweaks for how much the assets were correlated with one another (e.g., bonds and gold often move in the same direction, safe-haven utilities and risky tech stocks go in the opposite direction). The problem, Taleb explained, was that the past wasn't a good predictor of correlations during extreme events— the only ones that really matter (small daily market moves can't blow you up). It was a recipe for disaster, because bank managers using VaR were flying blind, making bets that carried hidden risks—a lesson many would learn a decade later when the Global Financial Crisis hit.

"VaR is a school for sitting ducks," he told his class.

It also spelled an opportunity. The increased use of flawed risk models, of hyper-leveraged hedge funds and investment banks, meant the financial system, more than ever, was a castle built on sand (or TNT). It meant more collapses, more blowups, more crashes. Taleb had been making money on crashes and blowups for nearly fifteen years, sometimes by accident. Increasingly he began to toy with the notion of a systematic trading strategy to exploit Wall Street's hidden, quant-contrived flaws.

He'd won his battle with throat cancer. Two years of radiation treatment eliminated the disease. But the brush with fate caused him to reconsider the course of his career. The pressure of trading— or more important, the pressure of avoiding the career-ending risk of blowing up—might have been responsible for his illness, he worried. He'd been considering starting up a hedge fund, which would give him more control over the daily grind. Importantly, it had to be a hedge fund that *could never blow up*.

That's when he got a fortuitous call from a reclusive tycoon named Donald Sussman. Sussman's hedge fund, Paloma Partners, had been shellacked in the market turmoil of 1998. He was a major investor in D. E. Shaw, a massive quant-driven New York firm that hemorrhaged money that year. Sussman learned through the grapevine that an obscure Lebanese-American trader-mathematician had actually *made money* in 1998. The same trader who had made millions in the great crash of October 1987. Such a trader, thought Sussman, could help protect him from future debacles.

He reached out to Taleb and pitched him on the idea. He told Taleb he'd seed him with $50 million to start and give him office space at Paloma's headquarters in Greenwich, Connecticut, a town that was quickly becoming a hub of America's booming hedge fund industry. Taleb would call his hedge fund Empirica Capital, a nod to his focus on observed, empirical evidence and experience rather than theoretical, quantitative castles in air.

As Taleb geared up to launch the fund, Neil Chriss at NYU's Courant told him about a new student in the program named Mark Spitznagel who'd worked for years as a pit trader in Chicago and a prop trader in New York. Taleb was impressed that a meathead pit trader would be interested in mathematical finance and thought he'd be an ideal partner at his new fund.

"Can he start today?" Taleb asked.

"Ha, we'll see," Chriss replied.

Chriss called Spitznagel. Fortuitously, it turned out he was familiar with Taleb's textbook, *Dynamic Hedging*, which he believed had helped him make the conceptual transition from the bare-knuckle, intuitive arena of pit trading to the complex mathematical world of derivatives.

"You should talk to Nassim," Chriss said.

Later that same day, Taleb rang Spitznagel and asked him if he could meet in his office in the Courant Building that evening.

"Sure thing," Spitznagel said. "See you soon."

After class that night, Spitznagel climbed the stairs to Taleb's office. The two quickly discovered they were cut from the same cloth, finishing each other's sentences as they discussed their interest in dirt-cheap trades that had the potential for explosive gains or their fondness for the writings of the Viennese philosopher Karl Popper. Spitznagel agreed with a handshake to team up with Taleb. His "learning sabbatical" at Courant, which had lasted roughly two days, was over. Empirica launched a month later.

CHAPTER 6

THE TURKEY PROBLEM

Brandon Yarckin was always a creature of contradictions. As a teenager, he was short and skinny. But his head was so large his friends joked that he looked like an orange stuck on a toothpick. When he joined his middle-school football team, the only helmets that would fit him were high-school varsity-size. He was innately conservative but reveled in daredevil skateboard tricks. After entering Duke University at seventeen, having already amassed a full year of credits from advanced-placement classes in high school, he decided to major in economics—and immediately decided the central tenets of modern economic theory were bullshit.

"The first lecture was about efficient markets," he recalled, referring to the theory that the prices for all markets immediately reflect all available information, hence making them thoroughly *efficient*. The theory is a corollary of the random-walk hypothesis in which the future of the market is unknowable, a random flip of the coin. "The professor spent an entire class talking about the market being efficient. I raised my hand with skeptical questions. It seemed stupid to me. It didn't make any sense. Why are people even in markets?"

It is a conundrum that has twisted the brain of many an economics student. If markets are always instantly efficient, why do traders exist? In part, the theory goes, the traders *are* the vehicle for making the market efficient. If a stock is too high, they sell it. If a stock is too low, they buy it. But *too high* or *too low* seem to inherently violate the efficient markets hypothesis, which also proposes that traders cannot consistently beat the market. How could they if the market was always right?

Despite Yarckin's skepticism, he graduated in three years with an economics degree and in 2000 found himself in New York City interviewing for jobs at major financial institutions. He turned down an offer from Morgan Stanley. Then he got an appealing offer from Cantor Fitzgerald doing sales—pitching clients on various trades— from an office on the 107th floor of the World Trade Center. He was about to accept when he got another offer from KBC Financial Products (*financial products* are Wall Street code words for fancy derivatives). KBC was an elite brokerage that had just been spun out of D. E. Shaw, the giant New York hedge fund that had inflicted so much pain on Donald Sussman in 1998. It was picked up by KBC Bank, a Belgian firm trying to make inroads into America's booming financial industry.

Yarckin took the KBC job. A year later, every Cantor employee who reported to work at the World Trade Center on the morning of September 11 was killed.

At KBC, Yarckin was at the center of New York's metastasizing derivatives industry. His job was to find the other side of a trade for KBC's clients. If a client called and said, "I want to buy ten thousand put options on IBM," it was Yarckin's job to call everyone he knew at the desks of other firms to try to find sellers of ten thousand put options. More important, Yarckin had to find trades that were cheaper than his competitors', a skill he quickly mastered.

In 2001, Yarckin flew to Tampa Bay to attend an options conference. During a break, he lined up for lunch. In front of him stood a trim balding man with a salt-and-pepper beard—Nassim Taleb. The two started talking and, after gathering their trays of food, sat down together at a table. Taleb, as usual, did most of the talking.

After returning to New York, Yarckin made himself familiar with Empirica and its head trader, Mark Spitznagel. He quickly realized Empirica would be an ideal client. Over the course of the next few months, Yarckin repeatedly nagged Spitznagel to let him handle orders for Empirica. The two hit it off. They had many shared interests, such as the political philosophy of libertarianism and skateboarding. Soon the pair were daredeviling together along the treacherous byways of Central Park and its kamikaze taxi drivers. Yarckin in short order became Empirica's biggest broker.

Taleb and Spitznagel had gotten off to an impressive start in 2000. Almost as if they were, God forbid, *lucky*. They were practically printing money as the dot-com bubble collapsed in spectacular fashion. At times they were making a profit almost *every day*, ending the year with a gain of nearly 60 percent—a dramatic performance when many other hedge funds were sputtering. Donald Sussman, at the time Empirica's only investor, was very pleased with his little experiment.

The office, parked on the outskirts of Greenwich, was a tiny affair, with a small trading room overlooking an expanse of trees. The hum of planes from the nearby Westchester County Airport was a constant white noise in the background, vying with the classical refrains of Bach, Mahler, Wagner. An oft-muted TV tuned to the financial markets channel CNBC hung in a corner. The walls were largely blank except for a giant dry-erase whiteboard always dense with illegible math equations, and a small pen-and-ink drawing of Karl Popper, aptly described in Gladwell's *New Yorker* profile as the patron saint of Empirica. (George Soros was another Popper acolyte.)

One of the philosopher's most important ideas, the Falsification Principle, asserts that science doesn't advance by proving theories true—it advances by proving theories *false*. Hence the European belief that all swans are white was proven false when sailors discovered black swans in Australia. "No number of sightings of white swans can prove the theory that all swans are white. The sighting of just one black one may disprove it," Popper wrote in his 1934 book, *The Logic of Discovery*.

The theory is a recipe for caution, especially for a trader dabbling in complex derivatives—Buffett's weapons of mass destruction. You may think you know all about the world around you, where it's going, why. Falsification showed that, in fact, you might not—and Black Swans might be lurking around the corner to prove how wrong you are.

To illustrate the idea, Taleb liked to use the example of a turkey on Thanksgiving. He called it the Turkey Problem. Every day of its life, a turkey is fed by a farmer. The bird (a special one capable of abstract thought) theorizes that this will continue forever, that the farmer has a great love for turkeys. Until Thanksgiving, the turkey's Black Swan—its ruin problem. The English philosopher Bertrand Russell used the same analogy, though he chose a chicken for his trusting doomed bird. Even further back, the über-skeptical Scot David Hume asserted that no one can know *with absolute certainty* that the sun will rise tomorrow, a claim that became known in philosophy as the Problem of Induction. This way of looking at things reduces our ability to predict future events from 100 percent to some lower statistical measure. For example, we can claim we believe the sun will rise with 99.9999 percent certainty, based on all the mornings in the past when the sun has risen. But we can never say it with 100 percent certainty. Who knows, maybe a black hole cooked up in a mad scientist's lab will swallow up the solar system in a nanosecond.

Inspired by debates over issues such as the Problem of Induction and the Turkey Problem, Empirica was very much like a laboratory experiment operating in real time as Taleb and Spitznagel searched for the optimal strategy to cash in on crashes while limiting losses. Using computer programs with names such as Igor, the firm would download hundreds of thousands of option contracts every night. The next day, the program would recommend a series of trades. Taleb and Spitznagel found an edge in trading against traditional order flow by big institutions and knowing how various dealers were positioned—which might provide advantageous prices. By tracking how dealers needed to trade around and lighten up on big positions they'd acquired from their customers, Spitznagel could figure out where to get the best deals. For instance, if Goldman Sachs had a client that wanted to sell $1 million worth of far-out-of-the-money S&P 500 put options, Spitznagel's contacts on the Street, knowing he was always in the market to buy such puts, would alert him to the potential trade. Hedge funds and other investors sold puts to banks for a number of reasons, but mainly because they are simply raising cash with the sale—selling puts was a reliable way for a fund to make money (just as long as the market didn't crash). The sellers couldn't believe their luck. "Who are these suckers, these idiots buying this crap?" they thought. "No way is the market crashing twenty percent in the next month." Empirica was becoming a reliable idiot to take the other side of those *sucker* trades.

"This was a discovery process, this was a lab, we were figuring stuff out," Spitznagel recalls. "We were all over the place." Spitznagel manned the trading desk. Taleb worked on math problems and met with investors.

At times Spitznagel reverted to his mad-dog pit-trader persona when hammering out deals with brokers over the phone. "That's fucking bullshit and you fucking know it!" he'd shout, red in the face, when told a price for a basket of options that he knew was a rip-off. "Don't call me again for a week!," slamming down the phone.

Empirica's strategy of betting on crashes was designed to work in combination with other strategies to balance out a firm's risk profile. Too much risk in stocks? Add a dash of Empirica. It wasn't a stand-alone strategy. No one would put all their cash in an Empirica-like hedge fund, twiddling their thumbs for years waiting for a crash.

It was also entirely unique. For months, even years, the strategy could look like a loser. Like Klipp said, you have to look like an ass and feel like an ass. Then, suddenly, it would be phenomenally successful. Spitznagel likened it to a pianist who could barely play chopsticks transforming overnight into a virtuoso with the skills of a Rachmaninoff.

Taleb and Spitznagel had wildly contrasting approaches to trading. Spitznagel operated purely by the book, following the precise system they'd painstakingly formulated and tested—the Black Swan protocol. Taleb was more shoot from the hip, trading at times by gut feeling rather than a set formula, in the hopes of front-running a spurt of volatility. *How bearish am I today?* Taleb might ask himself as he settled down before his Bloomberg machine. He'd grow agitated when Spitznagel played music from one of his favorite composers, Mahler. "Mahler is bad for volatility," he'd complain.

Down the hall, a new hedge fund bankrolled by Sussman was starting up—Amaranth Advisors. Empirica shared a bathroom with the firm. Six years later, it would blow up from bad bets on natural gas, losing nearly $7 billion in a matter of days—at the time the biggest trading collapse in modern financial history, surpassing Long-Term Capital Management's epic debacle. Luckily for Sussman, he'd abandoned the fund a few years before, saying it had gotten too big.

Taleb continued to teach at NYU. After classes, he often held court at The Odeon, a trendy restaurant in Tribeca, exchanging thoughts and ideas with friends such as Aaron Brown and Neil Chriss on mathematics, philosophy, chess, poetry, physics. Spitznagel attended once, and hated it. For him, the conversations were too theoretical, speculative, and philosophical—not grounded in the cold, hard reality of how the world really worked.

Empirica's chart-busting performance in 2000 started making the rounds at Wall Street's watering holes and watercoolers. The fund had performed exactly like a hedge fund should—zigging when the rest of the world zagged. It was, literally, a pure hedging fund. Outside investors started clamoring for a piece of the action. Taleb made for a peculiar front man. One of his quirks was a manic dedication to bicycling. Nearly every day, weather permitting, he'd bike the ten or so miles from his home in Larchmont to the Paloma office in Greenwich. Often, he didn't change out of his tight-fitting bicycle shorts into a suit, much less jeans, even when meeting prospective investors. One day, Yarckin brought in a group from KBC. There was Taleb in his bicycle shorts, beard peppered with crumbs. As they asked him about his strategy and market forecasts—standard questions any investor might ask a fund manager they were considering giving millions of dollars to—Taleb grew exasperated.

"Who fucking cares," he snapped. "Don't ask stupid questions."

They did not invest.

It was the beginning of a great boom in hedge funds as institutional investors such as pension funds began piling in. Hedge funds had long been viewed as the Wild West of the investing world, run by gunslingers like George Soros or Paul Tudor Jones, who placed billion-dollar bets based on gut instinct. But increasingly, with the rise of mathematical trading strategies crafted by a new breed of traders known as "quants," hedge funds were gaining a higher level of respect in the more levelheaded corners of Wall Street. In 1999, just $189 billion in assets were managed by hedge funds. By 2007, just before the Global Financial Crisis struck, hedge funds managed $2.3 trillion (the total stood at $5.1 trillion in 2022).

Despite the new institutional love for hedge funds, Empirica's engine began to sputter in 2001. The market regained its footing and volatility plunged. The stress of losing money day after day began to weigh on Taleb. He and Spitznagel engaged in epic shouting matches about arcane mathematical theories such as the implications of the Pareto-Levy distribution, a quantitative method to measure extreme phenomena. The feuds didn't impair their growing friendship and mutual respect, though, and often the two would take long walks in the woods outside the Paloma campus, swapping ideas about how to improve the Empirica strategy.

> > < <

A week before the September 11 attacks, Taleb published his first book for a general audience, *Fooled by Randomness*. A tour de force of eclectic mini-essays spanning behavioral psychology, statistics, philosophy, ancient history, and more, the book at its core was a dagger aimed at the heart of the tale told by Wall Street's chest-pounding Masters of the Universe. That tale, in its most basic form, was this: We're smarter than you, give us your money. *Bullshit*, Taleb declaimed, over some 250 pages. Most of these so-called geniuses were simply lucky, the beneficiaries of random chance. The coin had flipped in their favor more than 50 percent of the time—a trend that would eventually come to an end, incinerating investors' money in the process as the hedge fund managers decamped to the Bahamas in their private yachts. The market was random. Those who thought they'd detected a pattern, and traded on it, were fools. (Taleb never claimed that no investors had any skill, just that *most* didn't.)

Malcom Gladwell said the book "is to conventional Wall Street wisdom approximately what Martin Luther's 95 theses were to the Catholic Church." It quietly became a cult hit among hedge fund managers and traders, most of whom assumed they were the ones with genuine skill, not dumb luck—until they, too, blew up.

Among the many quirks of the book is the introduction of a pair of fictional characters who represent alternate approaches to trading— Fat Tony and Nero Tulip. Fat Tony is the Brooklyn-born trader who, as his name suggests, operates from the gut. He uses intuition and a hard-won bullshit detector to repeatedly defeat the business-school elites with their Wharton degrees and gaudy mansions. Characteristically, he tilts toward the gritty, seedy side of Wall Street, part Gordon Gekko, part Al Capone.

Nero Tulip—a thinly disguised Nassim Taleb—is the buttoned-down intellectual who designs a trading system that can never blow up. Like Taleb, Tulip is a mathematician with a specialty in statistics. Like Taleb, he becomes a floor trader on the Merc. Like Taleb, he moves to a New York investment firm. Like Taleb, he has an "early moment of glory." Like Taleb, he teaches a seminar, on "probabilistic thinking," at NYU.

Tulip's trading style also bears a strong resemblance to Spitznagel's Klipp-esque strategy of immediately cutting losses. "Nero rapidly exits trades after a predetermined loss," Taleb wrote. "I love taking small losses," Tulip proclaims.

There were also traces of Taleb in Fat Tony, the streetwise foil to professorial Tulip. Like Taleb, Fat Tony scoffs at traders who think they can predict the market and loves to take the other side of their misguided wagers, betting on a blowup.

Taleb also gestured at Empirica's crash-bang strategy.

"In the markets, there is a category of traders who have inverse rare events, for whom volatility is often the bearer of good news," he wrote. "These traders lose money frequently, but in small amounts, and make money rarely, but in large amounts. I call them crisis hunters. I am happy to be one of them."

> > < <

One Tuesday afternoon, during a layover in London, Taleb was having lunch with a friend when he got a call from Spitznagel. "Some amateur pilot just flew a plane into the World Trade Center," Spitznagel told him, echoing the initial widespread assumption that morning—September 11—that the Al Qaeda terrorist attack was a random accident.

Seventeen minutes after the first strike, as emergency responders rushed to the scene, a second Boeing 767 crashed into the south tower of the trade center, making it instantly clear that this was no accident. By 10:30 a.m., the Twin Towers lay in ruins, mangled heaps of metal and glass. A new phase of modern world history had begun—the Age of Terror. To most Americans, it was the Black Swan of Black Swans.

The markets closed almost immediately after the attacks began, and stayed closed for a week. That meant Empirica couldn't cash in on its positions, which had rapidly surged in value that morning. When the New York Stock Exchange reopened on Monday, September 17, stocks crashed. The Dow industrials fell 684 points, at the time its biggest one-day trading loss. By the end of the week, the Dow was off 14 percent. An estimated $1.4 trillion in market value had evaporated.

It would have seemed an ideal market for Empirica. But fears of another terrorist attack were rampant. Some of the firm's investors, including Paloma, didn't want to cash in. Empirica could have made a fortune, protecting their investors from big losses, but it didn't. Rather than sell their options and capitalize on the market's sudden nosedive, Taleb and Spitznagel held on to them just in case another attack came and the market crashed all over again—a big mistake, as it turned out, because fears of a follow-up attack faded and the market quickly rallied. At the time, the size of one's portfolio hardly seemed to matter. America, led by the Bush administration, was steeling itself for its forever war against terrorism.

Still, Taleb and Spitznagel were taking notes for the next crash, whenever it came along. Lessons were being learned as they continually modified their trading protocols.

After September 11 and the publication of *Fooled by Randomness*, Taleb started gaining a wider reputation as an iconoclast trader and skeptic. On November 23, he gave an interview on CNBC, the financial news channel—his first of many national TV appearances. The host, Ron Insana, introduced Taleb.

"He runs the crisis-hunting hedge fund Empirica Capital and is author of a new book called *Fooled by Randomness*."

Insana seemed perplexed by Taleb's idiosyncratic take on the market. "Most get blindsided by unexpected rounds of volatility. You make a business of trying to play the volatility and offer your clients a hedge against unforeseen acts. How do you do that exactly?"

"It's not a very complicated trading strategy," Taleb said. "I mean, making money on volatility is very simple. If you see the S&P or the Dow Jones moving more than two hundred points, twenty points for the S&P, two hundred points for the Dow Jones, you know that there is volatility. The problem is that there are not that many of these days."

Insana asked Taleb how he could predict these big events.

You don't, Taleb said. "You've got to be patient, rule number one, very patient, as patient as you can. . . . You bleed. It's like losing a piece of skin every day. You have to sit down, there's a long volatility strategy, and bleed."

Taleb likened the strategy to having a gift shop but not knowing when Christmas is going to come. "The Christmas season comes randomly, but you're going to pay the rent day after day after day."

"In short, you like to buy insurance," Insana said.

"It's more than insurance," Taleb replied. "It's aggressive insurance."

> > < <

One day in late 2001 Taleb made an appearance on a New York radio station. In the station's office, he ran into the writer Susan Sontag. Someone told her the exotic-looking bearded gentleman in the studio had written a book about randomness. Curious, she approached him. When she discovered he was a trader, she declared she was *against the market system* and stomped away as Taleb sputtered in confusion.

Later that day, Taleb met a man he'd soon come to idolize: Benoit Mandelbrot. The maverick French mathematician, inventor of fractal geometry, and pioneer of chaos theory, was giving a lecture at NYU's Courant Institute about two seemingly disconnected topics—fractals and finance. Taleb was intrigued. He had no idea how finance could have anything to do with fractals.

Fractals, Mandelbrot had shown over decades of research, pop up everywhere. In science, engineering, in clouds, flowers, and snowflakes. A key idea behind fractal geometry is self-similarity (or self-affinity). By way of explanation Mandelbrot had asked, years before in 1967: How long is the coast of Britain? Viewing the rocky shore from a plane, or staring at it with a magnifying glass, you'll see the same zigzag pattern of rough undulations. The answer to the question, therefore, depends on the size of your ruler. The veins in a leaf look like a branch that looks like a tree, a rock can look like a mountain, etc.

Fractals are determined by power laws, the mathematical expression of the nonlinear. As you move from the leaf to the branch to the tree, you are making big nonlinear jumps in scale.

That was bad news for financial models. Mandelbrot had argued—for decades—that the traditional models used in finance that depend on Gaussian mathematics—i.e., bell curves—were highly flawed. Deployed by nineteenth-century mathematician Carl Friedrich Gauss for astronomical measurements, the bell curve (commonly known as the *Gaussian*) had become ubiquitous in financial and economic models such as Value at Risk. It measured phenomena that had smooth step-by-step transitions, with most samples falling within the safe confines of the middle of the bell curve.

The bell curve didn't capture the extreme volatility that can occur in a fractal world—the world of power laws, sudden jumps, wild leaps. Much of Mandelbrot's work was based on power laws driving all sorts of phenomena, from cotton prices to income distributions to population densities in cities. Rather than adding up in linear fashion (1 + 2 + 3 etc.), which fit well within the bell curve, things governed by power laws can make dramatic, unexpected moves that live in the tails of the curve.

Mandelbrot—his big-eared, balding basketball-size head glistening over an Apple laptop perched on the podium—told the NYU audience filled with quants, traders, and finance professors that if the bell curve truly captured the reality of the stock market, big crashes in the market like Black Monday would never happen. It was a problem, he said, that went back a century to the work of a neurotic French economist in Paris.

"Prices of course go up and down, that was known to everybody, and there are all kinds of nice maxims about it," Mandelbrot said in a thick French accent. "In 1900, an incredible genius looked at the problem. His name was Louis Bachelier. Nobody noticed him. He had a very miserable life. But he wrote in 1900 a [dissertation] in mathematics, believe it or not, called 'The Theory of Speculation.' Speculation meant speculation on the stock market or bond market. And he introduced for the first time in loose and incomplete fashion Brownian motion," he said, referring to the nineteenth-century observation by Scottish botanist Robert Brown that the motion of pollen in a liquid is a random process.

"Now, the idea of Bachelier was more or less that prices vary at random. You can't predict them. You toss a coin. If it's heads, your price goes up. It's tails, price goes down. And you go on and on and on. Now, much later a whole theory of the stock market occurred on the basis that this model of Bachelier's is indeed a representation of reality. And the size of these increments of price, this size is what's called volatility. The model assumes constant volatility."

Mandelbrot displayed a chart showing a historical series of variations of financial prices, some real, some fake based on simple models he'd created. "All these phenomena have a very strange characteristic. They have very big peaks all the time. And the peaks don't arise by themselves. They arise in the middle of very great volatility, then there are periods of very, very low volatility. There are periods where volatility suddenly changes. Volatility, as you try to grab it in these sequences, either the fake or the real ones, is something very, very elusive. In fact, it's impossible to grasp."

According to the Gaussian (or bell curve) models, such big jumps in volatility should never happen, Mandelbrot said. "As you see here," he said, "they happen all the time. One gets in a situation where the large values dominate everything very strongly."

Over the last decade, only ten days really mattered in terms of gains and losses. "The great fortunes were made in a very few days. And great ruins happened in very few days. So one gets into a situation which is very, very unsettling. That is, in this context, only the very few rare events count overwhelmingly. The rest count hardly at all."

Taleb was mesmerized. Mandelbrot was describing the exact experience he'd had as a trader in which only a few big days had mattered. After the talk, he introduced himself and asked Mandelbrot why he bothered himself with the mundane world of finance—a world Taleb viewed as a great place to make fuck-you money before moving on to higher, ethereal worlds of literature, theory, and philosophy.

"Data," Mandelbrot said, smiling, "A gold mine of data."

Taleb's career had centered on the study of uncertainty, volatility, and its impact on option prices. He'd written a whole book about it. But he'd never realized there was a connection between fat tails and fractal geometry and all the fascinating math behind it. Here was a whole new way to think about randomness and Black Swans, he realized.

Taleb in short order became a close collaborator with Mandelbrot, who lived just a few miles away from his home in Larchmont. In 2006, they cowrote "A Focus on the Exceptions That Prove the Rule," an article that's a snapshot of major themes contained in *The Black Swan*. "The traditional Gaussian way of looking at the world begins by focusing on the ordinary, and then deals with exceptions or so-called outliers as ancillaries," they wrote. "But there is also a second way, which takes the exceptional as a starting point and deals with the ordinary in a subordinate manner—simply because that 'ordinary' is less consequential."

More often than not, rather than discussing the nature of uncertainty and Black Swans, their conversations revolved around literature, history, art, and the vast array of fascinating people Mandelbrot had encountered during his long career (Margaret Mead, Noam Chomsky, Robert Oppenheimer, Stephen Jay Gould, and John von Neumann, to name a few). Mandelbrot, who died in 2010, would have an outsize influence on *The Black Swan*. In fact, the book is dedicated to him.

But Taleb's new insights into fractal forces at work in market crashes didn't help him where it really counted at the time—at Empirica.

> > < <

Empirica was bleeding. It lost 8 percent in 2001. Over the next two years, it suffered from a ho-hum turn-and-churn stock market that didn't swerve up or down much at all. Alan Greenspan's Federal Reserve, in response to the September 11 terrorist attacks, flooded the financial system with cheap money. Growth didn't surge, but it did inch higher, fueled by a ballooning housing bubble across the country—dry tinder for the coming Global Financial Crisis.

The day-to-day losses, the constant bleeding, were wearing on Taleb. Spitznagel told him not to focus on the daily profit-and-loss, a measure of the fund's incremental success or failure. Taleb watched it constantly. "You've got to love to lose," Spitznagel said again and again.

"Nassim would be euphoric when we were doing well and despondent when we weren't," Spitznagel recalls. "It was bad for his health."

There was another irritant that preyed on Taleb's mental health. Clients or prospective clients kept asking him why he couldn't match the performance of another successful trading firm that also claimed to have a cutting-edge option-trading strategy: Bernard L. Madoff Investment Securities LLC.

"If you're so smart, why can't you do the same as Madoff?" they'd ask. "How come he can do it, and you can't?"

Then they'd show him Madoff's performance—the uncanny 15 or 20 percent returns per month, every month, year after year. Taleb tried to replicate a strategy on his computer that would provide such unearthly gains. He couldn't.

"Those returns are impossible," he'd tell them.

"You're just jealous," they'd snap back. The returns, of course, were fictional. Madoff was running the largest Ponzi scheme in history, and in 2009 he went to prison, where he spent the rest of his life.

Taleb and Spitznagel continued to tinker with their strategy, but Taleb was steadily losing interest. The sprawling feature article by Malcom Gladwell in the *New Yorker* about Taleb and Empirica, called "Blowing Up: How Nassim Taleb Turned the Inevitability of Disaster into an Investment Strategy," ignited a burst of interest in the fund—and nursed Taleb's bruised ego. The article positioned him as the antihero of Wall Street and captured something of the jittery zeitgeist of the time. Just a few years before, the dot-com revolution had changed the world—seemingly for the better. America's economy was charging ahead full-tilt. Capitalism and democracy were spreading throughout the globe. Even Russia was holding elections. By 2002, all that was in doubt. The dot-com bubble had popped. Terrorists had laid the country low, and the U.S. had started a war of revenge in Afghanistan, with the Bush administration saber-rattling about Iraq. And the economy was crawling, slowly, out of a recession. Here was a guy who seemed to explain the insanity—things blow up all the time and no one can predict it! And all those fat cats on Wall Street? Charlatans fooled by randomness.

It almost made you feel good about yourself.

> > < <

Taleb looked out into the audience and wiped a trickle of sweat from his forehead. It was 2004. He was giving a talk in Rome about a topic he'd introduced in *Fooled by Randomness*: Black Swans. He bluntly told the audience, packed full of financiers, that they were clueless regarding the biggest risks they faced. By their sour expressions, he could tell they weren't taking his message well. They were, in fact, very pissed off. After the lecture, the chairman of the conference told the audience there'd be no questions for the speaker. Taleb, walking away from the podium, looked around nervously, half-fearing the organizers might toss him from the building.

Then the next speaker took the podium. It was Daniel Kahneman, a Princeton University psychologist who the previous year had won the Nobel Memorial Prize in Economic Sciences for his groundbreaking work, with Amos Tversky, showing a variety of curious biases in human decision-making under uncertainty. Kahneman's work ran counter to the long-standing assumption in economics, going back to Adam Smith, that humans are rational decision-makers driven by self-interest. Kahneman and Tversky showed that people are actually pretty confused about lots of things and often make irrational decisions based on such factors as (usually false) perceptions of fairness, overattachment to random figures, aversion to loss, and more.

For instance, people react favorably when told an operation has a 90 percent likelihood of success. But when told the operation has a 10 percent chance of failure, they react negatively.

Taleb's fears of forceful ejection were quickly relieved as Kahneman's first statement was that he would elaborate on the points made by the previous speaker, which he *fully agreed with*.

Taleb and Kahneman soon became fast friends, meeting in cafes or at Kahneman's Greenwich Village apartment, or taking long drives together—including one five-hour trip to Delaware during which they got lost and were then tailgated by an outraged driver whom Taleb had flipped off. The field Kahneman and Tversky pioneered, behavioral finance, was catnip for a human-rationality skeptic like Taleb, convinced as he was that most successful professional traders are more lucky than skilled, especially in areas of extreme risk. People's knee-jerk aversion to loss, to the 10 percent risk of dying on the operating table, helped explain why most traders would rather make small, daily incremental gains—with the risk of blowing up—rather than lots of small losses (loving to lose) and infrequent, massive jackpots.

That November, Taleb submitted a paper for a Pentagon-sponsored conference on risk. Called "The Black Swan: Why Don't We Learn That We Don't Learn?," it claimed that history is driven by big unpredictable events—outliers. "Our ability to predict large-scale deviations that change history has been close to zero," he stated in the paper. We're unable to see outliers coming because we base our future expectations on past events, like a driver navigating a road by scanning the rearview mirror.

Taleb had gotten a real-world look at a looming Black Swan earlier that year when a young *New York Times* reporter (and future Covid-19 anti-vax conspiracy spreader) named Alex Berenson walked into his office with a top-secret risk report for the government-backed mortgage giant Fannie Mae. The report, obtained by Berenson from a former Fannie Mae employee, showed that a sudden 1.5 percentage point increase in interest rates would cause the firm to lose about half its market value. The report also showed that Fannie Mae was levered at a 50 to 1 ratio—that is, for every dollar it owned it had $50 in debt, an explosive amount of leverage. Fannie Mae's models might have sparked fear in the institution's risk compliance officers but for the fact that interest rates had remained relatively stable.

Bullshit, Taleb told Berenson. "The fact that they haven't blown up in the past doesn't mean that they're not going to blow up in the future," he said. "The math is bogus."

Five years later Fannie Mae and its sibling Freddie Mac were bailed out by the U.S. government amid the meltdown in the American subprime housing market. They didn't fail because of a sharp increase in interest rates. Rather, Americans across the country were defaulting on their mortgages as housing prices plunged nationwide—a turn of events that wasn't even in the models.

While Taleb's profile as an iconoclastic trader was rising, he was hitting a low point as a manager of money. Clients watching the stock market shoot higher in 2003 would call in outrage as Empirica consistently bled losses. While the clients might understand Empirica's trading strategy, they found it difficult to endure emotionally. All they could see was the lost cash and how much they could have made if that money was in the market—or another hedge fund.

Taleb hit on a notion he'd learned from Kahneman called *anchoring*. It worked like this. Say you're shopping on Amazon and see a fleece jacket that costs $500. Seems like a lot for a jacket. Then you see a similar jacket that costs $1,500. Suddenly that $500 jacket doesn't seem so expensive. Retailers exploit this bias all the time by offering discounts. Selling a $500 jacket with a 50 percent discount makes it seem like a bargain.

Taleb decided to ask clients to give him a figure for how much they were willing to lose in a year, like an insurance premium for crash protection. He later gave them reports showing how much better they did than they'd estimated. "It was a wonder pill," he later wrote. "Clients became excited as they treated the money not lost as if it were a profit."

To shake things up, Empirica moved to a small office on the

Upper East Side of Manhattan—making Taleb's bicycle commute from Larchmont even more hair-raising. Spitznagel had taken up skateboarding again and loved to ride to the office from his apartment on 68th Street and Central Park West. One day, a taxi ran a red light just as he was barreling downhill through an intersection. In a panic, he dived off the board and bounced along the road. As the taxi sped away, Spitznagel pulled himself up from the ground and dusted himself off.

"Dude, you almost died," a cyclist standing beside him said. A wheel of the taxi had missed his head by inches. Luckily for Spitznagel, he only suffered a separated shoulder and a cracked watch.

Perhaps in compensation for the extreme risk aversion practiced at Empirica, Spitznagel had acquired a taste for life-threatening hobbies. Every weekend, he'd fly to Los Angeles where his wife was pursuing an acting career. There, he'd engage in what had become his favorite pastime: *soaring*. He'd drive out to the desert and hop into an engineless sailplane, which was towed into the sky by another plane. Released, it would bob and weave in wide circles on the high desert thermals and updrafts over the Sierra Nevadas. Spitznagel loved the feeling of being in control in a situation that seemed totally out of control.

Taleb, for his part, hated that feeling. And he was feeling it more and more at Empirica. The drip-drip torture of daily losses while waiting for the inevitable, elusive crash was driving him crazy. He was also beginning to worry that the stress was undermining his health. Could the cancer relapse? In the summer of 2004, he took Spitznagel aside in the new office.

"I need to exit Empirica, Mark," he said.

"Are you fucking crazy?" Spitznagel sputtered. He truly believed in the strategy, that it had massive potential. "Don't you realize what we can do with this? I can't believe you want to walk away from this."

It was over. Taleb and Spitznagel had sat elbow to elbow for nearly five years, exchanging ideas about trading, philosophy, statistics, life. The friendship was entirely work-related. They never took a non-work-related trip together. Spitznagel took pains to stay far away from Taleb's eclectic social circles. But he would miss the daily intellectual stimulation, the heated discussions, the long walks around Manhattan's streets, the arm-waving arguments.

In short order, Taleb began plotting his next move. He got to work writing another book. He would call it *The Black Swan*, which memorialized and made famous his view that the future is unpredictable and that massive, overwhelming events determine history—and the performance of portfolios.

But not everyone agreed that the market was a random and fickle roulette wheel. In Zurich, Switzerland, a brilliant scientist claimed he'd unearthed the secret forces behind crashes—that he had, in fact, a crystal ball.

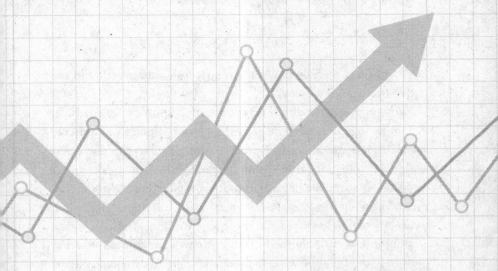

CHAPTER 7

DRAGON HUNTER

The road shifted into a streaming gray blur as Didier Sornette, complexity theorist, econophysicist, and stock market visionary, raced furiously along a Los Angeles freeway on his Kawasaki Ninja ZX-12R motorcycle. It was 2006. The UCLA professor was pushing himself to the edge, hitting 100 miles an hour as he cruised past an 18-wheeler in a flash, bursting along the open highway and opening up the throttle, 125, 150 . . .175 *miles an hour*. . . .

Sornette loved tempting risk. Even more, he loved taming it— *dominating* it. Growing up in the south of France, he'd gained an appetite for managing danger riding in a helicopter alongside his father, an employee of France's electricity giant EDF. His father's job was to monitor power lines using an infrared camera mounted on the helicopter. This required extreme control and daredevil maneuvers that put him within inches of the deadly lines. To demonstrate his skill, he once had Didier stand on the ground and raise his hand in the air as he carefully lowered the copter's landing skid onto the tip of his young son's finger.

Early on, Sornette displayed an uncanny aptitude for math. In 1977, at the age of twenty, he earned a place in France's elite École normale supérieure in Paris, the nation's top mathematics and physics academy. He graduated with a degree in physical sciences four years later and quickly got a tenured position at France's National Center for Scientific Research, known as CNRS. Soon after, while serving his compulsory year in the French military, he conducted research on how turbulence in water affects submarines—his first exposure to the mind-bending mathematics behind dynamic systems and chaos theory.

In the early 1990s, working with the French state-owned aerospace manufacturer Aérospatiale, Sornette began studying methods to detect and predict the rupture of Kevlar pressure tanks on Europe's Ariane rockets, which were designed to deliver communication satellites into orbit. To test the rocket's resilience, Sornette and his fellow scientists subjected the tanks to increasing pressure and used acoustic gauges to detect what were essentially tiny earthquakes in the Kevlar. At a certain point the earthquakes rapidly magnified, producing a catastrophic rupture. Applying methods he'd learned studying Mandelbrot's fractal geometry, he was able to identify mathematical patterns in the acoustic emissions—the tiny earthquakes—that predicted certain failure.

It struck Sornette that financial crashes—and the bubbles that often precede them—are akin to market "ruptures." After years of studying rocket pressure tanks and turbulence, he began to realize that these and other complex systems have similar patterns that he could measure on scales ranging from minute to tremendous—and that could potentially act as early warning signs for catastrophes. To illustrate the idea, Sornette used the analogy of a climber on a rope. As the climber ascends, tiny filaments of the rope break due to either the climber's weight or some kind of friction. But the climber doesn't notice these small breaks—until suddenly, there's a rupture, and the climber falls. If the climber had a method to detect the breaks, he or she would know to get off the rope.

Around the same time Sornette was studying pressure tanks, another physicist at CNRS, Jean-Philippe Bouchaud, had also developed a taste for finance. After leaving the research center in 1992, Bouchaud launched a firm whose name, Science & Finance, captured the intersection of physics and markets. Sornette joined in 1995, and the two collaborated on a paper that applied his crash-detection formula to the stock market. Called "Stock Market Crashes, Precursors, and Replicas," the paper identified a pattern of positive-feedback loops in which buying compounds at an ever-greater unsustainable rate, leading to a bubble—and a crash. "This model analyzes a situation of pure speculation, based on the tendency [of] traders to imitate each other," they wrote. "When a series of buy orders, say, are issued, an acceleration of demand results, which is self-strengthening. This acceleration cannot be sustained indefinitely and, at some threshold, a crash ends this sequence."

Sornette left Science & Finance a few years later. In 2000, it merged with Capital Fund Management, which went on to become one of the world's largest, most successful hedge funds.

> > < <

Even as he was applying his crash model to markets, Sornette began studying another catastrophic phenomenon: earthquakes. It began with a chance meeting at UCLA with the geophysicist Leon Knopoff, a pioneer in the study of earthquakes. Sornette grew fascinated by the confounding physics of quakes and the ever-elusive challenge of predicting them. He wondered if the fractal method he'd used to predict ruptures in Ariane rockets could be applied to earthquakes. Knopoff was intrigued by his work and invited him to UCLA. So in 1996, Sornette packed his bags and moved to Los Angeles to become a professor of statistical physics at the university (all the while maintaining his position at CNRS). Southern California appealed to Sornette's wild side. He rode motorcycles at suicidal speeds, frequently indulged in windsurfing, and flew to Hawaii to ride the big waves.

It was the 1990s, and it seemed the entire country had become enthralled with stocks. The market was in a sustained bull run as the dot-com bubble began to inflate and day-trading became a nationwide fad. Sornette, recalling his work with Bouchaud at Science & Finance, began to pursue an in-depth analysis of financial crashes. Collaborating with a group of finance experts at UCLA's Anderson School of Management, including Olivier Ledoit and geophysicist Anders Johansen, he helped write a series of investigations into the structure of crashes and bubbles with imposing titles such as "Predicting Financial Crashes Using Discrete Scale Invariance" and "Significance of Log-Periodic Precursors to Financial Crashes."

In the summer of 1997, Sornette noticed something odd—a crisis pattern in the stock market that looked remarkably like the signals before a rupture in an Ariane pressure tank. He called up Ledoit. A crash in the market was coming, Sornette said, a fairly remarkable claim, since, despite some wobbles here and there, stocks, fueled by the day-trading boom and emerging dot-com bubble, seemed relatively calm. Even more remarkable, Sornette said the crash would come in a few months, around the end of October. Ledoit told Sornette they should memorialize his prediction. Together with Johansen, the geophysicist, the three wrote a patent application detailing the model (it would come to be known as the Johansen-Ledoit-Sornette, or JLS, model), and filed it with the French patent office.

Then Sornette and Ledoit decided they might as well try to make money on the crash. In mid-October, they bought $30,000 worth of far-out-of-the-money put options. (The exact same contracts Universa buys.) Then they waited. Markets remained calm. Then, on October 27—a sudden crash. The Dow industrials fell 554 points, its third biggest point loss ever. It was the Asian flu, the same collapse that delivered a jackpot to Spitznagel.

Sornette and Ledoit cashed in, making a fast 300 percent profit.

They could have made more, because they only sold part of their position. Sornette was predicting a much bigger crash, one that would have delivered a 10,000 percent gain. They held on, waiting for more turmoil. It didn't happen. In fact, the market rallied the following day and soon the freak crash of October 27 was a distant memory.

Sornette subsequently discovered that he could also apply his method to predict market rallies off of bear-market lows, what he called an "anti-bubble" of irrationally low prices. In January 1999, he forecast that the Nikkei index would soon recover from some fourteen years of doldrums, rebounding by 50 percent by the end of that year—which it did.

His financial research culminated in the 2003 book *Why Stock Markets Crash: Critical Events in Complex Financial Systems*. An astonishing high-wire act of historical market analysis, the book applies concepts taken from complexity theory, fractal geometry, network theory, behavioral economics, evolutionary biology, chaos theory, the study of earthquakes, and more to the study of bubbles and crashes. As he had first argued in his 1995 paper with Bouchaud, bubbles begin rationally, with investors purchasing a stock in a company they believe will grow earnings in the future. More buyers come in, causing *more* buyers to join, chasing and pushing prices higher and higher, leading to an irrational herding effect that inflates the bubble. The stock (or the broader market itself) becomes unhinged from its underlying fundamentals, and the bubble rapidly expands. Sornette's model, he claimed, can detect the later stages of this phenomenon as it careens into an explosive crash.

Think of a balloon. Uninflated, it's hard to prick it with a needle. Blow it up a little bit and it's still impervious to the needle. Blow it up a lot, and the tiniest prick will cause it to pop. That's the dynamic Sornette's model detects. When a financial bubble is super inflated, it can explode at any moment, with very little pinprick pressure causing the crash.

The math behind the Johansen-Ledoit-Sornette model was first discovered by Sornette in the 1990s when he was diagnosing those critical rupture points in pressure tanks on the Ariane rocket as well as a method to predict earthquakes. The phenomenon, which had parallels in Mandelbrot's fractals, was something he said was *bigger* than standard power laws—it was a *super*-power law marked by diz-zyingly fast up-and-down oscillations.

The French physicist was claiming to have unearthed a phan-tom. A phenomenon that, according to prevailing economic and financial theory, couldn't exist. The market, according to this the-ory, behaves like a random walk. It was the theory first proposed in 1900 by Bachelier, the neurotic French mathematician described by Benoit Mandelbrot at NYU. Sometimes called a drunkard's walk, the theory claims that markets—all markets—are completely random and therefore unpredictable. Imagine a drunk staggering away from a light pole. Each stagger goes in a different direction, sometimes toward the pole and sometimes away from it. By the math, it's impos-sible to predict how far from the pole he'll be by the end of the night. For investors, this means never trying to time the market because it's impossible to predict whether it will go up or down over any mean-ingful time period. You can't know with any confidence whether the next flip of the coin is going to be heads or tails. It's always fifty-fifty. The random walk was the other side of the efficient markets coin that had frustrated Brandon Yarckin during his class at Duke. Since the market is always instantly incorporating all known information into prices, its next move is a coin flip, entirely impossible to predict.

Sornette agreed that, most of the time, the random walk theory holds for markets. But there are times, he said, when it *is* possible to predict what will occur. The most important time: when it's in a bubble. He called these events "pockets of predictability." Standard models fail to capture the extreme movements seen in crashes, such as Black Monday of October 1987. The models typically claim that the chance of such crashes is statistically impossible, occurring once in a billion years (or more). That means the models, while fine for most trading days, don't work in crashes. "If the largest drawdowns are outliers, we *must* consider the possibility that they may possess a higher degree of predictability than the smaller market movements," Sornette wrote in *Why Stock Markets Crash*.

Despite all the fancy math, few believed Sornette had cracked the bubble code. How do you *know* it's a bubble? Maybe prices are accurately reflecting collective expectations of phenomenal future profits. Most economists believed you could only know if something was a bubble *after* it popped. Alan Greenspan, then chairman of the Federal Reserve, said it was impossible to identify bubbles as they're inflating. Referring to the dot-com bubble, he said in an August 2002 speech in Jackson Hole, Wyoming: "As events evolved, we recognized that, despite our suspicions, it was very difficult to definitely identify a bubble until after the fact—that is, when its bursting confirmed its existence."

Wall Street has always been rife with visionaries claiming to have discovered hidden patterns in the market's warp and weft. The Elliott wave principle, propagated in the early twentieth century by accountant Ralph Nelson Elliott, claimed to predict market cycles and trends by pinpointing extremes in prices and investor psychology. Such cycles, the theory goes, move in discernible waves that slosh up and down—bubbles and crashes. Sornette himself has said that his model in ways parallels Elliott waves.

But while technical analysis had at times enjoyed short-term success, over the long run there was little evidence investors could use it to accurately predict the market. Sornette, for his part, claimed his method was far more rigorous, based on advanced methods taken from physics, and provable with objective, testable data. Other scientists, however, had tried the same game over the years—and failed. A prediction Sornette made in 2002 that U.S. stocks would remain trapped in a bear market for the next few years, when in fact they ramped up into bull territory, didn't help his cause. It also didn't stop him from continuing to try to tease out the secret signals hidden inside bubbles and crashes.

> > < <

In 2005, Sornette visited the Swiss Federal Institute of Technology, commonly known as ETH Zurich—the MIT of Europe—for a seminar. Afterward, several ETH professors invited him for dinner. During the meal, they told him a position had recently opened up at the institute. "Why don't you apply?" they asked. Months later, he packed his bags in Los Angeles and moved to Zurich, which became his permanent home.

With the unusual title of professor of entrepreneurial risks, he continued to focus on fine-tuning his model, which he came to describe using the shorthand LPPLS, short for log-periodic power law singularity. In October 2007, he gave the keynote address to a gathering of hedge fund luminaries at the luxurious Grand Hotel in Stockholm. The title of his speech was the same as his book: "Why Stock Markets Crash."

During his speech, he made a startling prediction. Based on results from the LPPLS model, he forecast that the Chinese stock market, which had soared more than 300 percent in the past few years, was a bubble on the verge of collapse.

Attendees were incredulous. Forecasters had been predicting the China economic miracle would burst for years, and they were all wrong. And Sornette was forgetting something. The Beijing Summer Olympics were coming up in 2008. The country's central planners would never allow a collapse to happen beforehand. Sure enough, soon after the conference, Chinese stocks began to wobble along with other markets worldwide amid growing contagion from the U.S. subprime housing market, triggering billions in losses across the globe. By the following October, China's Shanghai stock market had lost 80 percent.

Building on the success of that prediction and others, in August 2008 Sornette launched the Financial Crisis Observatory at ETH to develop additional quantitative methods to detect financial bubbles and, hopefully, predict when they might burst. He'd grown exasperated by all the excuses for why no one—not the shoulder-shrugging bankers, or the head-scratching economists, or the don't-look-at-me hedge fund managers—could have seen the Global Financial Crisis coming. Just three years before, Sornette had published a paper diagnosing a massive bubble in the U.S. real estate sector and accurately predicted it would pop by the middle of 2006. While he didn't predict the ensuing chaos that occurred as the real estate collapse ramified through the financial system via a hidden explosive network of derivatives, he did finger the fuse that lit the bomb. (Many others did as well.)

Sornette around this time started to become increasingly hostile to Nassim Taleb's Black Swans. The entire notion behind the Black Swan—that extreme earth-shaking events are impossible to predict—he believed, was radically misguided. It caused people to throw up their hands and stop trying to figure out the future—or understand the past. "The Black Swan concept is dangerous," Sornette told me. "It puts us back at the time of pre-science where the wrath of nature, the lightning, the storms were the expression of the anger of the gods."

Sornette had long been familiar with Taleb. The Frenchman was a resource for *The Black Swan*. Indeed, Taleb credits him in the book ("Didier Sornette, always a phone call away, kept e-mailing me papers on various unadvertised, but highly relevant, subjects in statistical physics"). Sornette soon concocted his own exotic beast for the land of the super extreme: the Dragon King, a term he invented in 2009 to compete with Taleb's tempestuous waterfowl. Dragon Kings, he said, were outliers with specific properties that, in extremis, can be detected—those tiny earthquakes leading to a massive rupture, identified by the LPPLS model—and used to predict when they might blow up.

The Dragon King is a double metaphor—referring to an event that's both extremely large (a king of a country who has by far most of the nation's wealth) and born of unique origins (a mystical dragon). The most extreme events aren't caused by the same mechanisms that affect normal events. They require amplifying processes that can make them go critical, leading to monstrously large phenomena, a singularity that ruptures and explodes with devastating force. The 2008 financial crisis, Sornette wrote, "provided one of the most prominent examples of a Dragon King, spreading across continents and affecting the world economy."

The challenge was detecting the hideous beasts with the ambitious goal of taming them. Using his LPPLS model at the Financial Crisis Observatory, Sornette began scanning hundreds of financial assets around the world for signs of the dragon. As word of his new monster began to spread, he became known in the Swiss press as *der Drachenjäger*—the Dragon Hunter.

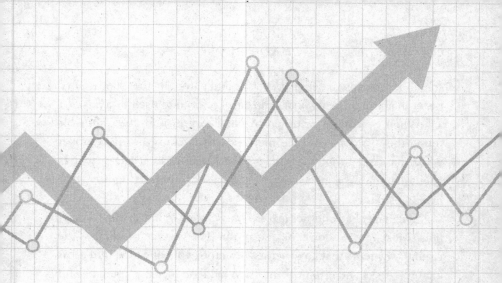

CHAPTER 8

THAT WAY LIES MADNESS

Mark Spitznagel ripped down the steep incline of a ski slope on Whistler Mountain, his snowboard gliding over the fresh, deep powder. He and his wife, Amy, were enjoying a post-Empirica round-the-world ski-bum-fest. They traveled to Whistler in British Columbia, Aspen, Squaw Valley, resorts in Austria and Switzerland. They'd decided to start having children, and this was their final free-wheeling hurrah before settling down.

Tempting risk—physical risk—was a trait Spitznagel shared with Sornette, who also loved skiing and surfboarding, as well as rocketing down L.A. freeways at 175 miles an hour (Spitznagel preferred daredevil skateboarding or engineless soaring over mountains). Not Taleb. He hated motorcycles, which he thought were recklessly dangerous. Taleb was a creature of the city: of cafes, bookstores, concert halls. He liked to call himself a *flâneur*, a French word that could be interpreted as a loafer, a stroller, a dreamer, or one that always is somehow associated with silk scarves and patent leather shoes. You'd never in a million years hear Spitznagel refer to himself as a *flâneur*.

When Spitznagel returned to New York in mid-2005 after his round-the-world ski tour, he met up with Yarckin, the KBC broker who'd handled Empirica's trades. They immediately began to talk about launching a new hedge fund based on the Empirica tail-hedging strategy.

Spitznagel had another investment scheme in mind: movie residuals. Most movies don't make a profit. That makes residuals—the regular payments that go to actors, directors, etc., once the film turns a profit—risky and often worthless. What if an investor could pay for those residuals up front, taking the risk of making nothing but with the potential for a massive upside from a blockbuster?

The odds were similar to those behind the out-of-the-money put options Empirica gobbled up—in reverse. Most of the options expire worthless, resulting in a small loss, but in a crash they can yield fantastic gains. Residual options pay off in the rare blockbuster. For every hundred *Battlefield Earth*s you might get a *Jurassic Park*.

Actors and directors, of course, were well aware of the risk. Some might prefer to get the guaranteed up-front cash rather than gamble on the bonanza, Spitznagel thought.

He'd gotten the idea after meeting movie producer Lynwood Spinks, known for films such as *Cliffhanger* and *Ghost Rider*, in Beverly Hills during a long lunch at the Ivy, an iconic celebrity hangout. In 2004, Spinks had launched a company called Relativity Media alongside an up-and-coming movie financier, Ryan Kavanaugh. Kavanaugh was trying to bridge the gap between Wall Street and Hollywood via a gimmick that made him attractive to the math geeks of Wall Street. He used a so-called Monte Carlo model that ran thousands of simulations to predict a film's success. Say a studio was planning to film a sci-fi epic starring John Travolta directed by Steven Spielberg. The model would crunch through box office returns of Spielberg and Travolta as well as recent sci-fi successes and failures. Using the results, Kavanaugh could estimate how much a studio should pony up—if anyone should at all.

Kavanaugh was combing Wall Street for sources of cash. Spitznagel was intrigued. Yarckin began shuttling back and forth between New York and Los Angeles and raising cash commitments for a fund that would use option-pricing models Spitznagel had perfected to price the residuals. Things seemed to be moving ahead nicely until Spitznagel backed out. (Yarckin and Spitznagel were lucky to separate themselves from Kavanaugh. After briefly looking as if he might become one of Hollywood's top producers, associated with such blockbusters as *Mama Mia!* and *The Social Network*, he drove his company into bankruptcy amid myriad allegations of fraud.)

A better opportunity had opened up. Neil Chriss, the NYU professor who'd put Spitznagel together with Taleb back in 1999, told him about a unique position at a secretive proprietary trading outfit at Morgan Stanley, the giant New York investment bank. It had a ho-hum name—Process Driven Trading, PDT for short—and a spectacular secret. Though few had heard of it, PDT was one of the most profitable trading operations Wall Street had ever seen.

PDT was the ultimate quant shop. Staffed with Ph.D. mathematicians, electrical engineers, computer programmers, and physicists, it had launched in the early 1990s when a quirky, brilliant mathematician and poker aficionado, Peter Muller, decided to see if a trading strategy he'd worked out on paper might succeed in the real world. It deployed a complex strategy called statistical arbitrage. Arbitrage is an age-old investment technique that looks for discrepancies in identical or nearly identical assets. Jay Gould, the notorious New York banker, used it to make a mint on gold in the 1800s. If gold in New York was cheaper than gold in London, he'd buy in New York and sell in London. It was a virtually riskless trade.

PDT practiced the strategy at high speed on stocks. Its computer models scanned the markets for correlations between shares of companies. For instance, when GM went up, Ford usually did, too—Americans were buying lots of cars. But they didn't always move in perfect unison. So if GM took off, leaving Ford in the dust, PDT might buy shares of Ford in the expectation that it would quickly catch up. Of course, PDT's models were *a lot* more complicated than that, and the trades didn't work all the time. But they worked often enough that, executed thousands of times a day, a profit was made nearly every day, like at a casino that takes so many bets on roulette it never loses in the long run.

By the late 1990s, PDT had become the most profitable trading operation at Morgan Stanley, its performance at times keeping pace with the hedge fund powerhouse on Long Island, Renaissance Technologies, considered by many the best-performing trading machine of all time. PDT went *years* without a monthly loss. Paranoid that copycats would mimic his strategy, Muller, so successful that he was earning more than Morgan's CEO, was obsessive about keeping its existence secret. Many senior managers at the firm didn't even know it existed. He wouldn't let Aaron Brown, a risk manager at Morgan Stanley at the time, learn anything about the strategy or underlying risk, claiming that a risk manager once stole some of his code.

Muller stepped away from full-time management of PDT in 1999, though he stayed on as an adviser. After a string of lackluster returns (which, for PDT, meant bananas profits but not super-duper bananas), he decided to take the helm again in 2006. He was looking for new strategies that could boost performance. PDT specialized in stocks and hadn't branched out into most other parts of the market. What about options? His friend Neil Chriss told him about an outstanding options trader whose firm, Empirica Capital, had recently shut down.

After a few meetings with Muller, Spitznagel agreed to join PDT. It was an odd fit from the start. PDT had something of a cult vibe. Team members would jet off for retreats in the woods or remote islands. Many had been there from the group's start in the early 1990s. Muller wore gold chain necklaces and sang folk songs in Greenwich Village bistros—decidedly not Spitznagel's scene. He'd even descend now and then into the city's grubby subway stations and sing, his electric piano case spread open as if he were busking for change.

Months after Spitznagel joined in early 2006, a few PDTers

jumped ship for a rival hedge fund. To Muller, it was a betrayal. Even worse, it was a threat. The models he and others had developed over the years were trade secrets as valuable as KFC's secret recipe. He decided to ask every employee to sign a non-compete agreement, which meant they couldn't pursue any of the strategies they deployed at PDT for a set number of years.

It was a blatant non-starter for Spitznagel. He didn't learn his strategy at PDT. He'd created it himself alongside Taleb. But Muller insisted, and Spitznagel left after less than a year, before he'd fully started his trading program.

It didn't matter. All along he'd been talking with Yarckin about launching their own fund, taking the strategy built up over years at Empirica, using what worked, discarding what didn't, and making it better. Even during his stint as a ski bum, Spitznagel would stay up late into the night programming on his laptop, tweaking the models and examining the data. It was an obsession. Now he was beginning to get a premonition that the time was ripe for the Black Swan strategy. The stock market was hitting records even as a bubble in the U.S. housing market appeared to be blowing up. He didn't want to miss what could be a once-in-a-lifetime opportunity. During long afternoons skateboarding through Central Park at suicidal speeds, he and Yarckin plotted out the details. On park benches, during strolls through the park's endless walkways, they discussed different elements such as office space, staffing, insurance, prime broker relationships, futures clearing agreements—the nuts and bolts of a professional trading operation.

Spitznagel named the firm Universa, based on the notion that fat tails (and Black Swans) are a universal trait of financial markets, a phenomenon discovered by Mandelbrot and other mathematical trailblazers. A corollary to the insight was that most investors were blind to the fact. Highlighting the firm's philosophical and practical distance from Wall Street's stifling groupthink, they decided to set up shop in Santa Monica, California. The location had the added benefit that Spitznagel and his wife, who'd moved back to New York, could raise their nine-month-old son outside of Manhattan, which they'd come to loathe. Mindful of earthquakes, Spitznagel chose a relatively small bow-trussed building with a loft for his private office and a conference room overlooking the trading floor below.

Universa launched to little fanfare in February 2007. Nearly all of its cash came from just two investors, an endowment, and a pension fund. Months later, a pair of hedge funds at Bear Stearns bloated with billions in subprime-mortgage assets imploded. It was the opening salvo of the Global Financial Crisis that would rock the world's economy.

> > < <

Spitznagel was wondering if he'd made a big mistake. He'd been taking lessons in qinna, an ancient Chinese martial art technique focused on locking an opponent's joints and muscles so that they couldn't move. Spitznagel was fascinated by the Daoist idea of weakness overcoming strength, of taking down an opponent with just a few fingers. He'd hired a Chinese kung fu master to come to the office once a week to teach him the method. Now he couldn't move. His body was locked in place. It was confounding. *How could this happen?* Even worse, his opponent was *an old man*. He was practicing in the loft conference room of Universa's new headquarters in Santa Monica. It was a hard lesson to learn that a man decades older than he could exert total control over his body.

He was also learning another hard lesson. Outside its initial pair of investors, others weren't interested in what Universa had to sell. After launching the firm, Spitznagel and Yarckin had hit the road to wrangle money for their new fund. They called the strategy the Black Swan Protection Protocol. Things did not go well.

A guiding principle behind the BSPP strategy was that it was designed to deliver its most explosive profits in a market that went down a galloping *20 percent* in a calendar month. The problem: The market had only done that *once* in recent memory—on October 19, 1987, Black Monday, when the Dow Jones Industrial Average crashed 22.6 percent (and Taleb made his first fortune).

That can't happen, they were told, again and again. Black Monday was a freak anomaly from another age. The market didn't even crash that much when the dot-com bubble burst.

Many investors had also developed an unswerving faith in the power of the Federal Reserve to protect them from big crashes. By lowering short-term interest rates when times were tough, the Fed made it easier for borrowers to get access to cheap loans, giving the economy a jolt. Under Alan Greenspan, that protective measure was known as the "Greenspan Put," a reference to a put option that gains when a stock falls. Since Ben Bernanke was the new Fed chairman, it was now known as the "Bernanke Put." The sentiment among pension funds and on the Street was: Who needs Universa when I've got the awesome power of the Federal Reserve at my back?

Another roadblock was the prevailing belief on Wall Street that the market and the economy were in a long run of low volatility. Dubbed the Great Moderation after a 2004 speech given by Ben Bernanke in Washington, D.C., the theory gave investors hope that big crashes and recessions were a thing of the past. Some called it the Goldilocks economy—not too hot, not too cold. One explanation for the shift could be random good luck, Bernanke said in his speech. Not likely, he pronounced. Instead, it was central bankers (such as himself) who'd helped provide the calm waters that were lifting all boats. "My view is that improvements in monetary policy, though certainly not the only factor, have probably been an important source of the Great Moderation," Bernanke proclaimed.

"If the economy is in the midst of a long-term shift into not-too-hot-or-cold moderation," investors said, "why should I give money to a firm that lives and dies by crashes?"

Spitznagel was also bedeviled by rumors about Empirica. If the strategy was so good, why shut it down? Did investors pull out? Did it blow up? He didn't think it mattered, even though he knew it had only shuttered because Taleb got fed up with the tedium of the daily losses and because of his health concerns. Universa was *his* fund, not Taleb's.

Other skeptics winked at the fact that if the market fell 20 percent, everyone would suffer the same catastrophe. And that would be just fine—for them. "All I need to do is track my peers," they said. It was, unfortunately, true. Fund managers are typically judged not by whether they make money for their investors, but by how well they perform compared to a benchmark of similar fund managers. If a tech-fund manager loses 10 percent, but the benchmark fell 12 percent, he gets a nice bonus—he outperformed by two percentage points! The downside of this, for investors, is that managers have a strong incentive to copy one another, behaving like a herd moving in the same direction. There's safety in the herd—and little incentive to take risks that might make one stand out in a bad year. Most professional investors, Spitznagel believed, were little better than sheep in wolves' clothing.

In other words, these managers were telling Spitznagel and Yarckin that their fund was worthless to them. In fact, it was a dreaded line item, with no expected return for most years, that would make their performance look *worse*—even if it might dramatically improve their performance in a bad year.

More often than not, the prospective investors didn't even understand what the fund did. "We do tail-risk hedging," Spitznagel would tell them across the expanse of a dark oak conference table. "The Black Swan Protection Protocol Fund buys far out-of-the-money options that produce explosive returns in crashes, fat tails . . ."

Tail risk? Options? Black Swans?

Blank stares.

It was as if they were speaking a foreign language.

"I had to sit and explain this to people who run hundreds of billions of dollars," Yarckin recalled. "Most people who run all kinds of money don't understand basic math, basic risk-management skills. I had to explain how options work in convertible bonds. These guys are running *billions*."

Another obstacle facing Spitznagel and Yarckin was that their strategy didn't fit within the standard Wall Street model for measuring risk and return. Commonly known as Modern Portfolio Theory, the approach relies on a simple, seemingly common-sense platitude: Don't put all your eggs in one basket. The idea, pioneered by American economist Harry Markowitz in the 1950s, claims that by diversifying your portfolio, you reduce the risk of getting harmed by bad news that can impact a single company or industry. And doing so results in what some claim is the only free lunch in economics: You maximize your returns. Say you own Ford Motor and Exxon. High oil prices might hurt Ford (people are buying fewer gas-guzzling F-150s), but Exxon will post record profits. On Wall Street, Modern Portfolio Theory wasn't just a theory, it was like a papal edict issued from the nation's leading business schools and universities. Endowments, pension funds, mutual funds, major hedge funds—all bowed at the feet of MPT. Those who didn't were heretics. Universa was heretic number one.

In its simplest form, MPT directs investors to buy a broad basket of stocks. The best proxy for the market was the Standard & Poor's 500 stock index—five hundred of the biggest stocks trading on U.S. exchanges. Vanguard, one of the world's biggest fund managers, had become a giant by steering investors into cheap S&P 500 index portfolios. For most investors, this makes a lot of sense. They don't have the time, skill, or experience to pick stocks. Indeed, this holds true for almost *all* investors, according to a library full of studies on stock picking.

It seemed simple enough. But Wall Street's financial engineers, never satisfied with something so easy, started devising grab bags of portfolios that provided various levels of potential returns and risks. By fiddling with the figurative dial they'd created, they could boost the risk, heightening the theoretical return. Or tamp down the risk, lessening the return. All for a fee of course.

Reducing risk is typically accomplished by investing in bonds, which are usually a lot less volatile than stocks. Indeed, bonds often gain when stocks go down (although they don't gain much). Such a portfolio usually runs pretty smoothly, without a lot of bumps on the road, like a well-oiled Cadillac.

Spitznagel's message: Forget all that. You don't want a Cadillac—
you want a Ferrari. By holding a big chunk of bonds, you're throwing
away money as the market rises—as it almost always does. Why not
put almost all of your money in stocks—say 97 percent—and give
us the rest. When the market crashes, we've got your back. The little bumps, the 5, 6 percent drops, don't matter. What matters are
crashes—Black Swans. If you lose 20 percent in a month, you need
to make 25 percent to get back to where you started. Lose 50 percent,
and you need to make 100 percent just to get even. What if, instead,
with Universa, you didn't lose anything, maybe even *made money* in a
crash? It would be like buying fire insurance for your $500,000 house
and getting paid $5 million when it went up in flames.

It sounded good. But it didn't fit into the MPT box. For one thing,
Universa's returns were exceedingly lumpy. It could go years without
making money. From an MPT perspective, that was a nightmare.
MPT likes portfolios that are nice and smooth, that post steady, reliable gains—and so do portfolio managers judged each year by their
annual returns. A bad run of two or three years could be fatal.

Investors weighed the incremental opportunity cost—*good money
down the drain*—and turned up their noses.

Spitznagel and Yarckin scheduled hundreds of meetings in 2007.
They crisscrossed the country making pitch after pitch. Not a single
new investor bit on the Black Swan fund.

> > < <

Universa may have been notably unpopular, but Taleb's ideas were
catching on, spreading beyond the close-knit circles of Wall Street's
hedge fund traders, quants, and risk managers. *Washington Post* columnist David Ignatius, in a February 2004 editorial called "And
Black Swans," described Taleb's 2003 Pentagon paper as "remarkable" and applied it to the Bush administration's mistakes in Iraq.
"Iraq is like Long-Term Capital Management, in that smart people
sailed into potential disaster thinking they knew what they were
doing," he wrote.

Taleb also became a target. Joe Nocera, a prominent financial reporter for the *New York Times*, wrote in an October 2005 review of the paperback edition of *Fooled by Randomness*: "For me, the issue isn't so much that Mr. Taleb is wrong in his analysis. The problem is his fundamental nihilism. Taken to its logical extreme—something Mr. Taleb is happy to do—his stance strongly implies that it's pointless to even try to forecast things like stock prices or economic trends. Nor, he seems to be saying, should we even bother attempting risk management, since we always miss the big thing that winds up really mattering. And on both points, I think he's dead wrong."

While predicting stock prices or the ebbs and flows of the economy may be flawed, Nocera said, it's ridiculous to throw your hands up and do away with prediction entirely. "We should try not to be fooled by randomness," he wrote. "But we should not be as skeptical as the author of *Fooled by Randomness*. That way lies madness."

Of course, the claim that Taleb didn't bother to manage risk was absurd. His entire investing strategy at Empirica was organized around risk management. But it was fundamentally a different kind of risk management than practiced by the rest of Wall Street. True, he claimed people can't predict the earth-shaking events that will shape the future. Who saw September 11 coming (aside from Osama bin Laden and his band of terrorists)? Who saw Black Monday? World War I and its consequences? But that didn't mean "fly blind." Taleb argued that the problem is that we're fooling ourselves with our predictions and are taking *too much* risk. Black Swans lurk in the shadows, he warned—be careful!

In the spring of 2007, *The Black Swan: The Impact of the Highly Improbable* hit bookstores across the U.S. It was an instant hit, debuting on the *New York Times* bestseller list at number five. An entire chapter, "The Aesthetics of Randomness," was a paean to Benoit Mandelbrot, the French mathematician whose fractal geometry deeply informed Taleb's vision of extreme events and fat tails—a land Taleb dubbed "Extremistan." The mundane territory in the middle of the bell curve he called "Mediocristan"—the tame Gaussian world

Mandelbrot had shown mostly doesn't apply to the wild rock-'n'-roll nature of financial markets.

The physical world of stars, planets, and bodies—these were the residents of Mediocristan, dominated by the Law of Large Numbers (the more times you flip a coin, the greater the odds that the outcome approaches fifty-fifty; so as any sample size grows, the results bunch toward the middle of the curve).

The world of finance, and much else, operated in Extremistan, the land of power laws, big jumps, fat tails, bubbles, and crashes. If the world's tallest man joins a lineup of one hundred people, he's not going to move the average height in a meaningful way—that's Mediocristan. But if Jeff Bezos walked into a room full of a thousand people, the average income would swing dramatically. It would be as if a one-hundred-foot-tall man walked (awkwardly) into the room. That's Extremistan. Put a thousand authors in a room and average their sales. Then Stephen King strolls in. It's the land of extreme winner-take-all concentration. If two people have an average wealth of $10 million, odds are one of those people is worth $9.999 million, the other is worth $1,000. The tail event becomes the central, indeed the *only* thing that matters. Everything else is noise. The tail wags the dog, literally.

"The problem, insists Mr. Taleb, is that most of the time we are in the land of the power law and don't know it," a reviewer observed in the *Wall Street Journal*. "Our strategies for managing risk, for instance—including Modern Portfolio Theory and the Black-Scholes formula for pricing options—are likely to fail at the worst possible time . . . because they are generally (and mistakenly) based on bell-curve assumptions."

Taleb's book became a cultural touchstone and made the Black Swan something of a universal meme for *surprising bad shit going down*. In the fourteen years before the book was published, *black swan* appeared 16,569 times in a Factiva search (usually in reference to a piece of choreography in Tchaikovsky's ballet *Swan Lake* called "the Black Swan pas de deux"). In the fourteen years after its publication, it appeared 92,561 times. Black Swans filled the skies. In the wake of Covid-19, Lloyd's of London proposed a Black Swan insurance plan for governments to protect themselves against pandemics and other extreme events. "Despite rampant uncertainty in 2020 stemming from the Black Swan effects of the coronavirus pandemic, U.S. ferrous scrap pricing finished the year strong," *Platts Daily Briefing* opined. "Trump was a classic black swan event," Lionel Shriver observed in the *Telegraph*. There's a Black Swan wine, a Black Swan publisher, Black Swan yoga, even an exceedingly eccentric comic strip called Black Swan Man that portrays Taleb as a muscle-bound, costumed figure battling the evils of bitcoin and the Federal Reserve and tossing off advice such as "We must always be vigilant against the problem of induction."

Misconceptions about what exactly constitutes a Black Swan endlessly tortured Taleb. People asked: "Was September 11 a Black Swan?" Yes, for the people in the World Trade Center, no for the terrorists. "The Global Financial Crisis?" No, said Taleb. It was entirely predictable (a Gray Swan). Indeed, Taleb and Spitznagel had been forecasting a credit-fueled blowup for years. They just didn't know when the blowup would blow up.

Experts complained Taleb wasn't telling them anything new ("others have been here before," a *New York Times* reviewer pointed out dismissively). Everyone, they said, knows about fat tails. And it was largely true among the quant cognoscenti. But Taleb never claimed to have invented the concept. He was well aware of the discoveries of power laws and fat tails in financial markets by predecessors such as Mandelbrot, and says as much in his book. His claim was that while Wall Street's legions of quants might know all about fat tails and Black Swans, more often than not they put blinders on and use bell curve–based models such as VaR and Black-Scholes, the dominant model for pricing options, acting as if the extreme risks don't exist.

Aaron Brown said Taleb's most important contribution wasn't the claim that fat tails exist in finance, but rather the assertion that long-term outcomes are *dominated* by tail events. "Every quant knew that surprisingly large things happened from time to time, and that it was important to allow for them," he told me. "But before Taleb, everyone assumed that how you managed day-to-day events was the main thing; only after you got that squared away did you devote maybe five percent of your attention to the 'outliers.' Taleb demonstrated that if you got the outliers right you did well, and if you got them wrong you didn't survive long enough for your performance to matter."

Another key concept in the book was hindsight bias—the tendency people have to claim, after a Black Swan event, that they could see it coming all along. The political scientist Philip Tetlock illustrated the concept in his 2016 book *Superforecasting: The Art and Science of Prediction*. He recounted how in 1988, when Soviet president Mikhail Gorbachev was implementing a series of major reforms such as glasnost (a more open society), he asked experts to estimate the odds that the Communist Party would lose its grip on the country in the next five years. Several years later, after the Soviet Union collapsed, he asked the same experts to recall their estimates. "On average they recalled a number 31 percentage points higher than the correct figure," Tetlock wrote. One expert who'd put the odds of collapse at 20 percent recalled forecasting it as 70 percent.

At the heart of Taleb's *The Black Swan* lurked a paradox, an uncomfortable contradiction—but a necessary one. Black Swans are by nature undefinable, uncontained, incomprehensible, unpredictable, uncertain, chaotic, random, wild, out-of-control crises. By naming this phenomenon, by describing it, defining it, Taleb was trying to do what he himself knew was impossible—to put the Black Swan in a box. To tell a story about it. It was a minor violation of another key concept in the book that Taleb called the Narrative Fallacy. "The angle I take concerns narrativity's simplification of the world around us and its effects on our perception of the Black Swan and wild uncertainty," he wrote. The human brain craves order—needs it. As Joan Didion wrote in *The White Album*, "We tell ourselves stories in order to live. . . . We live entirely, especially if we are writers, by the imposition of a narrative line upon disparate images." And so we impose patterns, structures, fragile frameworks onto a world constantly roiled in chaos. "The more you summarize," Taleb wrote, "the more order you put in, the less randomness. Hence *the same condition that makes us simplify pushes us to think that the world is less random than it actually is.*" It's a mistake constantly made by journalists and economists, causing them to make strong assumptions in areas of profound uncertainty, Taleb argued.

In a similar fashion, it's the problem the Indian novelist Amitav Ghosh, in his 2016 nonfiction book *The Great Derangement: Climate Change and the Unthinkable*, said explained why modern literary fiction was incapable of incorporating extreme events such as global warming into a believable narrative. Literary fiction craved sensibility, carefully constructed tales of cause and effect. It banished the incomprehensible—the unforeseen, unlikely disasters that are relegated to the less-respectable genres of fantasy and science fiction. Literary fiction has as its domain the little life, the daily comings and goings and small-world problems of middle-class characters such as Flaubert's Emma Bovary and James Joyce's Leopold Bloom. (Outliers to this phenomenon might include epics such as *War and Peace* and *Moby-Dick*.) Ghosh wrote: "The central credo of this doctrine was 'nothing could change otherwise than the way things were seen to change in the present.' Or, to put it simply: 'Nature does not make leaps.' The trouble, however, is that Nature does certainly jump, if not leap."

Black Swans abound. But it's wickedly difficult to talk or think about them. The British philosopher Timothy Morton coined his own term for a similar phenomenon: the hyperobject. These slippery entities—primarily, to Morton, global warming—are so vast in time and space that traditional forms of human thought are incapable of grasping them. And yet, humans are constantly obsessed with them, which in part helps explain the off-the-chart success of *The Black Swan*, which sold in the millions and spent thirty-six weeks on the *New York Times* bestseller list. That success turned Taleb into a minor celebrity—a "mini-institution," Bloomberg trumpeted—and brought him speaking fees of $60,000 or more per appearance. "Overnight, [Taleb] went from lone-voice-in-the-wilderness, spouting off-the-wall theories, to the great seer of the modern age," the *Guardian* said.

But his sudden stardom wasn't enough to convince investors to pony up cash for Universa's Black Swan protection plan in 2007.

That soon changed.

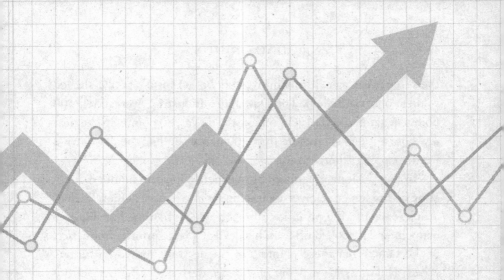

CHAPTER 9

A VERY DARK TUNNEL

Twitchy, nervous, sweaty, Spitznagel checked his BlackBerry for the twentieth time in the past thirty minutes. It was September 29, 2008, and he was stuck in a meeting with managers of a university endowment outside Chicago. He was monitoring news, emails, the state of the market. The American and European financial systems were spiraling, threatening to bring down the global economy with them. Lehman Brothers had collapsed, Fannie Mae and Freddie Mac had imploded (as Taleb had predicted years before), and banks were hemorrhaging cash. U.S. automakers were on the brink of ruin. Hank Paulson, the Bush administration's treasury secretary, had cobbled together a $700 billion financial rescue package to plug the gaping hole in the dike.

Congress was poised to vote on the bailout, and it wasn't clear which way the vote would go. Suddenly, at 1:43 p.m. Eastern time, the market plunged. The U.S. House of Representatives had rejected the rescue package. Terrified investors bolted for cover like shelled soldiers on a battlefield. The Dow Jones Industrial Average fell 100 points in a minute. By 1:45 p.m., it was down 580 points. In the next few hours, it had shed more than 700 points, ending the day down a head-snapping 7 percent.

In Santa Monica, Yarckin sat mesmerized by the numbers flickering on his screen. Universa's trading room was eerily quiet. He had a sick feeling in the pit of his stomach that something horrible was happening. He looked up from his desk at a large print reproduction of the famous Japanese painting of fragile ships tossed by furious waves, Hokusai's *Great Wave off Kanagawa*, hung by Spitznagel the previous year. A reproduction of a black swan painting by Belgian symbolist William Degouve de Nuncques hung on another wall.

As the market crashed, Spitznagel rushed from the meeting to his hotel room, fielding phone calls from anxious investors and managing the fund's positions from his laptop alongside his traders back at the Santa Monica office. The CBOE Volatility Index, or the VIX, a measure of volatility known as the Fear Index—and something of a proxy for Universa's profits—surged to its highest level in its twenty-eight-year history. The value of Universa's positions was exploding. It was a thunderstorm and Universa was the only firm with umbrellas. It was, in effect, setting the price for umbrellas.

After the market closed, Spitznagel scrambled to catch a late-night flight back to L.A. and get ready for the next day. It was the moment he'd prepared himself for ever since he'd started learning to lose from Everett Klipp on the floor of the CBOT in the 1980s. The risk of a market collapse was no longer a vague Black Swan looming distantly in the night sky. Universa's Black Swan Protection Protocol, which had gotten its first new outside investments only that March, by September was providing market insurance for $1 billion—that is, protecting $1 billion in investor assets against a crash. By the day of the Congress-sparked crash, it was protecting $1.5 billion. More was coming.

On October 8, the Federal Reserve, European Central Bank, and

Bank of England each slashed interest rates as the financial system continued to seize up. The Fed funds rate went to 1.5 percent, its lowest level in four years. The next day, the stock market appeared relatively serene following weeks of turmoil. Maybe the rate cuts were giving investors confidence? Then, at 3:00 p.m., it crashed. Again. Investors dumped shares en masse. The New York Stock Exchange saw its busiest day of trading ever to date, with 8.3 billion shares changing hands.

"There is a downward spiral of fear," Richard Sparks, a stock analyst at Schaeffer's Investment Research, told the *New York Times*. "We're witnessing complete panic," Trevor Callan, a California financial planner, said. "We're in the middle of a very dark tunnel," Brian Fabbri of BNP Paribas told the *Wall Street Journal*.

The Dow industrials fell below 9,000 points for the first time since 2003, wiping out the bull market of the previous five years. The Dow had plunged 1,874 points in a week, or 18 percent—its worst week ever. The Dow Jones Wilshire 5000, the broadest measure of the market, had wiped out $2.5 trillion in value in seven trading days and $8.4 trillion after hitting an all-time high the previous year.

By the end of trading on October 9, the S&P 500 had dropped 22 percent for the month. It was the crash Spitznagel & Co. had been telling investors they'd protect them from for the past year and a half. Most had said it wasn't possible.

The far out-of-the-money options Universa had been gobbling up on the cheap were suddenly wildly valuable. In late September, when the S&P 500 was trading around 1200, Universa had purchased put options that would pay off if the index fell below 850 by late October—a highly unlikely collapse. Most traders put little value on such options and sold them to Spitznagel for about 90 cents. Now the options were worth somewhere around $60. Universa sold most of its positions in the high $50 range.

After trading closed that day, Yarckin dragged Spitznagel out of the office for a beer to commemorate the grim occasion. As they walked to a dive bar around the corner, they marveled at all the people strolling obliviously down Santa Monica's Second Street Promenade in the California sunshine as if nothing were wrong. The ritual they were about to perform of knocking back a cold one was far from a celebration—the world was imperiled, and they knew it. "Be careful what you wish for," Spitznagel said as they raised their glasses for a toast.

> > < <

Big money was suddenly banging down Universa's doors. No one knew how bad the market would get. They only knew that it kept falling, and they wanted a parachute (though it's usually not effective to start shopping for parachutes after you've jumped from the plane).

After some two decades of trading, Spitznagel was finally a Big Dog like his pit-trading heroes at the CBOT. But it was a victory hollowed out by anxiety. The global economy was in a tailspin as a result of all the bad behavior he and Taleb had been warning about for years. That meant real harm to real people. Hardly time for chest-thumping declarations of victory. "I am very sad to be vindicated," Taleb told a British newspaper. "I don't care about the money."

But the money was very real and very large for Universa, which in all made about $1 billion on its positions during the initial phases of the Global Financial Crisis, in contrast to the billions lost by other hedge funds. Since the firm charged a management fee of 1.5 percent of the assets the firm protected and 20 percent of the gains, that meant it cleared roughly $200 million on that $1 billion bonanza, on top of the 1.5 percent fee.

By the end of 2008, Universa's Black Swan fund was protecting $4 billion in assets. It was mostly new money from new investors, not profits made on its Black Swan trades. Universa returned most of its gains to investors so they could either sock the money away for a rainy day or, for the bolder, use the windfall to scoop up pummeled stocks on the cheap.

Reporters suddenly wanted to know all about the secretive Black Swan trader in Santa Monica. Nearly every article featured the "*Black Swan* author" Nassim Taleb. The implication (or so Spitznagel thought) was that Universa was Taleb's fund—that Taleb was making investment decisions and Spitznagel was merely along for the ride. At first, he enjoyed the obscurity, happy to let Taleb hog the spotlight. But he began to worry investors might get the wrong idea. The fact was, Taleb had virtually no influence on Universa, aside from the research he continued to do on the math of fat tails, or when he was giving speeches to wealthy audiences who might take an interest in Universa.

In all, Spitznagel and his team made a 115 percent gain in 2008, compared with a 39 percent loss by the S&P 500 (the actual gain on Universa's trading position was in the thousands of percent). An investor starting the year with $1 million in the S&P 500 finished with $610,000. For that investor to become whole, the index would have to gain 64 percent—a feat it wouldn't pull off for nearly four years. The same million in Universa turned into $2.15 million.

Of course, no investor put 100 percent of their wealth into Universa—they put a sliver of it (Universa recommended 3 percent). An investor with that allocation would have lost about 8 percent overall in 2008—far better than the 39 percent gutting of the S&P.

Copycats plunged into what the Wall Street press had taken to calling "black swan funds." A strategy that hadn't existed before Taleb and Spitznagel launched Empirica in 1999 was suddenly one of the financial world's hottest products. It was flattering. The two iconoclasts had created a new asset class. How many traders could say that? It was also vexing. Now Spitznagel had to compete with fund managers he was certain were less than competent at trading but perhaps more adept at one of Wall Street's more primary skills: salesmanship.

Of course, Universa wasn't the only hedge fund to make billions during the Global Financial Crisis. A small group of opportunistic traders had identified a way to short the U.S. housing market. John Paulson, a high-rolling hedge fund manager who liked to place massive bets on mergers and acquisitions, made $15 billion in 2007 on a housing-related gambit. Michael Burry, a neurologist turned hedge

fund manager, posted a gain of nearly 500 percent by shorting derivative products tied to U.S. housing. Because hardly anyone thought
the U.S. housing market could implode, making that bet before the
implosion started was extremely cheap.

In some ways, those trades were similar to Universa's. They were
bets on volatility—in housing prices. The financial instrument that
traders like Paulson utilized was called a credit default swap. Think
of it like an insurance policy on a mortgage. If the mortgage holder
defaults (or if ten thousand mortgage holders default), the swap pays
off, just like a put option pays off if the price of a stock falls to a certain price.

Paulson and Burry had identified a systemic weakness in the
U.S. housing market and had devised an ingenious way to profit
when it blew up. Spitznagel and Taleb, by contrast, had identified
weaknesses *in the financial system as a whole*. The widespread use of
derivatives, the application of faulty risk-management tools such as
value at risk, the explosion of leverage, the Federal Reserve's lax monetary policy, the transformation of the investment banking industry
into a drunken Wild West hedge fund–mad casino—all had turned
the global financial system into a house of cards. Few shared their
views, and that meant they could make their bet—like Paulson's and
Burry's swaps—on the cheap.

The difference: The Paulson-Burry bets were onetime bonan-
zas. The housing market collapsed, they made a fortune. They never
repeated that performance. Indeed, Paulson suffered huge losses in
the years that followed. Their bets were similar to the phenomenally
successful trade Bill Ackman made in early 2020, which also used
cheap swaps to wager on a crash—a onetime, unrepeatable wager.

Universa, by contrast, could keep making its bet over and over
again, forever.

>   >   <   <

"The system is very unstable," Taleb said, facing a room of private
bankers. Capitalism was on the ropes, he said—and could collapse.

As Universa's reputation soared, so did Taleb's. The Global Financial Crisis seemed the quintessence of a Black Swan (even though Taleb claimed it was an entirely predictable "Gray Swan"). He was in great demand, and he was taking advantage of it.

In late 2008, he took the stage at Florence Gould Hall, the primary venue for the French Institute, on East 59th Street in New York City. Sans tie as always, clad in brown slacks and a blue jacket, he seemed something akin to a dapper biblical prophet proclaiming doom as the foolhardy fat cats were routed from the temple. It was just one week after the stock market had crashed on Congress's fateful bailout vote, a month after the collapse of Lehman Brothers. Doom was in the air.

He made his apocalyptic pronouncements in a calm, steady voice, occasionally gesticulating toward the crowd with a sweep of his hand. Financial markets, and the world itself, were far more volatile than many believed, as giant institutions toppled like dominoes. His concern with Black Swans, he said, extended beyond financial markets to the scientific method itself. Wild, unforeseen, chaotic moves happen all the time. But the financial geniuses on Wall Street can't see them. Their sophisticated models are backward looking, and they rely on the bell curve. The fact is, Black Swans can wipe out entire portfolios—or entire banks—in the blink of an eye.

As the reverberations of Lehman's bankruptcy continued to roll through the markets, Taleb ramped up his attacks on Wall Street's financial engineers.

"We have a problem," he said in a sober voice, addressing the crowd of bankers. "The illusion of control. We have this idea of the world being understandable and predictable. But we do not understand the future.

"In the stock market," he continued, "the ten most volatile days in the past fifty years represent 50 percent of the returns. Just one day in the past twenty years in derivatives represents 90 percent of the returns. Black Monday."

The recent events had pushed the financial system to the extreme. Taleb told the bankers in the room that the multitrillion-dollar credit meltdown on Wall Street, by the time it was over, would wipe out all of the money the global banking industry had made.

Ever.

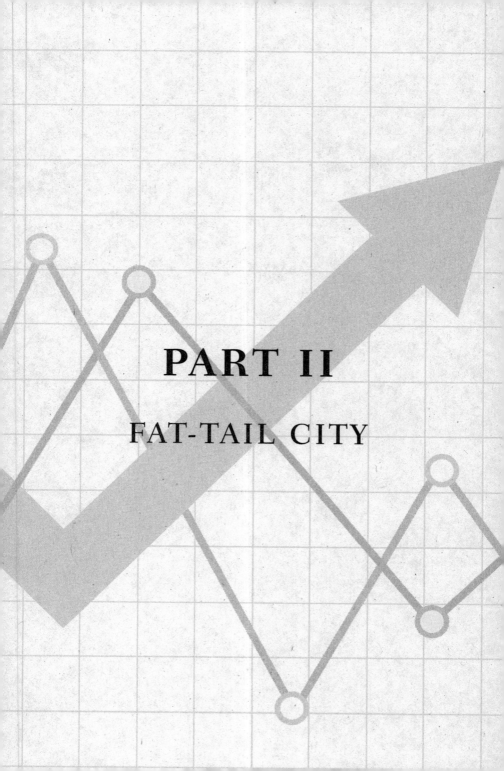

PART II

FAT-TAIL CITY

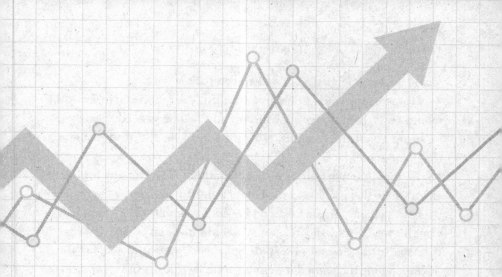

CHAPTER 10

DREAMS & NIGHTMARES

In January 2009, the world's top financiers, policy-makers, and so-called elite thinkers flocked to Davos, Switzerland, home of the World Economic Forum, to try to figure out how it all went wrong—and what to do next. Among the newly minted elite: Nassim Taleb.

On a Wednesday night at the forum, Taleb sat on a podium alongside Niall Ferguson, the British professor of history and bestselling author; Nouriel Roubini, known as Dr. Doom for having forecast the financial collapse; and behavioral finance Nobelist Danny Kahneman. The subject of their discussion: the fateful hours surrounding the collapse of Lehman Brothers and its role in the ensuing crisis.

Most agreed that while Lehman had made things worse, the problems in the financial sector were far broader and systemic. Ferguson, looking ahead, said the world was entering a "global lost decade." Things would be worst in the U.S., he added, leading to "the twilight of the American hegemony."

Then Taleb lobbed a verbal hand grenade.

"I was happy when Lehman went bust," he quipped. He'd made money on its bankruptcy via Universa and said he danced a jig when he heard about the calamity. "I hate traders," he added to hammer the point home.

Former Lehman traders were not amused. Now working for Barclays, which had purchased the defunct investment house, one trader wrote to a client, "Trading floor on fire about comments. . . . Seriously want his head." "Nassim Taleb may want to stock up on bodyguards," the *Wall Street Journal* observed. Spitznagel tried to downplay the dustup, telling the *Journal* it was a regrettable side of Universa's strategy that it tended to thrive when others were suffering.

Spitznagel found himself battling an altogether different and more powerful foe: Ben Bernanke and the Federal Reserve. In response to the financial crisis, Bernanke cranked up the financial stimulus dial to 100. Central bankers, having lowered short-term interest rates to near zero, had begun implementing a strategy known as *quantitative easing*, or QE. It sounds complicated. It's not. The Fed simply buys lots and lots of bonds. Mortgage bonds, Treasury bonds. Billions and billions of dollars' worth of bonds. That can stimulate growth in a few ways. For one, it can shrink the balance sheets of banks, which no longer have to hold those bonds. It can also make it easier for companies to get a loan, since the Fed is there acting as a buyer of last resort. By mid-2009, the Fed had purchased more than $2 trillion worth of debt.

Most economists applauded the move as necessary to keep the financial system from collapsing. Some likened the economy to a patient on an operating table requiring electric shocks to stave off a fatal heart attack.

Spitznagel said the patient might live—but would be sicker than ever. "With interest rates at zero, monetary engines humming as never before . . . we are back again embracing the brave new era of government sponsored prosperity and debt," he wrote in an opinion piece for *The Wall Street Journal*. Spitznagel was a disciple of the Austrian school of economics that decried government intervention in the economy. Its outlook contrasted with that of the supporters of English economist John Maynard Keynes, who prescribed government-funded financial stimulus to help rocky economies recover from times of recession or depression.

The Austrian view, elaborated by economists such as Ludwig von Mises and Friedrich Hayek, prescribed harsh medicine for failing businesses. Or rather, no medicine at all. "Let all the lame businesses fail—no bailouts," Spitznagel wrote. "The distortions must be removed or else the precipice from which the system will inevitably fall will simply grow higher and higher."

One significant risk of all the stimulus, Spitznagel believed, was that it would trigger persistent inflation, especially in assets such as stocks. In the summer of 2009, responding to investors' concern about the risk, he launched a new fund designed to profit from rising prices. He'd buy call options that would gain in value with commodities such as corn, crude oil, and gold, likely beneficiaries of an inflationary environment. It would also short Treasury bonds, which would inevitably take a hit from inflation as interest rates shot higher.

Spitznagel wasn't alone in his expectation of an inflationary spiral. Warren Buffett feared rising prices and said the Treasury bond market was in one of the biggest bubbles he'd ever seen. "The prospects for significant inflation have increased, not only here but around the world," the Oracle of Omaha said in 2010. Taleb said he expected *hyper*inflation.

They were all wrong. Runaway inflation didn't take off the way many expected. There were some periodic bouts of price spikes, but they were usually short-lived or confined to certain fast-growing economies and China, whose seemingly unstoppable 10-percent-a-year growth—and all the demand that came with it—triggered a so-called commodity super cycle that sent prices for metals such as copper, steel, and iron into record territory.

One argument for why inflation remained largely under wraps was that the Global Financial Crisis was caused by the collapse of the financial system, rather than weakness in other parts of the economy, like manufacturing. That made it difficult to stimulate consumption because banks weren't lending—burned by the crisis, they hoarded cash. That's why some economists, such as *New York Times* opinion writer—and frequent Taleb punching bag—Paul Krugman, said the Fed wasn't providing *enough* stimulus and the Obama administration wasn't spending enough to revive the sick patient. "Banks aren't lending out their extra reserves," he wrote in a May 2009 opinion piece. "They're just sitting on them."

Another reason why inflation remained relatively tame: Wages for most Americans remained stagnant amid tepid economic growth. People were out of work, hiring was weak, so businesses didn't have to crank up wages to lure workers. There was no spark to ignite the inflationary bonfire. The so-called wage-price feedback loop in which workers with higher salaries buy more stuff, pushing prices for that stuff higher, leading to demands for higher wages—a factor in the sky-high inflation seen in the 1970s—didn't happen. This was partly the result of the decline in union membership and the erosion in labor power since the 1980s. Competition from China was another factor as manufacturers offshored production at record rates. Wage growth in the 2010s in America was virtually nonexistent through much of the decade, according to the Economic Policy Institute. Median household income in 2015 was $70,200, no higher than it was in 2000, "marking a 15-year period of stagnation, an episode of unprecedented duration in the past five decades," the Pew Research Center said.

While the real economy suffered enormously following the financial crisis, hitting both wages and housing prices, the stock market surged. Households with significant stock investments benefitted greatly (on paper). But the feedback into the real economy from asset inflation that Bernanke was betting on didn't happen, or it happened much more slowly than hoped for. Such wealth disparities did enormous harm in the U.S., with rising resentment against elites and persistent despair among the many families, small towns, and struggling workers left out of the party.

So while Spitznagel's new inflation fund may have been a dud (he unwound it a few years later), his larger point—that loose monetary policy and fiscal stimulus don't come without substantial negative side effects, such as inflated assets that mostly benefit the wealthy—was valid. What's more, as inflation remained head-scratchingly low throughout the decade, the Fed never turned off the taps. It kept rates low and QE humming all through the 2010s. Stimulus went into hyperdrive after the Covid-19 crack-up. When the punch bowl is inevitably pulled away, there's bound to be an epic hangover. In 2022, as the Fed began ratcheting rates higher to fight creeping inflation, many on Wall Street began to wonder if they needed to stock up on aspirin—or something much stronger.

> > < <

As Nassim Taleb's taxi turned down 1 Rocket Road, the expansive warehouse hove into view: SpaceX, Elon Musk's Los Angeles rocket-development facility. It was late in the afternoon, July 24, 2009. Taleb checked his email. "Welcome to LA!" his literary agent and the organizer of the proceedings, John Brockman, had written:

> <u>Here's some specifics re: the agenda:</u>
> **FRIDAY NIGHT**
> *6pm Cocktails—Mezzanine Level*
> *7pm Dinner—Mezzanine Level—Studio 5*
> **SATURDAY MORNING**
> *7:30 Breakfast Mezzanine Level—Studio 4*
> *8:30 Depart by bus to Space X (about 20–30 minutes)*
> To accommodate Craig Venter who can only arrive at Space X in the afternoon, if possible, I will move Elon Musk's talk and tour of the facility to 4pm, instead of during the lunch break.
> *7:30 Dinner—Spago*
> *176 N Canon Dr Beverly Hills, CA 90210*

With the blockbuster success of *The Black Swan*, Taleb had gained entry into one of the most elite intellectual salons in America, Brockman's Edge Foundation, an informal collection of (mostly male) scientists and thinkers that included Richard Dawkins, Steven Pinker, Danny Kahneman, and Murray Gell-Mann (discoverer of the quark) as well as tycoons such as Google founders Sergey Brin and Larry Page, Amazon's Jeff Bezos, Microsoft's Bill Gates, and future disgraced financier Jeffrey Epstein. The idea behind the salon was simple: put a bunch of smart people together in a room, have them talk, and see what comes out on the other end. Sprinkle on some billionaire cash and maybe something big could actually germinate. It was a "forum for big, intriguing and/or disturbing ideas advanced by intellectuals who have a track record of major achievements in their fields," the *Guardian* wrote.

That week, the Edgies were gathering at SpaceX and the ritzy Andaz West Hollywood hotel to hear presentations about the latest advances in microbiology from experts such as Harvard Medical School geneticist George Church and Craig Venter, the biotechnologist who first mapped the human genome. Brockman had earlier sent Taleb a list of topics included in the so-called Master Class, a dizzying witches' brew of techno-wizardry: what is life, origins of life, in-vitro synthetic life, mirror life, metabolic engineering for hydrocarbons and pharmaceuticals, computational tools, electronic-biological interfaces, nanotech-molecular manufacturing, biosensors, accelerated lab evolution, engineered personal stem cells, multivirus-resistant cells, humanized mice, bringing back extinct species.

At the SpaceX facility, Church gave a talk called "Dreams and Nightmares." Attendees included venture capitalist Sean Parker, an original Facebook backer; Google's Larry Page; behavioral economist Richard Thaler; Stewart Brand, creator of the *Whole Earth Catalog*; someone from the White House; and a bunch of egghead scientists. Elon Musk ducked in from time to time to listen. Taleb introduced himself as a professor of risk engineering, which he said "doesn't explain what I do."

Church, a tall, wizardly man with a heavy white beard, explained that, contrary to popular belief, geneticists still hadn't mapped the entire human genome. That left gaps in scientists' efforts to detect what in DNA might be the cause of certain diseases, such as schizophrenia. (A complete map of the human genome was finally completed in 2022.)

Another lecture by Church later that day was called "Constructing Life from Chemicals."

"I'm going to describe some technology that may shock you. Do we really know what we're doing? Almost everything that I'll be mentioning could have unintended consequences that we might not be able to anticipate."

Church put up a slide that read: "Precautionary Principle. *If an action might cause severe or irreversible harm to the public, in the absence of a scientific consensus, the burden of proof falls on those who would advocate taking the action.*"

"You've got this precautionary principle," Church said. "There's a tendency, when you don't understand things, to do nothing. And that's defensible in some circumstances, and not in others. And I don't think we need to talk about it a lot."

Church moved on to what he called global terraforming as a method to combat the warming of the planet. One example was "ocean fertilization," seeding oceans with cheap forms of iron to absorb carbon dioxide, which can generate massive algae blooms. "Some people were concerned that we didn't really know what we were doing when we caused these big blooms in the middle of the ocean," he noted. "The point is, when you're doing this global terraforming, is what I'd call it, on the Earth, you're taking these kinds of risks. Not doing it, you're also taking risks."

The next topic concerned synthesizing DNA using a relatively cheap desktop fabricator. "Here you can make in one run something the size of smallpox," he said. "You can make a drug-resistant, vaccine-resistant smallpox, which wouldn't be too good. There's some enthusiasm for monitoring this."

A discussion broke out in the group about whether, in a matter of years, the technology would have evolved to the point at which a deadly pathogen could be synthesized in a high-school lab for a few thousand dollars.

"The reason why this falls into an important aspect of global existential risk," Church said, "is that they're replicating," referring to the pathogens. "Nuclear waste spreads, but it dilutes as it spreads. This *replicates*."

Taleb raised his hand. "The problem you're facing here is that when you say 'nuclear power' people are scared of it. But it's not multiplicative, and the errors are tractable," he said. "There's nothing more multiplicative than this"—i.e., exponentially spreading viruses. "This is a monster, all right."

"That's right," Church said.

"And it's a probability of one"—in statistics-speak, a one-hundred-percent gurantee—"that someone is going to invent something that scales. It's fat-tail city."

"The reality is there are a lot of ways to seriously mess with the world," Google's Larry Page said. "And most of them have not been done yet. The problem with defense against one of these things is you have to protect against all possible threats, which isn't very practical."

"It's the same problem as in finance," Taleb observed. "Before this crisis, people couldn't believe that the financial system was so messed up, so connected, right? Now, anything too connected in a complex system is going to break eventually. And we're too connected. Airline travel? We're too connected."

For days, listening to lecture after lecture about deconstructing, mixing, carving up, slicing and dicing DNA, Taleb went through a bout of severe emotional stress. Church was casually talking about top-down engineering of the building blocks of life—and of lethal viruses that could put an end to the human race. The visit to SpaceX would be Taleb's first and last Edge meeting. It marked the beginning of his deep concern about scientists tampering with genetics, which would later turn into a crusade against genetically modified organisms that put him squarely in the crosshairs of one of the world's largest corporations.

CHAPTER 11

FLASH CRASH

S hortly after 2:15 p.m. Eastern time on May 6, 2010, a trader at Universa's Santa Monica office placed an order with the firm's broker, Barclays Capital, to purchase fifty thousand put option contracts in Chicago's trading pits. The options would pay off if the S&P 500 fell to 800 by a certain date in June—a massive decline. The S&P was trading at 1135. Universa paid $7.5 million for that bet. If the S&P *did* fall to 800 by the June expiration date, the trade would be worth $1 billion.

In less than half an hour, the U.S. stock market would witness one of the most bizarre, volatile moments in its history—the Flash Crash, as the financial press later called it. In a matter of minutes, the Dow industrials fell one thousand points. It was a Black Swan, truly unforeseen, the most sudden, volatile market crash since Black Monday.

As stocks tumbled and volatility surged, put options Universa

had bought in April for $2 a piece if the S&P 500 fell below 1100—
it was trading at 1200 at the time—surged in value. In a snap, they
were worth $60 a piece as the index dropped as low as 1066. Univer-
sa's traders in Santa Monica raced to cash in on the company's bearish bets, selling their $60 options as other firms, scrambling to hedge
their losses, snapped up the über-expensive contracts. The opportunity was literally gone in a flash as the market swiftly rebounded
following the gut-wrenching downward spike. "If you blinked you
missed it," Spitznagel recalled.

Universa reportedly made $1 billion in just a single afternoon's
trading that day.

Soon after, chatter spread on Chicago's trading floors that Universa's big bearish bet at a time when the market was highly vulnerable might have helped trigger the cascade. A broker taking the
other side of the put option would have to sell stocks to hedge their
own position, protecting themselves from further declines. It eventually emerged that there was no single cause of the crash. There was
a lot of selling, very heavy volume, and technical glitches at stock
exchanges and brokerage houses. As the chaos spread, a large number of high-frequency trading firms—the computer-driven shops that
dominated markets by acting as market makers, buying when others sold and selling when others bought—turned off their machines.
That removed a huge chunk of buy orders from a market in which
everyone else was selling and created a bottomless vacuum that
sucked in sell orders like a black hole.

The Flash Crash offered a rare glimpse inside Universa's black box.
The firm's trade that day via Barclays Capital was incredibly bearish,
a bet not on a 20 percent decline in the S&P 500, but on a *30 percent*
decline. The payoff was *enormous*—$1 billion from a $7.5 million position it purchased that day and the $2 contracts Universa had bought
in April, which shot to $60 in minutes. That's exactly what Spitznagel
meant when he said Universa provided *explosive* upside protection.

> > < <

One day that summer Spitznagel and his wife were at the second home they'd bought in Northport, Michigan, the small town where Mark had spent the first decade of his life, when they spotted a vacant expanse of land across the bay. After inspecting what turned out to be a two-hundred-acre farm, which consisted of some rugged-looking cherry trees and a collection of dilapidated buildings, they decided to buy it for $1 million.

Then they had to decide what to do with it. They knew they wanted to farm the land, make something real connected to the area—and hedge against the total collapse of the financial system and global economy, a constant worry Spitznagel carried around in the darker recesses of his mind, one of the drawbacks of running a fund predicated on the sudden outbreak of chaos and disaster. After briefly contemplating winemaking, they settled on goat-cheese production. To learn more about the process, they visited goat-cheese makers in California and France, including world-class *fromager* Rodolphe Le Meunier. Soon after, they started buying—and breeding—goats. They'd eventually have hundreds, and the business—called Idyll Farms—would, in time, make some of the best goat cheese in America.

Taleb, for his part, began looking for places to stash his gains from Universa and the voluminous sales of *The Black Swan*. In the summer of 2010 he paid a visit to his native northern Lebanon to shop for olive orchards. "Healthy investments are those that produce goods that humans need to consume, not flat-screen TVs," he told the *Wall Street Journal* from near his family's ancestral home in Amioun. "Stocks are not a robust investment. Make sure you have a garden that bears fruits."

Taleb wasn't involved in Universa's day-to-day activities. He was jetting around the globe giving lectures, enjoying fine dinners at the world's top restaurants, revelling in the fruits of his fame. But he did like to fly out west for the Universa parties. Sometimes all the jet-setting got to him. Once, after showing up for a Universa Christmas bash, which involved driving around Los Angeles in limousines, he crashed in the spacious trunk of the limo for the entire night's festivities.

When Spitznagel wasn't trading options, herding goats, or trying out new goat cheeses, he was rubbing shoulders with some of the world's biggest investors, including those running sovereign wealth funds, the deep-pocketed funds that invest on behalf of governments. The days of fruitlessly trying to explain the Black Swan stategy to clueless fund managers were over. Universa was in talks with China's $300 billion fund, China Investment Corp., big Middle Eastern government funds, wealthy investors in European capitals such as London and Geneva, and giant pension funds across the U.S.

The firm was hitting on all cylinders, managing the risk of $10 billion worth of investments for its clients. That in itself meant a windfall for Spitznagel and his team. The fee structure Universa charged explains why so many on Wall Street aspire to be hedge fund kingpins. One-and-a-half percent of $10 billion is $150 million. Add that to the $200 million Universa made on its $1 billion Flash Crash trade, that's a total of $350 million for a firm of roughly sixteen people. (The fees were also a turnoff for some prospective investors who didn't like it that Universa took a chunk of the crash-bang insurance payout.)

Spitznagel, bluntly put, was getting wildly rich—and living like it. He bought a Bel-Air mansion from Jennifer Lopez and Marc Anthony for $7.5 million. A walled-and-gated French-style villa, it was surrounded by a moat and had a guesthouse, swimming pool, stream, and a garden with an arbor. One room the size of a New York studio apartment had been dedicated solely to storing J. Lo's shoes. The mansion stood a block away from a former home of Spitznagel's boyhood idol Ronald Reagan. Nancy Reagan still lived there, and he fantasized about strolling up to her home and knocking on the door.

Other fund managers, wanting their own J. Lo mansions and moats, did the math—and opened up copycat operations. "A growing number of money managers and financial firms are rolling out investment products designed to exploit big declines known as 'black swan' events," an August 2010 *Wall Street Journal* article said. Some twenty "tail risk" funds had launched just in the previous eighteen months.

To Spitznagel's horror, the article noted that some individual investors were considering setting up Black Swan portfolios in their day-trading accounts, citing a thirty-year-old transportation engineer who wanted to "pick up some extra money if things went crazy."

> > < <

Didier Sornette felt triumphant as he stepped to a lectern in a double-breasted gray suit, facing an audience of academics, financiers, and journalists. He had slain the dragon. Actually, *three* dragons. It was a crisp morning in Zurich, May 3, 2010. Sornette was about to announce the results of the Financial Bubble Experiment.

In late 2009, using the LPPLS model, he had forecast that four assets would form bubbles in the following six months. The twist: He didn't reveal his forecasts at the time. Instead, he submitted them to an open-access database, called arXiv, which time-stamped and encrypted them. Now he was going to reveal the results.

The test bubbles were in Brazilian stocks, a bond index, gold, and cotton. Three of the four market shifts had played out as predicted. Brazilian stocks and cotton had each entered bubble territory before tumbling more than 10 percent each. The bond index had cratered just before the forecast time period, indicating it was already emerging from a bubble when the test began.

The results were hard to parse. Cotton had tumbled more than 10 percent after a sharp increase, but the indicators implied that it remained in a bubble. And indeed it did—over the next year cotton surged 300 percent, along with a host of other commodities in what economists took to calling a commodity super-cycle largely based on insatiable demand from China. (Sornette, in a paper detailing his results, said cotton "was and still is in a bubble without showing a clear change of regime.") Gold also continued to ramp higher after its short-lived decline. It seemed Sornette's system had indeed identified some bubbles, but failed to accurately predict when they would pop.

The near-miss forecasts highlighted weaknesses of the LPPLS

approach. In October 1997, he'd also forecast a crash—and he was right. But the magnitude of the crash he'd expected was much greater than what actually happened. He seemed able to detect tremors; he just didn't know if it was the Big One or merely another temblor that would barely get noticed.

In December of 2009, Sornette presented the latest results of his research at the Financial Crisis Observatory in a talk to the American Geophysical Union in San Francisco. Fittingly, it was the annual Ed Lorenz Lecture given in honor of the pioneer of chaos theory and nonlinear geophysics. Lorenz became famous in the 1960s for his description of the butterfly effect in which the flapping of a butterfly's wings in Brazil can (theoretically) conjur a tornado in Texas.

Sornette began with an attack on his nemesis: the Black Swan.

"This is the evidence . . . that crises are *not* Black Swans, as my friend Nassim Taleb describes in his famous book, which is now a paradigmatic representation of financial crises. They are dragons," he said. "What does it mean? If you think of the Black Swan story . . . they are basically unknown, even unknowable, until they occur. A great earthquake according to this view is nothing but a small earthquake that didn't stop. Impossible to predict. There is nothing that you can diagnose in advance, it cannot be quantified. There is no predictability. In the case of the financial crisis there is no responsibility. The wrath of God! And there is only one unique strategy. Only buy insurance," a reference to the Universa strategy.

Not so with Dragon Kings, which can be quantified, Sornette declared. "There is a degree of predictability."

Financial crashes display unique and identifiable mathematical characteristics totally unlike what happens during a typical trading session. A phenomenon that can cause a normal day to turn into a catastrophe, he claimed, is super-exponential growth combined with positive feedback loops. Price declines cause more declines triggering more and more declines until a critical moment is reached—a panic, a crash, a blowup. Sornette called such an event a *finite-time singularity*. He displayed a slide of phenomena with similar positive-feedback characteristics: the formation of black holes, turbulence in plasma, large earthquakes.

Or the size of cities. He brought up a chart showing the relative population of cities in France. All fit comfortably well on a slanting line showing that most cities stayed within a normal boundary, the safe confines of the bell curve. Except for one: Paris, the Dragon King among French cities. "This is Paris," he said. "There are special mechanisms at work that have led to the growth of cities."

The dream: By identifying these special mechanisms at work inside Dragon Kings, he could predict them. The overarching goal wasn't to always try to predict the future, a visibly impossible task, but rather to identify "pockets of predictability where there is this condensation of complexity." In other words, a crash crystal ball—albeit one that might be slightly cracked.

"These are some of the examples that I have encountered in my career chasing, hunting for these Dragon Kings," he concluded.

Sornette and a few assistants decided that if the forecasts were so accurate, why not make some money on them—just as he had in October 1997 when he predicted a crash? They opened up an Interactive Brokers trading account and put in $100,000 of their own money. Sornette won't reveal his results but says the investment was "extremely successful." But it became a distraction from their research, so he decided to stop it. "We were becoming a hedge fund," he told me.

Sornette says he gets asked the following question all the time. "If you're so successful, why aren't you running a big hedge fund?"

"I get this from students, my colleagues," he said. "Think about what this question means. It implies that the pinnacle, the ultimate success of an individual, is to run a hedge fund. Of course not! My position is one of the best positions on the planet. I'm completely free to explore the infinite universe of ideas."

The stress of running a hedge fund is bad for one's health, he added—at least one opinion he and Nassim Taleb might agree on.

> > < <

In late July 2011, Spitznagel took a Bloomberg reporter on a ride in his new nautical toy, a twin-engine Chris-Craft Corsair 28, across Grand Traverse Bay in northern Michigan, just offshore from the farm he'd purchased the year before. The reporter observed that at more than eighty kilometers an hour, the heavy boat left a big wake. "Turbulence is where Spitznagel, the founder of hedge fund Universa Investments, thrives," the article observed.

"Investors are pouring into doomsday black swan funds, [which] entice investors with the chance of a huge pay-off if a crisis hits," said the article. Assets in Black Swan funds had surged to $38 billion from $500 million before Lehman's collapse in 2008.

A big chunk of that $500 million had been in Universa. Indeed, so-called Black Swan funds *didn't exist* before Universa (aside from Empirica). Many that started up in the wake of the crisis were flying blind. Spitznagel had spent years refining the strategy, building relationships with options dealers on the Street, working out how to cut down transaction costs, building sophisticated computer models. One of Universa's advantages was that it effectively became a brokerage house for options, acting like a middleman providing liquidity to investors when they wanted it (investors being the ones selling the options). Many trading outfits, when it came to far-out-of-the-money put options, only wanted to sell them. It was, for the time being, free cash, since they usually expired worthless. Universa was happy to take that trade, at a fair price. Spitznagel's intricate models told him how much the options were worth, and he was extremely hardheaded about getting the price he wanted.

Part of the Universa strategy that went under the radar was the daily grind of building its Black Swan portfolio of crash protection. One trick Spitznagel used, going back to his days at Empirica, was to *sell* options—puts and calls—with strike prices close to the value of the underlying stock. Say Microsoft was trading at $100 a share. Universa might sell options that would gain in value if the stock moved up or down $5. Spitznagel reasoned that such options were pretty fairly valued—they weren't cheap, like the crazy, no-one-in-his-right-mind far-out-of-the-money options he bought every day. They might even be *over*valued, meaning it was profitable to sell them. And he felt he was better than his counterparts when it came to trading them. The profits he made on the strategy helped fund the crash-bang portfolio.

It's one reason why he boasted that Universa provided the best bang-for-the-buck strategy on Wall Street, because it helped lower the amount of money investors had to pony up for the protection. If a client wanted Universa to insure $1 billion against a 20 percent drawdown—or a loss of $200 million—for two years, that would require about $30 million (3 percent of $1 billion). The $30 million didn't go into the market immediately. Universa only invested part of it and used the rest to maintain the trade over the course of the next two years as the options behind it expired. Sometimes the client spent the entire $30 million and got nothing in return, like an insurance premium. But when the inevitable crash came— when the fire burned the house down—they got what they paid for, Spitznagel believed.

> > < <

Mark and Amy Spitznagel beamed as they greeted guests at their Bel-Air mansion. It was March 2012. They were hosting a $2,500-a-plate fundraiser for the longshot presidential campaign of libertarian Texas congressman Ron Paul, who shared a common enemy with Spitznagel: the Federal Reserve. Taleb, who said Paul was the only candidate he trusted in the race, appeared and gave a brief speech. "Who wouldn't want to debate monetary policy in the house where J. Lo once slept?" quipped a local columnist about the event.

Taleb's and Spitznagel's support for Paul—to whom Taleb would dedicate a later book, *Skin in the Game*, alongside his political polar opposite, Ralph Nader—came largely from their shared disdain for the Fed and other forms of government intervention. Paul, of course, didn't win the Republican nomination, which went to Mitt Romney.

Not only was Spitznagel convinced the Fed was doing irrepara-ble harm to the economy by keeping monetary policy exceedingly loose, he was deeply concerned about government bureaucrats tampering with the system's complex levers. One issue he constantly came back to concerned *time preferences*. Investors—or generals or central bankers or stranded sailors—who want an immediate victory might give up the advantage of waiting for a better opportunity later. A central banker who cuts interest rates to give the economy a pop now is robbing the future of potential growth. Spitznagel believed he knew a better path to maximizing outcomes, including for one's portfolio. He called this "roundabout investing," or taking the long route to whatever your goal is, rather than dashing straight toward it. He liked to point to the example of Robinson Crusoe, from the Daniel Defoe novel, the shipwrecked sailor who went hungry while spending precious time making a fishing rod. Loving to lose meant big gains down the road.

It was a lesson Spitznagel learned not only from the futures pits of Chicago but also from his years studying the writers from the Austrian School of Economics—Carl Menger, Eugen von Böhm-Bawerk, Ludwig von Mises, Friedrich Hayek. In a nutshell, the Austrians emphasize personal freedom and free markets against what they describe as the tyranny of central planners. Pure capitalism versus (they say) wealth-destroying socialism. The followers of Keynes, by contrast, argue governments can rescue economies from recessions and depressions by lowering interest rates or spending more. Think FDR's New Deal in the 1930s during the Great Depression or Hank Paulson's $700 billion bank bailout in 2008. Market forces, they argue, can fail, leading to long-term economic and social harm. When they do, governments need to jump in to fix the problem.

There is, clearly, much more to it. The Austrian School, long ignored in favor of Keynes, gained prominence in the 1980s during the time of the anti-big-government Reagan administration and Thatcherite Britain. It became fashionable on Wall Street, the beating heart and home of free-market capitalism. Traders influenced by the Russian-American free-market champion Ayn Rand and Hayek's *The Road to Serfdom*, the core economic text of the movement, came to despise

Alan Greenspan (who ironically loved Rand and praised the Austrian School) and his surprise interest-rate moves that roiled markets.

Spitznagel's diagnosis of Keynes and central bank interventions is far more nuanced than the typical trader's *fuck the Fed* attitude. It also, much like Taleb's Black Swan theory, bears strong resemblances to the sit-and-wait trading strategy he followed. If ever there was a "roundabout" approach to investing, it was Universa's love-to-lose method, always with that explosive payoff waiting in the wings.

Spitznagel laid out many of these ideas in his 2013 book, *The Dao of Capital: Austrian Investing in a Distorted World*, a medley of autobiography—with tales of CBOT trading and Klippisms such as "love to lose"—history, Eastern philosophy, trading insights, military strategy, economic theory, a critique of *Robinson Crusoe*, even a diversion into the arcane realm of forestry.

Soon after the book came out, Spitznagel and Yarckin decided to make a big move, literally. Annoyed by California's high tax rates, they decided to move Universa's headquarters to Miami due to its more business-friendly policies (i.e., lower taxes). In 2013 Spitznagel unloaded the J. Lo mansion for $10 million and set out, once again, for the East Coast. Around the same time, he also purchased a home in the upscale Detroit suburb of Bloomfield Hills and enrolled his two children in Cranbrook, a private school once attended by Mitt Romney.

Spitznagel and his wife had decided against living in Miami (he would rent a hotel room at a Four Seasons near Universa's office). They wanted to get away from another sprawling city such as L.A., and Detroit was closer to where Spitznagel had grown up. Deep down, he always felt a kinship with the more conservative, buckled-down mindset of the Midwest. Somehow the idea of living in Detroit meshed with his always-contrarian mentality. *Who the hell would want to live in Detroit?*

Disturbed by the city's endemic urban blight, Spitznagel in the summer of 2014 cooked up a plan to alleviate at least some of it. He transported twenty goats from Idyll Farms to a crime-ridden neighborhood in the northwest part of Detroit and opened up an urban farming experiment. Spitznagel hoped to turn it into a major philanthropic operation, providing cheap goat meat, milk, and cheese to the community. He was also hoping the goats would nibble on the out-of-control weeds and other vegetation in the overgrown yards of the abandoned homes that dotted the neighborhood.

Locals loved the goats. Unfortunately, Spitznagel never asked the city for permission, convinced they'd reflexively say no, and they promptly booted him and his goats back to Idyll Farms.

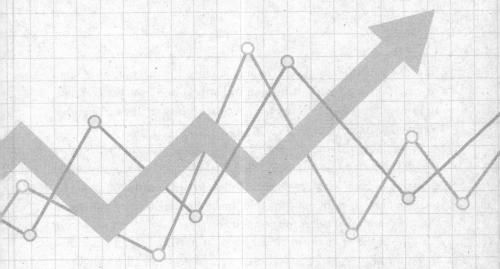

CHAPTER 12

THE DISORDER CLUSTER

N assim Taleb was on edge as he waited alongside Brandon Yarckin backstage in the grand ballroom of the Bellagio Hotel & Casino in Las Vegas. It was May 2014. Luminaries of the investing world had gathered at the palatial Bellagio for the annual SALT Conference, an event hosted by SkyBridge Capital, the $11 billion New York fund of funds managed by Anthony Scaramucci (who'd go on to serve as communications director in the Trump administration for eleven days).

Scaramucci's SALT conferences had become one of the financial industry's biggest events, mixing funds looking to raise cash with major investors from around the world. Past speakers had included hedge fund titans John Paulson and Steven Cohen as well as former Presidents Bill Clinton and George W. Bush. The speakers this year included famed astrophysicist Neil deGrasse Tyson, L.A. Lakers legend Magic Johnson, former British prime minister Tony Blair, and film director Francis Ford Coppola. Lenny Kravitz was scheduled to entertain the nearly two-thousand-strong horde of bankers and fund honchos in after-hours festivities with hits such as "American Woman" and "Fly Away."

Appaloosa Management's David Tepper, the top-performing hedge fund manager of 2013 with $3.5 billion in winnings, warned everyone to keep a healthy chunk of cash in their portfolio. "Don't be too frigging long right now," he told the audience. "It's nervous time." (Stocks went up another ten percent that year.)

One of the main draws: A debate between Taleb and Larry Summers, former head of the National Economic Council under President Obama, treasury secretary for Clinton, and onetime chief economist for the World Bank. Scaramucci moderated. (Taleb, who'd grown a reputation for having a hot temper and a violent disregard for economists, had pledged to Scaramucci that he'd play nice in the debate, as if Larry Summers were a shrinking violet requiring tender care.)

Yarckin was there to meet prospective investors tantalized by Taleb's fame. Appearing at such events—Taleb had been the keynote speaker at the previous year's SALT conference in Singapore—had become one of Taleb's primary functions at Universa. His draw as a public speaker helped the firm advertise itself to the world's biggest financiers at major conferences such as SALT. Few may have heard of Universa, but everyone knew who Nassim Taleb was.

As Taleb, sporting a pink shirt and blue coat, sans tie, waited for the event to begin, Summers entered the backstage waiting area. Stone-faced and icy, the MIT- and Harvard-educated economist barely acknowledged Taleb's presence, a foretaste of the tense clash of intellects to come.

Scaramucci, known to friends as the Mooch, gamboled across the stage, all energy, and introduced the pair. Taleb and Summers took their seats in matching jet-black leather chairs.

"When you look at the global economic landscape, what do you like? What worries you?" Scaramucci asked.

"I don't think it's plausible to think we're at the end of financial instability," Summers said. "Even if we appear to have relatively low volatility."

Taleb saw danger. The problems that had caused the Global Financial Crisis of 2008 still lurked beneath the surface. "When you have a crisis like we had, it was a very good painkiller to stop the bleeding, but it did not address the cancer," he said. "We have a lack of skin in the game, greater than any point in history."

The remark was an early reference to a more sweeping theory about risk management Taleb was formulating—*skin in the game* (and the title of his next book, published in 2018). The idea, at least for banks, was that management needs to have a much deeper, personal financial commitment to their firms. If the failure of a bank could cause management to go bankrupt as well, institutions would be much safer. As it stood, management faced few repercussions, if any, when a bank blew up, especially the "too big to fail" kind that socialized risk by passing it off to the taxpayer. That's why banks remained too large, too fragile, Taleb said, and the risk of collapse was greater than ever.

Summers's hackles went up. He was a chief architect of the Obama administration's bailout of the financial system and reforms put in place to shore up bank balance sheets. "Major financial institutions are much better capitalized," he said. "The mistake is to not recognize that things were done to put the pieces back together."

Taleb didn't agree. Like Spitznagel, he'd opposed the bailouts and thought the system would have been better off if more banks had been allowed to fail—and more bankers sent to jail. No major bank executive suffered in the crisis, he argued. The risk-takers were thrown life preservers. Because they didn't have skin in the game, bankers had turned their firms into high-stakes casinos that rewarded them with all the upside, with virtually zero risk on the downside. In later years, Taleb would go on to describe this as the "Bob Rubin trade," a reference to the former Clinton administration treasury secretary Robert Rubin who pocketed $120 million in compensation from Citibank in the years leading up to its implosion during the Global Financial Crisis, and wasn't forced to give back any of that cash stockpile. Rubin didn't have "skin in the game" that would have motivated him to press the bank to take less risk.

"These people are using the system," Taleb complained. "Let's go back to where banks were boring."

Summers disagreed that no one paid a price, noting that nearly all major bank CEOs lost their jobs. (Left unmentioned was their lucrative severance packages.) "I'm not for government running financial institutions. I'm for making them much more failure-proof and more safe for failure when they do fail. What are you for?"

"I'm for punishment," Taleb responded.

>   >   <   <

Weeks after his confrontation with Summers at the Bellagio, Taleb traded barbs with Didier Sornette at the New York Academy of Sciences in downtown Manhattan. Seated elbow to elbow on a platform before the audience, Taleb seemed relaxed in jeans and a jacket, eagerly anticipating the drinks promised after the debate. Sornette, in a more traditional button-down white shirt and striped gray suit, appeared tense. The debate pitted Taleb's extreme skepticism about forecasting against Sornette's finely honed mathematical models he claimed could predict extreme events—Black Swans versus Dragon Kings.

"This cup is fragile," Taleb began, pointing to a picture of a porcelain teacup on a projector. "It is fragile because it doesn't like volatility. And it has very specific attributes, sensitivity to volatility."

His implication: Don't be the teacup. And your trading strategy definitely better not be like the teacup. The first mistake people tend to make in risk management and probability theory is focusing too much on forecasting the future—the course of interest rates, economic growth, or currency valuations—he said, rather than the nature of one's exposure to risk (i.e., a trading position). "What people tend to study is a random variable," he said. "There's that conflation between a variable and the exposure."

The problem: The variable is extremely hard to compute. "Instead of wasting my time trying to compute the statistical properties, which I'll never get, I can change my exposure."

Measuring specific risks and making forecasts didn't matter when unpredictable Black Swans can smash you or your portfolio like a fragile teacup. You need to have *zero* (or near-zero) risk of getting smashed. Exposure—the nature of the investments in your portfolio and their sensitivity to extreme events—mattered. "I could care less about risk," Taleb said. "I care how it affects me."

He showed a slide displaying what he called the Disorder Cluster: uncertainty . . . variability . . . imperfect, incomplete knowledge . . . chance . . . chaos . . . volatility . . . disorder . . . entropy . . . time . . . the unknown . . . randomness . . . turmoil . . . stressor . . . error.

"Everything in nature likes these things or doesn't like these things to some degree," he said.

He was taking a page from his latest book, *Antifragile*, published in 2012. The book, another bestseller, examined a range of phenomena that are either destroyed or improved by the Disorder Cluster, i.e., extreme volatility. Something that's *antifragile*, a Talebian neologism, is made stronger when encountering disorder, chaos, volatility, etc. Like *The Black Swan*, the book had its roots in the crash-proof trading strategy Taleb had developed alongside Spitznagel at Empirica—all those out-of-the-money put options love volatility, the more the better.

When Taleb finished, Sornette stood from his chair and pointed to a slide with the heading "WHY? HOW? WHEN?" It displayed a list of world historical events, including: the French Revolution, the Spanish flu of 1918, the collapse of the USSR, the Challenger Space Shuttle disaster of 1986, the dot-com crash of 2000, and the financial crisis of 2008.

"What do these different systems have in common?" he said in a thick French accent. "I would claim that these and many others went through dynamical processes that make them knowable and to some degree predictable, to some degree. So what is the underlying process that I would like to discuss? Well, I view the world of these extreme events through the lens of the term I introduced, which is [a] Dragon King."

A Dragon King, he explained, is a dynamic process that moves toward massive instability, known as a phase transition. As an example, he showed a slide of water heating to one hundred degrees Celsius—the boiling point.

The bad news is that Dragon Kings occur much more frequently than traditional statistical models would imply. The good news, he said, is that this behavior can be predicted as a system approaches what he called bifurcation—the sudden shift in the phase transition, the leap from water to steam. "Close to bifurcation you have a window of visibility," like a plane flying from clouds into the sunshine. "I'm thinking of the world in terms of change in regime."

Another slide showed results from the Financial Crisis Observatory since 2008.

"This type of knowledge I think should empower us to go to the next stage, which is control," he said. "I'm happy to report . . . that we have been able to show that in some circumstances when we understand the dynamics of the system, when the system shows this power-law distribution of events with a Dragon King, by very tiny perturbations at the right moment, we can actually control this Dragon, kill it, slay the Dragon King. A fantastic achievement!"

Sornette finished and took his seat beside Taleb, who was grinning like a Cheshire cat.

After mischievously gifting Sornette with a copy of *The Black Swan*, Taleb put a question to him. "Do you think September 11 was a Black Swan event?"

"No," Sornette replied.

"For someone in the building, was it a Black Swan event?"

Sornette shrugged.

"For the pilot of the plane, was it a Black Swan event? My whole thing is, a Black Swan for the turkey is not a Black Swan for the butcher."

Then Taleb said something he knew would yank Sornette's chain. Supposedly, he, Taleb, had come up with the Dragon King concept years ago. He called such phenomena *Gray Swans*, extreme events that have some degree of predictability (he claimed the Global Financial Crisis was a Gray Swan). He added that while he agreed to an extent with Sornette's analysis, its fatal flaw was that a small change in the inputs to its super-exponential model can have dramatic results—an event that happens every 10 million years can happen every six hundred days with a tiny tweak of the dial. The upshot: While Sornette's analysis was mathematically rigorous, it was not capable of making the precise predictions required to manage risk.

Taleb's primary point wasn't about the model or the difference between Black Swans and Gray Swans and Dragon Kings. The key issue was *how you trade* and *what you trade with*—your exposure to the market.

"I was a trader for twenty-one years," Taleb said. "I had hair when I started. One thing you learn as a trader is that it's not your opinion that will ever make you money or make you bankrupt. You know what will really make it or break it for you is how you *express* your opinion. The financial instrument or the strategy is vastly more important than whether you guess right. You see. For example, if you use options and they're convex you can be wrong 99 percent of the time and still be okay." (Put simply, something that's convex benefits from volatility.)

Making forecasts was a waste of time. The trick was to figure out a trading strategy that didn't depend on forecasts. "You divorce yourself from the statistical property of the underlying [assets] by having smaller losses when you're wrong and much bigger profits when you're right, and this is what matters a lot more. And this is not what's understood by people who casually look at statistical data and think it maps directly to performance."

Sornette was visibly agitated. "The king effect," he said. "Maybe you know the king effect? You have the king family in many countries which is way beyond the population, the king effect. It is not just a Gray Swan. The king effect. Dragon King."

"It is a Gray Swan!" Taleb insisted.

"Let me speak," Sornette snapped. "I let you speak. Let me speak. Dragon, dragon, like animals, mystical animals with special properties. That's exactly what are the Dragon Kings, predictable, but outliers. Second point. Excuse me Nassim, you're not going to like it. You confuse a little bit the power laws. You are speaking about power laws in terms of statistics and indeed the fragility of estimation with respect to fat tails. I'm speaking of a different type of predictive model which is fundamentally dynamic, *not* statistical. That is the underlying theme of everything I showed."

Sornette was saying that Taleb's analysis was based on the wrong kind of math—statistics. His Black Swans were a snapshot in time, a single *static* picture of an extreme event. Sornette's method, based on physics, was *dynamic*. It evolved and captured movement as systems changed and accelerated from state to state. Taleb looked at the market and saw nothing but fat tails, and the only response was to stay away and buy a lot of insurance. Sornette claimed his model showed how the market emerged from one regime (stable) to another (bubble, super bubble, and crash)—and that he could trade on it.

Taleb wasn't buying it.

"I told you I started trading when I had a lot of hair. And progressively I lost my hair. And during this period I've seen a lot of people trying to fit dynamics . . ."

"You see I'm still keeping my hair," Sornette quipped. "And we are trading."

> > < <

Despite jittery investors such as David Tepper, the stock market remained resilient through the rest of the year. The jitters returned in the summer of 2015, as markets around the world wobbled following reports of a slowdown in China, a crucial economic engine driving growth worldwide. Heavy selling began in China on August 24, a Monday, pushing the Shanghai index down 9 percent. Shortly after trading began in New York, the Dow industrials crashed, falling 1,089 points in just six minutes, then the largest intraday point loss in its history, surpassing the 2010 Flash Crash.

Traders in Universa's Miami office swept into action. By the time the dust settled in the following days, Universa had clocked a $1 billion gain. Spitznagel didn't think the decline had much to do with China, which he saw as a fuse that lit a much bigger bomb. He was convinced the stock market was in an unsustainable Fed-induced bubble. Investors were in for a lot more pain. This was just the beginning.

He was wrong. While U.S. stocks were lackluster in 2015, finishing the year down about 1 percent, the market charged ahead again in 2016 and 2017.

But was Spitznagel getting angry calls from investors screaming at him for wasting their money (as had happened to Taleb at Empirica)? Not quite. An important feature of Universa's strategy was that it allowed investors to benefit from gains in the market even as it protected them from steep losses. And the cumulative benefit, according to Spitznagel, was better than any other risk mitigation strategy in the world. In a 2016 article in *Barron's*, he compared the historical returns of a plain-vanilla tail-hedging strategy with other strategies designed to lower an investor's risk—gold, ten-year Treasury bonds, and the Swiss franc (a historically safe currency).

Among the three alternatives to tail-hedging, gold won. The data showed that since 1974, when the market was down more than 15 percent in a year, gold returns ranged from 70 percent to 5 percent, with an average of 30 percent. The problem was that in other years the returns for gold varied a lot, ranging from a blowout of 125 percent to a loss of 30 percent, averaging under 7 percent. Also, you need a lot of gold to provide enough protection, about two-thirds of your stock holdings. That means you're giving up a big chunk of gains when the market is rising. "This is like skydiving with a parachute that may or may not deploy," he noted.

The returns for bonds and the Swiss franc in a crash were negligible. That is, they provided hardly any protection at all.

Universa's tail-hedging strategy, however, made more than 1,500 percent when the S&P 500 lost more than 15 percent in a year. What's more, since the strategy only required a small slice of an investor's holdings—say 2 or 3 percent—the amount of cash left over for stocks or other risky assets was much higher than in a portfolio with gold, bonds, or francs. A standard bond hedge, for instance, typically required a 30 or 40 percent position in fixed income.

Spitznagel's point: Universa investors could do very well in bull markets because they got a lot more of the upside than investors seeking protection in Treasury bonds or cash.

That didn't mean it was easy. Universa traders found the job hard and often tedious. Coming in every day—and losing money—*for years*. A big incentive for traders is the year-end bonus, which is often calculated as a percentage of the profit the trader made in a calendar year. That gave traders the fortitude to come into the office every day and engage in an activity that was, by any measure, extremely stressful. At Universa, there often wasn't a profit.

Traders were told to think like employees of a private tech company with a boatload of options that will only be valuable when it goes public. You might have to wait for years, but when it happens, you'll be rich.

Spitznagel remained extraordinarily bearish, always waiting for another crash around the corner—fully expecting it. That didn't mean he was timing the market or making a call on a crash that would hurt his investors if it didn't happen. It almost seemed like a magic trick—Universa investors could make money in bull *and* bear markets. After all, that's what hedge funds said they did—that's what the *hedge* in hedge funds was there for. Many didn't.

> > < <

In August 2015, Taleb traveled to Medford, Massachusetts, home of Tufts University, to give a lecture for its annual conference on political risk. Following the talk, Nadim Shehadi, an expert in Eastern Mediterranean studies, quizzed him onstage about which threats in the world worried him most. What about ISIS, the brutal Middle East terrorist group spawned during the Iraq War that had lately been waging war in Syria? "There's a panic in the West about ISIS jihadists who return from Syria," Shehadi said.

"I have no clue about that," Taleb said. "This is so minor currently as a source of risk."

Such risks get a lot of ink in newspapers, but they don't represent a systemic societal threat. "If you look at the risks we face on a daily basis, the real risks are not ISIS, that's bullshit," he said. "The real risk was Ebola. Because Ebola can spread. Ebola can accelerate and spread. And the next Ebola we will be facing, the first time in history, is an epidemic that flies on British Air. And, of course, Delta. And gets bad food on United. And bad treatment by flight attendants. So that's a problem. We never face it. So when people tell me, let's talk about risk, the first thing I talk about is—ISIS could accelerate it, or it could come naturally—is an epidemic."

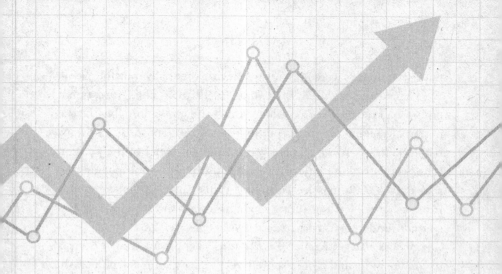

CHAPTER 13

VOLMAGEDDON

In the summer of 2016, Universa received an email from Ron Lagnado, a senior portfolio manager for the California Public Employees' Retirement System, better known as CalPERS. Lagnado was interested in learning more about how Universa operated and wanted to set up a call.

CalPERS was America's largest public pension fund, with more than $300 billion in assets at the time. Even a tiny slice of that pie would be a windfall for Universa. It would also help it crack the stubborn, conservative world of pension funds. Many of Universa's assets came from endowments and private wealth managers, typically savvy investors who had a fairly strong grasp of the firm's strategy. Pension funds, however, were often skittish and vexingly conventional. Few wanted to stray from the pack into a strategy that seemed experimental. If Universa could turn CalPERS into a client, perhaps the precedent would give other pension funds the thumbs-up that tail-risk strategies were now kosher. It was potentially transformative.

Lagnado's boss, Ted Eliopoulos, CalPERS's chief investment officer, had recently seen a talk by Taleb and grown intrigued by the notion of making the fund's portfolio more resilient to Black Swans with a tail-risk strategy. There was a common belief in the pension fund world that the strategies were too expensive and couldn't be scaled to fit their massive portfolios. While you might make money in a crash, the bleeding during good times wasn't worth it. Eliopoulos started wondering if, perhaps, that wasn't always true.

He was also getting nervous. As stocks kept rising, CalPERS was becoming more and more exposed to the devastating risk of a crash. Stocks had been on a tear for seven straight years. A fateful presidential election was shaping up with Hillary Clinton squaring off against Donald Trump. Risk was in the air.

To protect itself, CalPERS's investment committee made a call. It sold $15 billion worth of stocks, about 5 percent of the entire fund, to ratchet down its risk profile. Some inside CalPERS, including Lagnado, said that was crazy. It was an obvious exercise in market timing. What if stocks went up in the next few years?

Lagnado and Eliopoulos became intrigued by the idea that if you could protect your portfolio against big shocks with something akin to insurance—a Black Swan tail hedge—you wouldn't have to reduce your exposure to the market. Maybe you could even *increase* it.

Their instinct ran counter to how many investors were feeling at the time. The long post-recession bull run seemed to be neverending. America had ridden the magic carpet of one of its longest economic expansions in history. More and more investors were starting to think they didn't need to keep funneling cash to tail-risk funds, and many were pulling out of the strategy. Universa copycats were shifting gears toward less aggressive hedges. Or they were simply shutting down altogether.

Despite the bull market, U.S. pension funds such as CalPERS were in dire straits. There was a massive gap—trillions of dollars—between what they'd promised their beneficiaries and what they had on their balance sheets. State pension-fund balance sheets showed total assets that were roughly 70 percent of what they owed—which some critics said was a wildly optimistic estimate based on rose-colored expectations for the market—a looming disaster for pension-dependent American retirees.

Inside CalPERS, some fund managers had begun questioning the fundamental assumptions behind their strategy, the don't-put-all-your-eggs-in-one-basket diversification approach that was the bedrock of Modern Portfolio Theory. CalPERS was underperforming the standard benchmark, the S&P 500, by some 2 percent a year, because a big chunk of its assets was in poor-performing Treasury bonds. If CalPERS had simply put all its cash in a low-cost S&P 500 index fund, it would have done much better. And while 2 percentage points a year might not seem like much, it had a devastating effect on the pension fund's long-run returns from a compounding perspective.

Things had to change. Perhaps tail-hedging could help. Eliopoulos told his number two, Eric Baggesen, to check it out. Baggesen delegated the task to Lagnado.

"I don't know if you've ever heard of these guys, but look into it," Baggesen told him.

A Wall Street veteran, Lagnado had started his career in the 1990s at Leland O'Brien Rubinstein Associates, a firm that gained notoriety for creating portfolio insurance, a key factor in the 1987 crash on Black Monday. He'd gone on to work for such banks as Bank of America and BNY Mellon before landing at CalPERS in 2014.

Lagnado had cautioned against the $15 billion stock sale in 2016 aimed at lowering CalPERS's risk profile. "You might get lucky, but if you keep doing this market timing at some point you're going to get it wrong," he complained. Nearly a decade before, in 2008, CalPERS had unloaded billions of dollars' worth of stocks at the height of the crisis. That meant it lost out when the market began to rally the following year. Lagnado worried they were making the same mistake again.

After several calls with Spitznagel and Yarckin, Lagnado and a team of CalPERS officials flew to Miami for a meeting in May 2017. It was largely a formality. Lagnado and his bosses had already agreed to invest. Universa passed the due diligence, and by August 2017 it had a $1.5 billion portfolio of CalPERS's market risk to protect. It was a figure set to increase every three to six months.

Stocks kept rising for the rest of the year. Then, in February 2018, the market crashed again in spectacular fashion. Volatility rocketed to the stratosphere in what came to be known as Volmageddon. Wall Street's relentless marketing machine was behind it.

As the post-financial crisis bull market had kept galloping higher year in and year out, Wall Street cooked up clever trading products that would benefit as long as the market remained smooth and steady. And why not? Volatility was near record lows aided by the Fed's seemingly bottomless punch bowl of stimulus. The new products took the other side of the VIX, the fear gauge that surged in market crashes. In other words, investors in these products were betting against the possibility of extreme volatility.

On February 5, a Monday, disaster struck those investors. The anti-volatility products coughed up more than 80 percent of their value in a single day. The Dow Jones Industrial Average saw its then largest intraday point decline on record. And the volatility kept coming like bursts from a machine gun. Through the rest of the week, the Dow swung at least one thousand points in all but one day. "It feels like I've been shelled all week by artillery," a trader told the *Wall Street Journal*. The action was so heavy, traders often didn't have time to go to the bathroom.

Universa, of course, cleaned up.

The following month, Spitznagel sent a letter to Universa investors to commemorate the ten-year anniversary of the Black Swan Protection Protocol. "As we ring the bells and reflect on how far we've come, I am reminded of an old Russian proverb that warns, 'Dwell on the past, lose an eye. Forget the past, lose both eyes,'" he wrote.

Just as he'd done in *Barron's*, Spitznagel compared six risk-mitigation strategies, including gold, bonds, hedge funds, and of course Universa. Over the past decade, a strategy with 25 percent in gold and 75 percent in the S&P 500 produced a compound annual growth rate of 8.5 percent; 25 percent bonds, 75 percent S&P produced 9.7 percent; and 25 percent hedge funds, 75 percent S&P produced 8.2 percent.

A strategy with just 3.3 percent Universa and the rest in the S&P produced 12.3 percent.

That compound annual growth figure is important, Spitznagel wanted his investors to know. Because it wasn't just that Universa performed more than two percentage points better than the other strategies over the decade, it did so *every year* (on average).

The impact is significant. If you put $10,000 into the Universa strategy (3 percent Universa, 97 percent S&P 500) in 2008 and left it there, by the end of ten years you'd have $31,700. That same $10,000 in the bond strategy, the second-best performer, would be $25,250—20 percent below the Universa return. Gold returned $22,600, hedge funds $22,000. As time went on, the difference between the returns the strategies provided expanded, year after year.

Even more damning, none of the other strategies, besides Universa's, performed better than the S&P 500 itself.

It was yet another lesson in Wall Street's colossal failure. How much money, brain power, PowerPoint razzle-dazzle, and endless hours spent on conference calls and meetings had been dedicated to strategies that couldn't beat Grandma putting all her dough in an S&P 500 index fund? In the end, Universa's story showed not so much how great Universa was, but rather that Wall Street's legions of investment advisers—its "helpers," as Warren Buffett disparagingly called them—were nothing more than a carnival show meant to separate investors from their money. Among the assets the carnival barkers managed was $35 trillion of retiree cash stashed in U.S. pension funds.

Buffett himself, in 2007, made a wager that hedge funds weren't all they were cracked up to be. Many experts at the time thought the Oracle of Omaha had made a bad gamble, since hedge funds as a whole had for years broadly beaten the market. He bet another firm called Protégé Partners that a select group of hedge funds—handpicked by Protégé—wouldn't beat the S&P 500 over a decade. After a quick start by the hedge funds in 2008, the S&P won every single year thereafter, gaining 126 percent compared with the average gain of 36 percent by the high-fee-charging hedge funds. The lesson: Investing "does not require great intelligence, a degree in economics, or familiarity with Wall Street jargon," Buffett wrote at the end of the bet in his 2017 letter to Berkshire Hathaway shareholders. "What investors . . . need instead is an ability to both disregard mob fears or enthusiasms and to focus on a few simple fundamentals."

Such as: Don't lose money.

"A strategy that worked in the past naturally isn't guaranteed to work again in the future," Spitznagel wrote in his letter, a concession to the possibility that maybe he'd just been lucky all along, a fool of randomness (which of course he didn't believe). "Yet, if a strategy didn't work in the past, isn't there something inherently unscientific about expecting that it will in the future?"

He ended on a chest-thumping note. "Our legacy to date speaks for itself."

>   >   <   <

That summer, Spitznagel, Yarckin, and Taleb flew to Sacramento to meet with CalPERS's senior managers. It was a marathon affair. Holed up for five hours in a large conference room, they met with all the heads of the investment groups for the country's biggest pension fund, and their voluminous staff. At times more than thirty people packed into the room. Spitznagel did most of the talking. The February Volmageddon jackpot helped make their case, since the gains from just that week had paid for the entire strategy through the year, with some left over.

One question kept coming up: What if the market didn't crash, but simply ground lower slowly, inch by inch, over time? Wouldn't they be wasting money on a tail hedge but not getting that fantastic bang for the buck?

Spitznagel conceded that in such a market, the Universa tail hedge wouldn't work. It was Universa's kryptonite. He pointed out that historically there was very little precedent for such a market. Bear markets, instead, are characterized by sudden crashes. You even get crashes during bull runs—Volmageddon was just one example. Somewhat paradoxically, he said, for investors a slow downward-trending market is the best of all possible worlds, because it gives them the ability to exit their trades. In a crash, you're stuck. Everyone's trying to rush out of the door at once. "Why would I give you protection against the best thing that can happen to you?" he asked the room.

The CalPERS team, led by Lagnado, had evaluated virtually every other tail-risk strategy on Wall Street. Nothing stacked up against Universa's track record or compared with how it managed the strategy and the crash-bang returns it historically provided, they determined. The pension fund wanted Spitznagel and his team to be the cornerstone of its new risk-mitigation strategy. (They assigned a smaller chunk of assets to a Universa competitor, a California firm called LongTail Alpha.)

Afterward, the Universa team gathered at Il Fornaio, a sleek local Italian restaurant, for dinner with CalPERS's senior managers. Spitznagel was seated beside Eliopoulos and Baggesen, who asked endless questions about Idyll Farms (Baggesen owned a farm of his own in Missouri). Yarckin was impressed by one of the fund's new top investment officers, Elisabeth Bourqui, a Swiss risk manager with two decades of pension asset management experience and a Ph.D. in financial mathematics from ETH Zurich, Didier Sornette's stomping ground. Supersmart, she had a strong grasp of Universa's approach, Spitznagel thought. He'd learned earlier in the year that Eliopoulos would be leaving CalPERS, and was under the impression that Bourqui was likely going to replace him. That sounded good to Yarckin, Spitznagel, and Taleb.

They flew back to Miami jubilant. CalPERS by that point had assigned some $5 billion in stock market risk for Universa to protect, a mammoth position that accounted for half of the portfolio in the Black Swan Protection Protocol. Lagnado and Baggesen said they wanted to ratchet it higher—to $15 billion, maybe even $25 billion.

Times were good and the future was bright at Universa.

> > < <

In January 2019, Universa got some surprising news. Out of the blue, Elisabeth Bourqui, who they'd been led to believe would oversee the investment from CalPERS after Eliopoulos left, had resigned. An email distributed to CalPERS's staff didn't provide any clarity:

> *Good morning,*
> *Elisabeth Bourqui has submitted her resignation as*
> *CalPERS Chief Operating Investment Officer (COIO)*
> *effective today.*

That was it.

The author of the email was Ben Meng, who'd worked at the pension fund back in the 2000s and had rejoined just that month. Spitznagel and Yarckin had never heard of him.

Meng, unbeknownst to Universa, had made a power grab inside CalPERS. He would be the new Eliopoulos, with control of the fund's entire portfolio. "Ben was pulling the strings behind the scenes," a person familiar with CalPERS said. "He was moving pieces on the chess board to put himself in power."

In short order, Meng began reviewing every position and strategy at the fund—a colossal task for an operation that by then included some $400 billion in assets as the stock market continued to rally. It was, indeed, a sensible move. CalPERS had been performing poorly for years and a review was badly needed. It was still recovering from the Global Financial Crisis when it lost nearly a quarter of its assets in its 2008–2009 fiscal year, putting pressure on the cities, schools, and state agencies that relied on the fund. Meng brought in outside analysts to help review the strategies.

Among the programs they flagged: the Universa tail-hedge program.

They concluded Universa was too expensive. It was a cash drag, a line item that would pull down performance. It also was an ant on the giant beast that was CalPERS's megaportfolio. It could never cost-efficiently scale up to a size that would move the needle, or so they said.

Other CalPERS advisers disagreed. Andrew Junkin, an executive of Wilshire Associates, told a meeting of the pension fund's board in August 2019 that the strategy was well worth the cost.

"There [are] some really weird numbers on this page that I thought it was worth highlighting," he told the board, referring to a sweeping report on the fund's strategies and performance. He referred the board to a line item titled *Risk Mitigation Strategies*. The firm had $200 million in those strategies, and they were down an eyebrow-raising 82 percent.

"That seems awful," Junkin said. "Remember what those are there for. They are sort of tail-risk hedging strategies. In normal markets, or in markets that are slightly up, or slightly down, or even massively up, those strategies aren't going to do well. But there could be a day when the market is down pretty significantly, and we come in and we report that the risk mitigation strategies are up 1,000 percent. It's possible the day that happens, you're going to ask yourself why you didn't have more of this stuff," he said. "It's sort of an insurance premium. You pay a little bit when the market is normal, and then when the market sells off, it should help support the fund."

Meng disagreed and decided to kill the strategy in a sweeping purge of outside fund managers. Universa didn't hear about the decision for months. Then, in November, Yarckin got a call from a person at CalPERS he'd never spoken with. *That's weird*, he thought.

"We have an important phone call we need to set up next week," he was told. "Don't be alarmed."

He was alarmed. Over the years he and Spitznagel had seen it before time and again—clients get nervous about a market crash, then, year after year, it doesn't happen. They begin to see the strategy as a needless expense weighing on their returns. On the call, Lagnado's boss, Eric Baggesen, delivered the bad news—CalPERS was out—adding that he was personally disappointed with the decision. He almost seemed embarrassed. CalPERS demanded that Universa redeem the entire position by the end of January.

It was a blow. CalPERS was Universa's largest client by far, accounting for half the assets they protected. The only conversations they'd been having up to that point were about how big CalPERS's position would get. Twenty billion? Twenty-five billion? CalPERS was asking Universa to unload a large amount of put options—the exact opposite of the fund's strategy of always *buying* put options.

"I just feel like I've let you guys down," Spitznagel told Baggesen. He knew the problem wasn't performance. Perhaps the problem was explaining the strategy to higher-ups at the fund. "Could we have done anything differently?"

"You guys did a great job," Baggesen said. "We just have to redeem a lot of managers."

Yarckin tried to convince CalPERS to let their current position ride. Much of it was on track to last through the following September. The pension fund refused. Spitznagel had no choice and gave the order to the firm's confused traders: Liquidate CalPERS.

At about the same time, a person in Wuhan, China, began to cough.

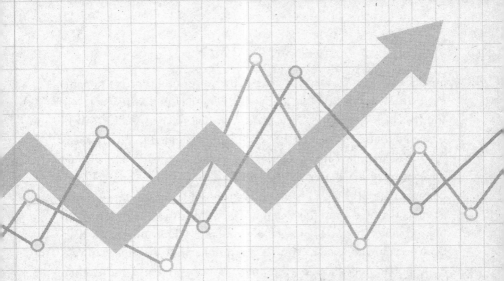

CHAPTER 14

THIS IS THE WORLD WE LIVE IN

"Holy mother of god," Harvard epidemiologist Eric Feigl-Ding wrote on Twitter, "the new coronavirus is a 3.8!!!" It was shortly before midnight, January 20, 2020. Feigl-Ding had reviewed a new unpublished paper on the virus, which estimated its R0—the measure of how many people a single person with the virus could infect—might be as high as 3.8. Given how fatal it seemed to be, that would put it on par with the most deadly viruses in the history of the modern world. "I really hate to be the epidemiologist who has to admit this, but we are potentially faced with . . . an unchecked pandemic that the world has not seen since the 1918 Spanish Influenza. Let's hope it doesn't reach that level but we now live in the modern 🌍 with faster ✈ + 🚢 than 1918. @WHO and @CDCgov needs to declare public health emergency ASAP!"

After the tweet, Feigl-Ding faced a fierce backlash from the epidemiological community, which accused him of panicking, of being an alarmist. In retrospect, of course, he was entirely correct to panic early. In a March 2020 article about Feigl-Ding's Twitter post and the backlash it sparked, *New York* magazine's David Wallace-Wells observed that if the rest of the world had responded to the outbreak with the same measure of fear and apprehension early on, it would have been much better off. "As I've written before about climate change, when the news is alarming, the only responsible response is to be alarmed—and raise alarm," he wrote. "And like runaway climate change, the threat of a global pandemic, which graybeards have been warning about for years, is a reminder that we should always build public policy around the precautionary principle, rather than waiting until uncontestable and inarguable evidence arrives that action is necessary. If we wait that long, it will always be too late."

Among those who took the new estimate very seriously was Nassim Taleb. He'd arrived at Universa's Miami office to attend a finance conference in the city. Taleb was already losing sleep over news of the novel bug circulating in Wuhan—the pop-up hospitals, the images of Chinese doctors clad head to toe in protective gear, the multimillion-person lockdown, the infected cruise ships.

After swimming laps at his hotel's indoor pool, Taleb puzzled over computer models projecting the spread of the virus. In a document called "Epidemiology Models," using commands such as "Now if f is nonlinear, then the operation in the computation of f may include serious biases in addition to uncertainty" and "Trick (Fragility): Do same for tails of distribution/ruin properties," he crafted interactive charts that let him toggle between various characteristics of the virus and its spread. He soon looped in Universa's quantitative team to run projections. It wasn't good.

One day he swung by the office to take a walk with Spitznagel and Yarckin along the waterfront. On the way, Taleb, sweating in his professorial jacket in Miami's eighty-degree heat, spotted a penny on the pavement in front of a parked steamroller—and picked it up, laughing at the inside joke about risk-oblivious hedge fund managers snatching pennies before the proverbial steamroller. Later that night, they huddled over dinner at Brasserie Brickell Key, an Italian restaurant with an encyclopedic wine list. Over Negronis and pasta, they swapped ideas about what the best response would be. Spitznagel feared government overreach.

"Governments have a tendency to make problems worse," he said.

Taleb, noting that the virus's R0 was well above one, said the risk of the pandemic getting out of control was extremely high. That meant extremely strong action by the government—shutting borders, imposing lockdowns, etc.—was necessary.

The stock market, meanwhile, continued to float on calm waters. The VIX fear index neared its all-time low mid-February.

Not everyone was complacent. A pair of new clients, increasingly nervous about the pandemic, decided to invest. One had invested just before the 2008 financial crisis, then pulled out after reaping a bonanza. The other firm had been in talks with Universa for more than a decade, and decided, finally, that it might be a good idea to have some downside protection.

Their timing was extremely fortuitous, of course. Because most other investors weren't worried about risk, and volatility was near record lows, Universa was able to quickly load up on dirt cheap S&P 500 puts and VIX call options—bets on a spike in volatility—before things went crazy.

> > < <

On January 23, 2020, the Bulletin of Atomic Scientists moved its Doomsday Clock twenty seconds closer to midnight—"closer," it said, "to apocalypse than ever"—a symbolic one hundred seconds to humanity's ruin. The group, founded in 1945 by Albert Einstein and others involved in creating the atomic bomb, cited climate change, the ever-present threat of nuclear disaster, and cyber-enabled information warfare as the most prominent factors forcing the heightened threat level. It was the nearest to doomsday since the watchdog group of scientists first published the metric at the dawn of the Cold War.

Not mentioned in the report: Covid-19.

Three days later, Taleb, Bar-Yam, and Norman released their memo warning that the novel virus emanating from China carried enormous risk to humanity.

By early February, the disease had spread to twenty-three countries, but in America there were only a few dozen known cases. Complacency reigned. Stock markets around the world hit records. M&A banker turned author William Cohan was getting nervous about the bubbly market. With stocks sky high and bond yields near zero, where to turn? To find answers, he called Spitznagel.

Winter is coming, the hedge fund manager warned. Blame the central banks. "Randomly go look at a screen and it's pretty crazy. Big caps, small caps, credit markets, volatility. It's crazy. Reach for yield is everywhere," he said.

Spitznagel told Cohan he had no idea when the party would end. "This is the world we live in. And we've got to deal with it," he said.

Contrary to how most outsiders viewed Universa, as a bear hunter, Spitznagel said he'd be "pretty hunky-dory if there's never a crash again." By providing explosive downside protection for his investors, they can "take more systemic risk" by being fully invested in stocks rather than putting a big chunk of cash into standard risk-mitigation assets like Treasury bonds. For instance, while those few new investors with perfect timing looked smart, they likely would have fared better had they been invested in Universa during the decade's long bull market.

Cohan, who reported on the conversation for *Vanity Fair*, wrote that he could "see the wisdom of [Spitznagel's] approach" and asked him how the little guy could benefit from his wisdom.

"I get asked this every day," Spitznagel replied. "Every day. And I should do something for them. But I have a handful of really big clients. Yeah, if I wasn't so preoccupied, I would do that. I should do that. I should do that."

> > < <

In late February, as Covid-19 continued to spread beyond China's shores—and luxury cruise ships—Spitznagel and Yarckin flew to New York to meet with clients. Tremors in the market had started to break out, indicating widening fear. The massive lockdown in Wuhan was rattling investors. As markets began to wobble, officials in Washington, D.C., tried to put on a brave face. On February 24, the Dow industrials fell more than 3 percent. "Stock Market starting to look very good to me," Donald Trump tweeted.

The next day, Spitznagel sat down with Bloomberg anchor Erik Schatzker in New York. "Your fund offers investors protection—an insurance policy, if you like, against low-probability outcomes," Schatzker began. "Is the coronavirus outbreak the Black Swan you've been preparing for?"

"It's hard to say," Spitznagel said. "I don't know if it is. I don't think any of us really know if it is. . . . There usually aren't monsters hiding under the bed. And sometimes there are. And I don't think we can really determine which is which until you know it's too late."

"It's hard to call any one thing the Ultimate Black Swan," Schatzker said. "I can think of some pretty horrible outcomes that we might retrospectively call the Ultimate Black Swan. But a pandemic seems to fit into that category."

"A prediction and forecasts shouldn't be part of your investment thesis," Spitznagel replied. "If it is, you know, you've got a problem."

If that's so, Schatzker asked, why do so many investors devote so much time and energy to making predictions?

The problem isn't so much the predictions, Spitznagel said, it's the way many investors attempt to protect themselves from the unpredictable—through diversification. "This is the Kool-Aid that we're drinking from modern finance, diversification, lowering the volatility of our portfolio is going to somehow protect us from things like this. But in fact, it doesn't. What it's doing is just making us poor at the end of the day—it doesn't provide enough protection when we need it."

Later that day, Spitznagel and Yarckin dropped by a class Taleb was hosting for his annual Real World Risk Institute, or RWRI (commonly pronounced *rew-ree* by acolytes), a group of some one thousand people from all walks of life—medicine, the military, policy-making, venture capital, banking, complexity theory, psychology, etc.—to discuss a host of topics around risk management. The topic that day: Covid-19 and how to respond to it.

The market was crashing again. After the RWRI session, Spitznagel and Yarckin walked the brisk streets of New York City—streets already ripe with fear as Covid cases started rapidly popping up in the outer boroughs—and began discussing contingency plans for the office if the pandemic worsened. Having worked out of Los Angeles, where the risk of an earthquake was an ever-present threat, and now Miami, a hurricane bull's-eye, they'd long been prepared for sudden disruptions. Universa rapidly shut down its Miami headquarters, and its traders set up shop at home. A few senior staffers continued to meet at the office, sitting at basketball-court-length distances. The market soon began to descend into one of the most gut-wrenching periods of volatility in its history—no less painful for being relatively brief. Spitznagel flew with his family to his remote log home in Northport. Over a Zoom meeting, he warned his trading team to be ready at any moment for a radical intervention by central bankers.

"We should absolutely expect to see a response from the Fed that will shock everyone, even us," he said. To drive home his point and add a dollop of humor during an otherwise grim moment, he shared a GIF of the fictional Wall Street maniac Patrick Bateman, played by Christian Bale in the 2000 horror film *American Psycho*, slowly peeling a mask from his face—a reference to a Fed-induced "face ripping" rally.

It didn't take long for the Fed to swing into action, though the face-ripping rally took a while longer. On March 3, it executed an emergency rate cut of a half percentage point. "The coronavirus poses evolving risks to economic activity," the central bank said. Stocks fell another 3 percent that same day. The rate on the benchmark ten-year

Treasury note fell below 1 percent for the first time. "There is skepticism about whether central bank actions can mitigate a virus-related shock," J.P. Morgan economist Bruce Kasman opined. "Rate cuts will not prevent the spread of the virus or offset the immediate economic costs of containment measures."

"I think financial markets will bounce back," Trump told reporters.

On March 12, the Dow Jones Industrial Average hemorrhaged 2,352 points, nearly 10 percent, its single largest percentage decline since Black Monday. Bankers and regulators began worrying that the entire financial system was seizing up, just as it had in 2008. At 5 p.m. on March 15, a Sunday, the Fed announced more rate cuts and a program to buy $700 billion in bonds. Instead of calming markets, the surprise move triggered panic. Investors began to fear that some kind of blowup or bank collapse, similar to 2008's Lehman meltdown, might be behind the Fed's action. Complicated moves in interest-rate derivatives were jamming up banks' balance sheets. Suddenly, they couldn't buy bonds because the new assets would add risk. Mortgage bonds, and the firms that owned them, started to collapse. Municipal bonds were treated like kryptonite. Volatility exploded. The VIX shot to a record 82.69.

Watching from Miami, Yarckin thought it might even hit 100. With volatility at records, Universa's traders were feasting like pirates who'd just captured a gold-laden Spanish galleon. The firm's systematized, quantitative programs provided traders signals for when to sell its suddenly highly valuable positions—and when to buy, as volatility shot wildly up and down.

Others were imploding. One popular trade had been to bet on a burst of volatility in Asia and relatively low volatility in the U.S. and Europe, assuming that Covid-19 would roil Asian economies while leaving the West largely unscathed. The opposite happened—Asia managed to contain the virus, while Europe and the U.S. bungled their response. Because of that, volatility in Asia remained calm while it spiked in the U.S. and Europe.

Funds that systematically sold volatility—betting that the market would remain steady—were self-immolating. Malachite Capital Management, a New York hedge fund founded by a pair of former Goldman Sachs derivatives traders, had for years been making the exact opposite bets that Universa made. The firm had been collecting premiums for selling puts on the S&P 500—pennies and nickels in front of the proverbial steamroller—racking up double-digit annual returns as the stock market quietly drifted higher year after year. The day after the VIX hit its record, Malachite went up in smoke. It suffered losses of $1.5 billion, more than double the assets on its balance sheet. It blamed the "extreme adverse market conditions of recent weeks."

Funds managed by Allianz Global Investors, which handled money for the German financial giant Allianz SE, had also been posting solid returns for years by taking the anti-Universa bet—selling put options that paid off in a crash. By late 2019, the funds were managing $11 billion. "We are acting like an insurance company, collecting premiums," Greg Tournant, manager of Allianz's Structured Alpha funds, said in a May 2016 marketing video. "When there is a catastrophic event, we might have to pay—very much like an insurance company."

Insurance companies work hard to make sure catastrophic events won't wipe them out—won't be a ruin problem. But the math behind Tournant's strategy—which he told investors included a measure of downside protection—didn't add up when the catastrophe struck in March 2020. In a matter of days, the funds lost a staggering $7 billion. One fund was down 97 percent for the year, a stark real-world example of gambler's ruin. Pension plans were battered. An Arkansas teachers' pension fund, which sued Allianz over the debacle, said it lost as much as $800 million. Raytheon Technologies, which also sued, said its pension fund lost $280 million of its $375 million investment. (Investors reached a settlement with Allianz in early 2022.)

Federal investigators smelled a rat. It soon emerged, among other allegations, that Tournant had rejiggered his hedging strategy in late 2015 without informing investors, according to the Justice

Department. In May 2022, Allianz Global pleaded guilty to fraud and agreed to pay about $6 billion in penalties and restitution to investors for misrepresenting the risk posed by the Structured Alpha funds. Tournant, who'd pocketed some $60 million since 2014, was arrested in Colorado and released on a $20 million bond. Lawyers for the manager, who pleaded not guilty, said the case against him was a meritless attempt to criminalize the impact of the "unprecedented, Covid-induced market dislocation of March 2020."

Of course, it was a Black Swan. No one could have seen it coming.

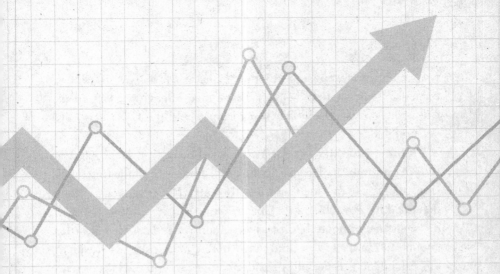

CHAPTER 15

LOTTERY TICKETS

As markets crashed in early 2020, Margaret Brown, a CalPERS board member, grew curious about how well the new tail-hedging strategies it had implemented in the past few years had done. She raised the question with CalPERS chief investment officer Ben Meng at a March board meeting.

"Ben, can you tell me how our left-tail investments are performing?" she asked, referring to the Universa bet (the left tail of the curve was the crash side). "Are they performing the way we thought they would in this economic downturn?"

"Yes, for any left-tail risk hedging strategy you're referring to, they should perform well in this kind of down market, as they were exactly designed to do," Meng replied. "And from what we know, most of these strategies are performing as anticipated."

Shortly afterward, Brown found out that most of the tail-hedging strategies the pension fund had invested in during the past few years had been terminated in January. She was furious. "Mr. Meng's response omitted that he had abandoned the Universa hedge," she wrote on Facebook. "The board must hold the CEO and CIO accountable."

It turned out Meng's reference to a tail-hedging strategy referred to a big position in Treasury bonds and some risk-mitigating stock investments. In a video address to CalPERS employees, Meng defended his move to cut its Universa investment with the standard pension-fund critique that it was too expensive and couldn't scale up enough to matter to the fund. "It is not economical to buy explicit tail-risk hedging, especially considering the cost and the lack of scalability of such an insurance strategy," he said.

"So, basically, we chose better alternatives for market-drawdown protection, and they turned out to be better alternatives in the recent market rout," he said. "Those two risk segments added more than $11 billion of our drawdown mitigation matrix."

Seeking to justify his decision, Meng mentioned a 2012 paper produced by AQR Asset Management, a giant Greenwich hedge fund founded by quant legend Cliff Asness, that panned tail-hedging strategies. Written by an AQR portfolio manager named Antti Ilmanen, it was called "Do Financial Markets Reward Buying or Selling Insurance and Lottery Tickets?" The study concluded that it was better in the long term to *sell* insurance (put options that benefit from a stock's decline) and lottery tickets (call options that gain from an increase) rather than buy them, a strategy that had just annihilated funds such as Malachite.

"Selling volatility on either the left tail (insurance) or the right tail (lottery tickets) adds value in the long run," Ilmanen had written. "Conversely, buying option-based tail-risk insurance against financial catastrophes and then holding lottery-like high-volatility investments results in poor long-run returns."

That went directly against the Spitznagel-Taleb strategy, which suggests "investors *underweight* rather than *overweight* low-probability events," AQR's Ilmanen wrote. The evidence "sides against Taleb."

Taleb, no surprise, disagreed. In a video posted on the website Naked Capitalism, he said the $11 billion gain Meng bragged about left out the opportunity cost of having such a large position in Treasurys in the first place. By owning a big chunk of bonds, the strategy misses out on gains in the stock market. "Effectively, we think, back of the envelope calculation, this so-called mitigating strategy would have lost something like $30 billion the previous year," he said. "So you make another $11 billion, you lost $30 billion before, not a great trade. And definitely not a great trade if you take that over long periods of time, where you lose in rallies and make back a little bit in a sell-off. That's not a mitigating strategy."

Soon after, Cliff Asness—whose firm had written several other reports attacking tail-hedging strategies over the years—and Taleb engaged in an epic insult-flinging Twitter battle. Taleb kicked things off:

@nntaleb

> AQR issued…flawed reports saying tail risk hedging doesn't work (in theory), options are 'expensive'
> Yet they did not reveal that
> 1)Their OWN risk premia strategies lost money
> 2)Their other public crap underperforms MKT.
> Insult to clients & the REAL WORLD
> Meanwhile Universa hedge portf outperformed SP while AQR crap and RISK PARITY junk underperformed.

Asness fired back:

@CliffordAsness

> I've avoided fighting with this insane person for a while, as while sometimes brilliant, he's often very wrong and clearly both nuts and a world-class terrible person. Didn't need that in my life. But sometimes the insane people eventually get around to you.

He went on to suggest that Taleb was "broken," full of "libelous vitriolic bullshit" and "evil mendacious intent."

@CliffordAsness

> Debate is good. But apparently he's incapable of having this debate without lies, deflections, accusations. He just tried to steamroll with bombast, bullshit, viciousness, and jargon.

Taleb again pointed to the underwhelming performance of a number of AQR funds. Asness said that was irrelevant and had nothing to do with tail-hedging strategies.

@nntaleb

> Perhaps Mr. Asness can show us empiricists, with the benefit of hindsight, which fund he wants us to pick to get the relative performance. PS - I have no interest in Asness, not even AQR, but they can't get away w/ nonsensical claims abt tail risk.

@Clifford Asness

> Getting famous and rich for saying 'bad shit happens sometimes' and then screaming 'see' when it luckily does soon after, even though you've lost all the money many times, and then using that pulpit to slander and abuse people is just gross. Just my opinion.

@nntaleb

> For the general public watching the road rage of Mr. Asness who misreplied to my last post: The claims [sic] by AQR is: tail risk is not needed by funds because there are ways to do it better. As we are finding out: the performance of AQR doesn't show it.

It went on. "Black Swan Author Spars with Quant Legend Over Tail Risk Hedges," a Bloomberg headline said. Spitznagel found it embarrassing. He didn't do Twitter, and he certainly didn't get into public sparring matches with other hedge fund managers. But he shared Taleb's contempt for AQR's tail-hedging research. Was it a surprise AQR couldn't replicate Universa's returns? He'd been perfecting the strategy for more than two decades. "Universa's 12 years of results speak for themselves," Spitznagel told *Institutional Investor*. "Backtests from naïve researchers are an unfortunate distraction."

What angered Spitznagel most of all was that AQR's research played a role in convincing CalPERS to throw away the windfall it could have made in March 2020. And that all the money it could have made in the coming years for its pensioners was up in smoke. In 2021, the pension fund was moving ahead with a plan concocted by Meng to use leverage—more borrowed money—to increase its diversification. That included boosting its allocation to private equity funds (while cutting its stock portfolio). Since private equity funds are in themselves a form of leverage (they typically use borrowed money to buy stuff), it was leverage piled on top of leverage.

As word leaked about Universa's chart-shattering performance in March that provided investors a 4,144 percent return—think of a $1 million stake turned into $41 million—the head-slapping folly of Meng's move to dump its tail hedge became all too apparent. Ron Lagnado, who'd overseen the investment in Universa, quit in disgust. He immediately joined Universa as director of research.

Meng came under withering scrutiny. He told the *Wall Street Journal* that he had no regrets about getting rid of the Universa hedge. "Knowing what we know, we would make the exact same decision," he said. Amid criticism for missing out on Universa's massive payday, he resigned in August.

CalPERS had likely given up $2 billion to $3 billion in gains by dumping Universa with historically bad timing. The following year, it put up poor results—again. In its fiscal year ending July 27, 2021, CalPERS had a return of 21 percent, gains driven largely by the historic stock market rally. It was the second worst performance of all pension funds tracked by *Pensions & Investments* for the period, a hair ahead of the Texas Municipal Retirement System. Its sister fund, CalSTRS, which managed the state's massive teachers' portfolio, earned 27 percent.

Investors, meanwhile, flocked to Universa, just as they had after the 2008 crash. Spitznagel was crowned as the latest Master of the Hedge Fund Universe. *The Wall Street Journal* called him a "hedge-fund star." *Forbes* opined: "Spitznagel's mathematical view of the world is in some ways similar to capitalism's ultimate optimist, Warren Buffett. His selling of immediate gratification for a massive payday far down the road, after all, is engineered to conjure cash and profit in crashes."

Forbes estimated Spitznagel was worth $250 million—likely an underestimate—and mused about whether his success would lure copycats, with the competition making the strategy less profitable. "It should," Spitznagel told *Forbes*. "But do I lose any sleep over it? Not a minute. . . . There's such a herd mentality in finance."

By the end of 2021, Spitznagel and his team oversaw some $16 billion in stock market risk, up from $4 billion when the pandemic hit—many billions more than they'd managed even before CalPERS pulled the plug.

Universa wasn't the only fund to benefit from the insanity of March 2020. There was, of course, Bill Ackman's Pershing Square, which pocketed $2.6 billion. A tail-risk fund from Saba Capital, run by former Deutsche Bank trading whiz Boaz Weinstein, gained nearly 100 percent in March alone by betting against junk bonds. A fund managed by LongTail Alpha, the other tail-risk firm CalPERS had given money to, posted a return on invested premium—the amount of money it had placed on its bets—of nearly 1,000 percent (CalPERS was reportedly in the process of unwinding its LongTail position during the crash and may have derived a modest benefit from the position).

Cliff Asness's AQR, meanwhile, like many hedge funds, was hemorrhaging. Through March 31, its assets under management had fallen, from the end of 2019, by $43 billion to $143 billion (and down from a peak of $226 billion in 2018). "Things are bad out there, but $43 billion is a death signal," a hedge fund manager told the *New York Post*.

The big post-March market rally didn't help. By late 2021, AQR's assets had dropped to $137 billion. Of course, the hedge fund had been around for a long time and had survived other longer-lived upheavals—for example, the dot-com bubble and the Global Financial Crisis. Odds were that Mr. Asness & Co. would live to trade long into the future.

> > < <

Didier Sornette hunched on his S 1000 RR BMW motorcycle and cranked the throttle—150 . . . 165 . . . 175 *miles an hour*. Rome swept by in a blur as he rocketed toward the town of San Cesareo. He'd left Zurich early that morning and was attempting to accomplish in one day what usually takes two or three: travel the entire 650-mile stretch from his home city in Switzerland to Naples in southern Italy.

Somehow, he did not die. As in L.A., Sornette continued to perform hair-raising exploits on his super cycles, now in Europe. And he also continued to hunt bubbles—his elusive Dragon Kings.

In 2020, he believed he was witnessing the formation of one of the biggest bubbles of his bubble-hunting career: electric-car maker Tesla. Elon Musk had been a master of bubbles, becoming a billionaire in the early 2000s just as the dot-com bubble was bursting. His coup? Selling PayPal—Musk was the largest shareholder with about 12 percent of the stock—to eBay for $1.5 billion. With Tesla, he was riding what Sornette called the Green Energy Bubble (Musk was one of its principal creators, Sornette believed). Musk was also dabbling in cryptocurrencies—another bubble, thought Sornette.

Sornette's monthly *Global Bubble Status Report* in February 2020 noted: "As the dragonhead of the Electrical Automobile companies, Tesla has persuaded many people that it is a new 'APPLE' of the coming decade and all other petrol-fuel mechanical car companies are just like 'Nokia.'" Calling Musk a "clever CEO with many creative marketing strategies," the report said Tesla is reminiscent of dot-com bubble stocks and "very dangerous for short-sellers." The report ridiculed the EV maker's biggest shareholder, Ron Baron, for predicting that Tesla would reach a $1 trillion market cap in ten years.

Tesla was in a bubble, but an "early positive bubble from the long-term view." Along with Tesla, bubbles were forming in green energy and electric automobiles. "Thus, a technical correction is inevitable," the *Global Bubble Status Report* said. When a correction comes, "the sky-high valuation of Tesla (lack of reasonable fundamentals to justify the price) will become the last dagger to sting the foam."

At the time, Tesla's market cap was $160 billion. Sornette wasn't calling for the bubble to pop yet. By late 2021, however, Tesla had surged above $1 trillion—nine years earlier than Baron had predicted. It was worth the eight next biggest carmakers in the world *combined*. Elon Musk had become the planet's richest person. *Time* named him 2021's Person of the Year.

Sornette saw trouble. "Our alarm signal suggests that Tesla might have a correction very soon," his November 2021 *Global Bubble Status Report* proclaimed. Warning signs were rampant. Big investors were selling, including Musk himself. The CEO had unloaded about $10 billion worth of his own company's stock.

Of course, by then, Zurich's precocious Dragon Hunter wasn't the only market expert warning about Tesla. Around the same time Sornette issued his November correction call, legendary investor Jeremy Grantham said Tesla would have to become "one of the most successful companies in the history of capitalism" to meet investor expectations implied in the stratospheric stock price. It would soon be facing stiff competition as every single major automobile company in the world dived into electric vehicles. "To live up to the expectations of the price will be impossible," Grantham said. Indeed, both market seers proved prescient as Tesla's stock touched its all-time high of $410 a share that November. By the end of 2022, as Musk grappled with his ill-fated takeover of Twitter, the stock had cratered to nearly $100 a share, a colossal wipeout of some $800 billion in investor capital. Musk, of course, was no longer counted as the richest human on the planet.

More broadly, Grantham said the stock market itself was in an epic "superbubble" with investors more euphoric than before the crashes of 1929 and 2008. "There's a bigger buy-in this time to the idea that prices never decline and that all you have to do is buy them . . . which suggests that when the decline comes it will be perhaps bigger and better than anything previously in U.S. history."

Dragon Kings loomed.

Sornette, like nearly everyone else with even a passing interest in finance at the time, had also grown intrigued by bitcoin, the computer-generated cryptocurrency. Bitcoin is "one of the largest speculative bubbles in human history," he and a fellow ETH professor said in a 2020 paper. A phenomenon they called the Social Bubble Hypothesis fueled its growth. Bubbles in this context are good for innovation, driving technology forward through social herding and scaling. As investors flooded into bitcoin—driving its overall value to $300 billion by 2018—the viability of it as a useful financial instrument increased. The bitcoin bubbles "were necessary to bootstrap and scale the protocol and cryptocurrency," the professors wrote.

Like Grantham, Sornette was expecting dramatic events—but on an altogether different scale. Way back in 2001—in a paper that examined global population growth rates, worldwide economic production, and international stock markets—he'd detected long-term patterns eerily similar to those found in bubbles and crashes. Making what seemed an insanely far-out long-term prediction, he argued that humanity was entering a new "regime" characterized by the end of centuries (if not millennia) of faster-than-exponential economic growth that would end sometime around 2050.

"In this respect, history tells us that civilizations are fragile, impermanent things," he wrote. "Our present civilization is a relative newborn, succeeding many others that have died." Factors that triggered civilizational collapse in the past: excessive levels of complexity, war, plagues, and environmental havoc. Too many people and too little fresh water is a common cause of collapse. As a consequence, Sornette wrote, civilization became vulnerable to environmental stressors such as prolonged drought or a dramatic change in the climate.

The historical record is replete with climactic instabilities, including multicentury-length droughts that started abruptly, devastating societies that were unprepared. Such events were "highly disruptive, leading to societal collapse—an adaptive response to otherwise insurmountable stresses."

The modern world of complex technologies and seemingly endless energy resources is a different beast from earlier, simpler societies, of course. Might we be able to "figure it out" and technologically hack our way out of the coming calamity? Can we grow out of it? Maybe, maybe not, Sornette said. Part of the problem is that the complexity and the innovations that drive growth are a primary factor conjuring the coming instability. Accelerating technological complexity "carries the roots of its own collapse in its womb," he claimed.

He noted that some complex systems do in fact develop a kind of robustness in the face of big perturbations, but they can also be "hypersensitive to design flaws or rare events." Organisms and ecosystems can be robust to large variations in temperature, moisture, nutrients, and predation—but they can also be catastrophically sensitive to small perturbations such as a strange genetic mutation, new exotic species, or a novel virus.

Society has largely benefitted from the ever-accelerating race for technological mastery, but, according to Sornette, the race is unsustainable because it's approaching a self-defeating level of supercomplexity. That's why our civilization "may be fragile with respect to a global change that may require a different dynamical regime."

As the 2020s kicked off with all their dystopian fireworks—Covid-19 and market crashes, political chaos and street protests—Sornette had no reason to abandon his prediction that a civilizational phase change was racing toward humanity. Indeed, with the worsening effects of global warming, geopolitical instability, the crisis of democracy, the rapid advances in AI, the lingering pandemic and its endless Covid variants, and more, his forecast—made more than two decades ago—seemed eerily accurate.

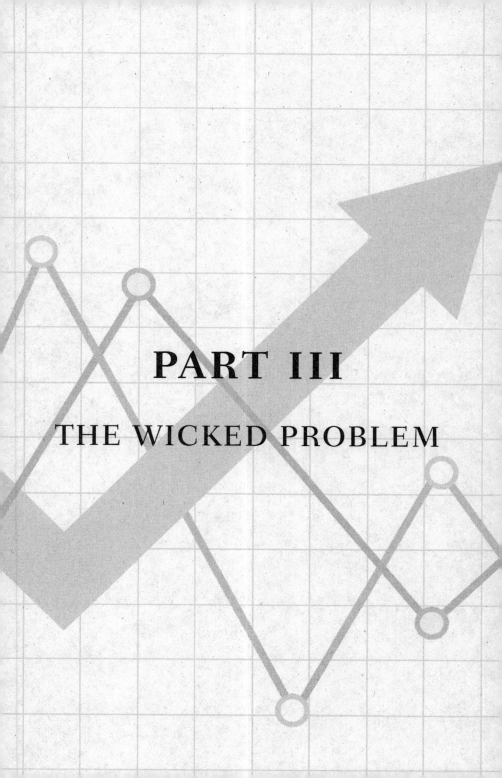

PART III

THE WICKED PROBLEM

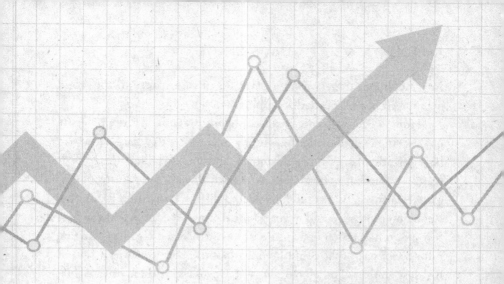

CHAPTER 16

THIS CIVILIZATION IS FINISHED

Rupert Read—dapper, trim, sandy-haired Green Party politician, Oxford-educated philosopher, spokesman for the activist environmental group Extinction Rebellion—breathed in the crisp Alpine air as he stepped off a train in Davos Platz.

Here he was in the very belly of the beast: Davos, Switzerland, home of the World Economic Forum's annual gathering of the planet's self-anointed movers and shakers, the millionaires and billionaires, the politicians and policy-makers. It was January 2020. Read had endured fourteen hours on a string of trains from London to the snowbound ski resort to avoid riding in a carbon-belching airplane (thereby passing up a one-and-a-half-hour flight from Heathrow). He reveled in the stunning views along the way, the picture-perfect French countryside, the jagged misty peaks of the Alps. But it was, no question, a pain in the ass. When he arrived, he quickly surmised that a great many attendees had jetted into town on private planes.

In his opinion, there wasn't a place for private planes in the world anymore. They all needed scrapping.

Hoping against hope, Read, a philosophy don at the University of East Anglia, had made the journey to Davos with what he knew to be a quixotic plan. If he could convince just a few billionaires to dedicate a nontrivial portion of their wealth toward the catastrophe of global warming, that could help accomplish what a dozen Extinction Rebellion protests could never do (he'd grown skeptical that the protest group had much of a future unless it received a game-changing infusion of cash that could help it expand). This visit was a sign of his desperation. The global elites at Davos, with their private jets, mansions, and limousines, were major contributors to global warming. Not to mention the fossil fuel–gulping corporations they ran. Read felt it was worth a shot, though. If just a tiny fraction of the world's super-rich would join a "Billionaires Rebellion," it could be game-changing.

In a private meeting hosted by Lord Adair Turner, chairman of the forum's Energy Transitions Commission, Read addressed some of the world's leading industrialists, including a high-ranking executive at an oil major. Civilization, he said, faced the risk of collapse if immediate action wasn't taken to sharply reduce carbon emissions. In the meantime, he said, the world needed to take adaptive measures to prepare for the destructive forces to come—the superstorms, the rising sea levels, the scorched crops. Starkly, he warned that it was probably already too late. What was needed was a massive redistribution of wealth to help those in the world's poorest populations who were most exposed to the coming onslaught. Sitting out in the audience, the Big Oil titan wasn't amused.

The executive was likely even more put off by Greta Thunberg, the teenage climate activist whose world-on-fire rhetoric made the smug Davos elite squirm. (The previous year, she'd made headlines when she told the audience, "I don't want your hope. I want you to panic.") In her 2020 address titled "Averting the Climate Apocalypse," she chastised world leaders for their failure to act:

"Any plan or policy of yours that doesn't include radical emission cuts at the source starting today is completely insufficient for meeting the 1.5 or well below two degree commitments of the Paris agreements. You say children shouldn't worry. You say just leave this to us. We will fix this. We promise we won't let you down. Don't be so pessimistic. And then, nothing. Silence."

Thunberg and her father, Svante, accompanied Read for the first part of his long train ride back to London. The professor gifted Greta with a copy of his book *This Civilization Is Finished*, based on a climate-emergency speech he'd given across the UK in previous years. Read and the senior Thunberg talked for hours about the effectiveness of nonviolent direct action, the protest strategy exploited by Extinction Rebellion throughout London in 2018 and 2019 that had garnered international attention (and from some, condemnation).

Read left Davos disappointed, though hardly surprised. The billionaires talked a good game about putting a stop to global warming, but the conversations got awkward when it came to real money. Especially if there wasn't the promise of a pot of gold at the end of the clean-energy rainbow. Much like the Thunbergs, he'd grown used to disappointment when it came to the world's meager appetite for taking on global warming.

Weeks after the conference, as Covid-19 began to rampage across continents, Read obtained a secret document from the giant U.S. bank J.P. Morgan—one of the world's largest funders of fossil fuel companies—spelling out the firm's mounting alarm about global warming. "We cannot rule out catastrophic outcomes where human life as we know it is threatened," the January 14, 2020, report said. "Although precise predictions are not possible, it is clear that the Earth is on an unsustainable trajectory. Something will have to change at some point if the human race is going to survive."

Skeptics might dismiss so-called Cassandras like Rupert Read or Greta Thunberg screaming civilization is finished, but this was *J.P. Freaking Morgan* wringing its hands about existential risk and ruin problems. Read leaked the report to the *Guardian*, which ran an article with the headline "JP Morgan Economists Warn Climate Crisis Is Threat to Human Race." (The *New Republic* had a catchier headline: "The Planet Is Screwed, Says Bank That Screwed the Planet.") Read hadn't needed J.P. Morgan economists to tell him global warming was an existential threat. He'd reached that conclusion years before.

In 2016, he'd begun delivering a speech across the UK ominously titled "This Civilization Is Finished: So What Is to Be Done?" It was a relentlessly grim indictment of humanity's response to the climate threat and a condemnation of the world's addiction to fossil fuels in the face of what he believed were civilization-destroying climate-driven calamities. That fossil-fuel-powered civilization, Read said, was in its death throes. In October 2018, he gave the speech to students and faculty at Cambridge University's Churchill College.

"What I want to say to you is slightly stark. It is this," he began. "That your leaders have failed you, your governments have failed you, your parents and their generation have failed you, your teachers have failed you. And I failed you. And what I mean by that is that we have all failed to warn adequately and prevent the dangerous climate change that is now here, and that is coming, and that is definitely going to get a lot worse. Definitely. And because of that failure I am afraid for you. I have fear for you. I fear that some of you are unlikely to grow old."

It was a shocking claim, one Read would take a lot of grief for, including from fellow climate activists who warned that such "doomist" language threatened to make people give up, rather than inspire them to action. Some said it risked making children suicidal. But there were others who privately agreed that his dire warning wasn't as radical or scare-mongering as it might seem. Confidence that the world would achieve the 1.5 Celsius degree maximum-warming target set in the 2015 Paris Accords was waning fast as carbon emissions continued to escalate around the world, with little sign of slowing or of governments taking meaningful action beyond the empty promises that enraged Greta Thunberg. Indeed, in 2018, it seemed the world was going backward. The Trump administration had dropped

out of the Paris Accords. Brazil had elected a far right wing president, Jair Bolsanaro, who promised to open up the Amazon rainfor-
est to more farming and industry. China continued to build coal-fired
power plants at a head-spinning pace.

Read's speech went viral among UK environmentalists. Gail
Bradbrook, a molecular biophysicist who, like Read, had been growing increasingly freaked out about the warming planet, heard the
speech delivered to freshman students at East Anglia. Bradbrook and
a small group of activists had been in discussions about launching
a new radical environmental group focused on global warming and
species extinction. They would call it Extinction Rebellion, XR for
short. It would use nonviolent direct-action techniques pioneered by
Gandhi and the U.S. civil rights movement to raise awareness of the
looming civilizational disaster. She wanted Read to help launch it.

Read told her XR should emphasize a philosophical approach to
climate action based on the precautionary principle. A common tac-
tic used by climate-change skeptics and deniers and corporations to
fend off action against the problem was to point to the uncertainty
of the science and the complex models it depended on. Even the
best models were chock-full of uncertainty about the impacts of rising emissions. How high would temperatures rise, and when? What
would the impact be—and would it really be all that bad? Do clouds
created by the warming atmosphere accelerate the atmosphere's
heating trend or slow it by blocking sunlight (bad news, they probably accelerate it)? In the face of such uncertainty, they said, why take
such drastic, expensive, economy-wrecking actions such as reducing
the use of fossil fuels until we have more information? Think about
the poor who want cheap power, too!

The precautionary principle was an end run around that argument. The science might not be precise, but the risks, including
mass human death and potential extinction, were too high *not* to
act. Reliable models at the time predicted that given current emission projections, the Earth's average temperature had a 10 percent
chance of increasing by six degrees Celsius from pre-industrial

levels by the end of the century, a truly catastrophic result with hair-raisingly high odds. Look before you leap across that deadly chasm, the principle cautioned. Or don't leap at all. Especially, Read felt, because the climate models might not be right. The risk might be far worse than they calculated. The possibility of an unknowably devastating tail risk in the climate models was what the skeptics routinely ignored.

Read and Bradbrook met in person for the first time on October 31, 2018, All Hallows' Eve, in front of Parliament in London for the official launch of XR. Their slogans: "This is an emergency!" and "We're fucked!" The news at the time was full of images of devastating flooding that immersed more than half of Venice under several feet of water. Greta Thunberg, then a little-known fifteen-year-old climate activist from Sweden, handed out leaflets that read "I'm doing this because you adults are shitting on my future." Only a month before, the *Guardian* had introduced her to the world. "Following Sweden's hottest summer ever, Greta Thunberg decided to go on school strike at the parliament to get politicians to act. Why bother to learn anything in school if politicians won't pay attention to the facts?"

As Thunberg faced the assembled crowd in a sun-drenched Parliament Square before the statue of the former Liberal British prime minister David Lloyd George, Read, clad in a green vest and tie and black jacket, black-rimmed glasses dangling from his neck, stood directly behind her, urging her on. It was her first address to an international audience. "There are no gray areas when it comes to survival," she said, nearby onlookers repeating her every phrase because the loudspeakers weren't strong enough for the large crowd that had gathered. "Either we go on as a civilization or we don't. We have to change."

After she finished, Read took the microphone. "Greta Thunberg everybody!" he cheered. "What an incredible hero she is. Lighting the way for the future."

Rupert Read, however, was not optimistic about the future. The future terrified him.

> > < <

As a child growing up in London, Read loved to travel outside the city to the Lake District, where his mother's family lived. He'd wander for hours, often alone, over the storied green hills that were once the inspiration of the Romantic poets William Wordsworth and Samuel Taylor Coleridge (and *Peter Rabbit* author Beatrix Potter). A diligent student, he did well in school and earned entrance into Balliol College at Oxford University. While there, he got to know another Balliol scholar, future UK prime minister Boris Johnson. After graduating in 1987, he moved to the U.S., where he earned a Ph.D. in philosophy at Rutgers University, specializing in the arcane writings of yet another influential Austrian thinker, Ludwig Wittgenstein.

America shocked Read—the rampant industrial pollution of northern New Jersey, the colorful sunsets caused by the chemicals in the atmosphere, the blatant divisions between rich and poor, black and white. He started becoming more politically radicalized and joined a protest against an annual pigeon shoot in Hegins, Pennsylvania, trying to get in between the hunters and the doomed birds. He joined the EarthFirst! Redwood Summer movement in California, protesting the destruction of the old forests from logging (part of the so-called Timber Wars of the 1990s).

Back in the UK by the mid-1990s, Read landed a job in the University of East Anglia's philosophy department. Norwich, the district where the school is located on the eastern coast of England, was becoming an environmentalist hotspot. In 2004, Read was elected councilor for Norwich's Green Party. He joined a civil disobedience movement to protest Trident nuclear missiles. Seeking more direct action, he once interrupted proceedings in the UK's House of Commons to protest the use of cluster bombs in Iraq. For punishment, he spent the afternoon in a tiny holding cell in the Palace of Westminster.

By the late 2000s, Read had started to focus on the climate. Reading voraciously on the topic, he stumbled across a 2001 report by the EU's European Environment Agency called "Late Lessons from Early Warnings: The Precautionary Principle 1896–2000." The report examined a selection of environmental, medical, and chemical controversies, ranging from nineteenth-century British fisheries to radioactivity to asbestos, and how the precautionary principle could be applied to them (global warming is barely mentioned, a follow-up in 2013 would address it). Read began studying the long and tangled history of the precautionary principle and became convinced it provided a template for taking on the growing threat of global warming and other looming risks and catastrophes.

The 2008 financial crisis unnerved Read. He was astonished by the recklessness of the banks and hedge funds. He thought it was a perfect instance of how the application of the precautionary principle might have kept bankers from running the world off a cliff. It was also when he first came across the works of Nassim Taleb.

In September 2012, Read invited a group of speakers to a University of East Anglia lecture series about philosophy and the Global Financial Crisis. Among the speakers he invited was Taleb, who gave a talk titled "Opacity, Asymmetries and Ethics," topics from *Antifragile*.

Afterward, Taleb and Read huddled in a local pub, where they sat sipping single malt whiskey. They hit it off, having a shared view that much of the world vastly underestimated the risk of Black Swans. Read accompanied Taleb to the nearby train station.

"Do you need your travel expenses covered?" he asked.

Taleb chuckled. "Rupert, you do realize that I bet against the banks?" he said, referring to his Universa winnings. "I knew they weren't taking tail risk seriously. As a result, I don't need to claim travel expenses from a university."

"Of course," Read said, laughing. "One more thing Nassim, before you leave, I don't understand why you don't talk about the precautionary principle. From where I sit and how I work, that really is what you're talking about."

Taleb's eyebrows furrowed as he thought a moment. "You know,

Rupert, you're absolutely right," he said. "We should write about it. You and me."

After returning to the U.S., Taleb began acquainting himself with the vast literature behind the precautionary principle. He didn't recall that George Church, the Harvard geneticist, had mentioned the principle in his presentation in 2009 at Brockman's Edge meeting at Elon Musk's SpaceX. But he did recollect his feeling of extreme unease verging on nausea concerning the topics discussed there, such as synthetically tampering with DNA and the potential that a vaccine-evading strain of smallpox might one day be created in a high-school lab—a risk he'd called "fat-tail city."

In short order, Taleb and Read got to work summarizing their views in what would eventually become the multiauthored paper "The Precautionary Principle."

> > < <

In April 2013, Taleb received a public letter from the musician and producer Brian Eno. The letter was sent via the Longplayer website, a thousand-year-long musical composition that began on December 31, 1999. Eno was part of the project.

Eno had designed the digital letter to be a chain. Taleb would craft a response and send it to another public intellectual, whose response would be sent to someone else. Eno's letter to Taleb was the first in the chain.

His letter concerned an endemic problem in modern society— we're shortsighted, focused on the moment, the quarterly earnings report, the next political campaign, tomorrow's weather. It wasn't always like that, Eno said. Olive farmers and cathedral builders thought across generations, planting farms that might not be productive for decades or groves of oaks to replace a chapel roof hundreds of years in the future. Modern humans seem to have lost the ability to think about generational risk. Take the nuclear disaster at Fukushima, the Japanese power plant that melted down when it was struck by a tsunami in 2011. Despite the severity of the disaster, there were no radiation-related deaths. That wasn't the message you heard in the media. "It became one of those little nuggets of received, and totally incorrect, wisdom: Nuclear=Fukushima=Catastrophe," Eno wrote. The unfortunate result: countries such as Germany decided to decommission their nuclear reactors and replace them with coal-fired power plants. "So the real catastrophe of Fukushima is in the future," Eno wrote, "waiting for us in the form of vastly increased atmospheric CO_2."

Eno wanted to revive the ability to think across future generations. It wouldn't be easy. "Those olive farmers and church builders . . . had something we don't: a sense that the future would quite likely be similar to the present. We, on the other hand, can be sure this won't be the case. So the question is this: how can we even think about designing for a future that we can't imagine?"

Taleb's response drew directly on the work he'd done with Rupert Read as well as lessons from *Antifragile*. "If I am hit with a big stone I will be harmed a lot more than if I were pelted serially with pebbles of the same weight," he wrote.

The big stone was Taleb's ruin problem.

"Now that we have this principle, let us apply it to life on earth," he wrote. "This is the basis of the non-naïve Precautionary Principle that the philosopher Rupert Read and I are in the process of elaborating, with precise policy implications on the part of states and individuals. Everything flows—by theorems—from the principle of nonlinear response."

Rule 1 – Size Effects. Everything you do to planet earth is disproportionally more harmful in large quantities than in small ones. Hence we need to split sources of harm as much as we can (provided these don't interact). If we dropped our carbon by, say, 20% we may reduce the harm by more than 50%. Conversely, we may double our risk with just an increase of 10%.

Other rules included: avoid large-scale, top-down, command-and-control systems, which are vulnerable to human error and can propagate harm widely; favor decentralized, local systems because the errors in those realms don't spread systemically; and favor nature over the man-made. "Nature is a better statistician than humans, having produced trillions of 'errors' or variations without blowing up." In complex systems "it's impossible to see the consequences of a positive action (from the Bar-Yam theorem), so one needs—like nature—to keep errors isolated and thin-tailed."

An example of the policy implications of these rules and principles concerned genetically modified organisms, or GMOs, Taleb wrote. GMOs are exactly what the name implies—organisms that have been genetically modified by the insertion of DNA from another species, such as a bacteria or virus, for some specific purpose. Tomatoes resistant to blight. Corn that can dish out poisonous toxins to harmful butterflies. Rice that can grow in the world's most arid deserts. Wheat that isn't (in theory) harmed by massive doses of weed killer. GMOs are different from grains (or animals) that are modified by crossbreeding, which is, from an evolutionary perspective, as old as life itself. The science behind GMOs was about three decades old. These concoctions might provide a short-term benefit and feed more people, but over the long run—across generations—the impact could be disastrous on a global level, a risk that should never be taken, Taleb warned.

Taleb sent his letter to Stewart Brand, creator of the *Whole Earth Catalog* and president of the Long Now Foundation, whose goal was to improve long-term thinking. Taleb, who'd briefly met Brand at the Brockman conference at SpaceX in 2009, was shocked by his reply. "The science of genetic engineering is far more precise than blind selective breeding, and for that reason it is even safer," Brand wrote. "I think that the ghost in the GMO story is a misplaced idea of contagion. Any transferred gene, people imagine, might be like a loose plague virus. It might infect everything, or it might hide for years and then emerge catastrophically. But genes don't work like that."

It turned out, to Taleb's immense surprise, that Brand had been a staunch advocate for GMOs for years. It wouldn't have taken much time to find out. Brand's 2010 book *Whole Earth Discipline: Why Dense*

Cities, Nuclear Power, Transgenic Crops, Restored Wildlands, Radical Science, and Geoengineering Are Necessary is a paean to outside-the-box techno-solutions to the world's ills, including GMOs. The book "gushes about technology in a way that might raise a blush even in a spokesman for Monsanto," a *Financial Times* review observed.

It was an old stance for Brand. "We are as gods," he wrote in the *Whole Earth Catalog*, first published in 1968, "and might as well get good at it."

This was not a view Taleb—or Rupert Read—looked fondly upon.

> > < <

In May 2013, Taleb and Read traveled to Hay-on-Wye, a sleepy market town in Wales, to attend a popular philosophy and music festival called HowTheLightGetsIn after lyrics in a celebrated Leonard Cohen song. In a debate about spirituality and nature, Read faced off against Benny Peiser, director of the Global Warming Policy Foundation, a London group known for agitating against taking action to address the very thing for which it was named.

Peiser told the audience that he came from an enlightened, humanistic tradition and complained that extreme environmentalists—troublemakers he called "Deep Greens"—undermine humanity by putting people on the same level as the rest of nature. In fact, he said, humans have a "special role" on the planet.

"I look at environmental issues from a social and a moral perspective," he said. "So I think that we are risk-takers. There is simply no way humans can avoid taking risk. It's trial and error. That's how we have evolved. That's how we are who we are. So therefore my view is that to err is human and to progress is to take risks. And that includes the balance between protecting the environment and intervening in the environment."

The climate crisis and other environmental harms are measurable risks, he said. We need to think carefully about the costs and trade-offs involved in fixing them. How bad is it really? The Deep

Greens are too obsessed with "gloom and doom," he complained, and want to shut down economic growth. That approach misses the point that growth is at the heart of environmental protection. Impoverished countries don't have the wherewithal to enact costly environmental policies. "It's a luxury to look after your environment," Peiser said.

"It's very important," Read responded, "to be clear here that when we are trying to think about ourselves in or as nature that we don't fall into the illusion of thinking that we can think of ourselves as fundamentally *separate* from nature. And *that* is exactly the mistake that Benny makes, right? The fantasy that we can think about ourselves, humans, in this Promethean form as being over and above nature, able to dominate it, take from it what you will, have a fundamentally rationalist attitude towards it—that's where the Enlightenment goes wrong."

There's your Deep Green fanaticism, Peiser said. "People who are zealots, who are dogmatics, who are extremists, always get it wrong. Even if they're right, they get it wrong," he said. "We are here because of fossil fuels. Britain wouldn't be Britain without coal, without natural gas, without nuclear energy, right? We wouldn't be here with just the sun and the wind."

That cold, hard pseudo-rational view is dangerously short-sighted, Read said, and doesn't take into account the future unborn generations who have no voice and who will pay the price for humankind's mistakes today. "When Benny says we've got to weigh things up, we've got to balance things, we've got to compromise things, we've got to take risks, what we must *not* do is gamble with the very future existence of our children's children."

> > < <

The following day, Read took the stage with Taleb. The subject: "How do you solve a problem like uncertainty?"

One area where uncertainty reigned, Taleb said, was humanity's dangerous experiments with the natural world. Exhibit number one: GMOs. "Nature tinkers slowly and over time. Some shmuck was telling you on Twitter," Taleb said, looking over at Read, "that GMOs are biological. That's bullshit all right. Nature discovered that it took one hundred million years how to make it. And now we humans with our arrogance want to introduce it top-down. Whatever we introduce tends to be fragile."

This is where the precautionary principle comes in, he said. "Necessarily, if I go against Nature, then I have to prove why I'm not harming Nature. It's not like *we* have to prove it. Someone might say you have no evidence that I'm harming Nature. I say no no no. It doesn't work that way. You need to produce the evidence you're not harming. Think about it. Evidence shows up too late in risk systems."

One way of thinking about it, Taleb added, was to consider the fact that there are far more slightly ill people in the world than very sick people (which he said is why Big Pharma is constantly developing treatments for the slightly ill). Since Nature has seen many more slightly ill cases, they don't require significant medical interventions—or any at all. Nature will take care of it—it doesn't require the precautionary principle. Very sick cases require quick, aggressive intervention.

"This gives a statistical structure to precaution," he said. "A little bit of rigor in the way we apply precaution. If I have a cold, don't treat it. If I have a headache, don't treat it. If I have cancer, see six doctors, not one."

> > < <

In the summer of 2014, Yaneer Bar-Yam, founder of the New England Complex Systems Institute, or NECSI, heard about Taleb and Read's work on the precautionary principle. He was intrigued. He called up Taleb, who was planning to come to a conference Bar-Yam was holding at NECSI's campus in Cambridge, Massachusetts.

"I think what you're onto here is fascinating, Nassim," Bar-Yam said. "Let's talk about it once you're here."

"Sure thing," Taleb replied.

At the NECSI campus, they began to swap ideas about how to advance the paper. Bar-Yam's specialty was complex systems. A property of complex systems is that it's very difficult to predict how they will react to new information or actions, a conundrum Bar-Yam had frequently written about. In certain classes of complex systems— and nature is the most complex of all—controlled experiments and models aren't sufficient to determine what will happen in the real world, he'd argued. Because it's so hard to determine specific outcomes, the focus needs to narrow down to one simple, crucial question: Is the threat local or global?

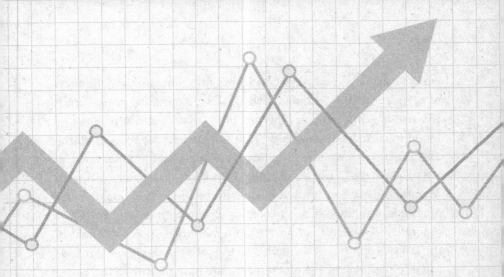

CHAPTER 17

TRANSITION TO EXTINCTION

Taleb had first met Yaneer Bar-Yam, a slender, cerebral man with a curly shock of hair and an enduring fondness for wool sweaters, when he attended a New England Complex Systems Institute conference in Cambridge in 2010. He'd been teaching Bar-Yam's textbook, *Dynamics of Complex Systems*, to his class at NYU, and saw interesting connections between Bar-Yam's specialty, complexity theory, and his own idiosyncratic Black Swan worldview. Bar-Yam, he came to believe, was the world's leading expert in complexity theory.

It was a big claim. No less an authority than Stephen Hawking proclaimed, "Complexity is the science of the twenty-first century." Not only founder of NECSI but also chair of the International Conference on Complex Systems, Bar-Yam had long been at the very forefront of the complexity pack.

The study of complex systems is an analysis of the interrelations and emerging properties of systems and their parts and their connections to the larger world (there are hundreds of definitions of *complex systems*, and not all align). That may sound vague, but it has real-life implications. The properties of an ant colony can't be found in an individual ant, but in the collective properties of all the ants functioning together, forming the complex system that is a colony. The nature of a spear-wielding Greek phalanx marching toward Marathon can't be captured in the psyche of a single hoplite—the phalanx is a thing in itself, a complex system with its own rules and properties. The nature of an NFL offense driving down the field in the last two minutes of the fourth quarter of a tied game can't be captured in the brain of the quarterback. You have to analyze the whole team, the coach, the defense, the rules of the game, and more to capture the dynamics of the system. The study of complex systems is anti-reductionist—you have to study the whole colony, the whole team. As complexity scientist Peter Dodds put it: "There's no love in a carbon atom, no hurricane in a water molecule, no financial collapse in a dollar bill."

Bar-Yam's career in math and science seemed predestined from the crib. Born in 1960 in Boston, he was taught math by his older sister while he was a toddler. His father, a survivor of the Holocaust, was a particle physicist who trained at Carnegie Mellon University and MIT; his mother was an expert on child development psychology.

In 1967, at elementary school, he saw televised footage of starving children, victims of the Nigerian Civil War. He never forgot the horrifying images, and later in life the memory of those potbellied children played a role in his decision to focus on practical solutions to poverty and starvation. He graduated from MIT in 1978. Six years later, he earned a Ph.D. in applied physics (also from MIT).

Bar-Yam founded NECSI in 1996. The institute quickly became a hotbed of academics who developed models to predict and solve thorny problems such as famines, pandemics, financial crashes, global warming, ethnic cleansing, economic crises—and much more. Researchers looked for patterns, signals in the noise, that could predict extreme, often harmful events, with the hope, at times, of stopping them in their tracks or taking measures to mitigate their impact. Or, at times, to make money off them.

Complexity science is intimidating due to its, well, complexity—but it's intensely fascinating because of the vast potential it has for solving real-world applications. Bar-Yam spelled out a number of those applications in his 2004 book *Making Things Work: Solving Complex Problems in a Complex World*. Themes included military warfare, education, health care, ethnic violence, and terrorism. A quasi-handbook for laymen showing how to put complexity theory to use, the book revolves around a singular insight: Any organization designed to solve complex problems needs to match (or exceed) the complexity of the problem itself. That means single individuals by definition are unable to solve very complex problems. Solving very complex problems takes a village. Bar-Yam wrote: "The underlying challenge of this book is the question: How do we create organizations that are capable of being more complex than a single individual?"

> > < <

Among Bar-Yam's most important areas of focus was the evolving, increasingly deadly nature of pandemics in a globalized world. In 2006, he coauthored a study of how even small increases in long-range transportation dramatically increase the risk of widespread breakouts. "Global mixing," as the paper called it, can result in sudden instability in a population—e.g., a deadly pandemic. Alarmingly, this can happen "with little warning as global mixing increases in frequency."

"Our results suggest the need for a concerted response, including medical developments, and, perhaps, societal changes," the paper concludes. "Due to increasing global transportation, human beings may cross the transition without much warning and suffer large pandemics unless preventive actions are taken that either limit global transportation or its impact."

The following year, Bar-Yam helped produce a mathematical model he claimed could predict the breakout of ethnic conflict.

Deploying methods to detect pattern formation, such as how chemicals interact, the model analyzed signals that could provide strong indications of future violence. For instance, the risk of violence was often high in regions of highly mixed groups where no one group could dominate. That opened the door to increased conflict.

"Our research shows that violence takes place when an ethnic group is large enough to impose cultural norms on public spaces, but not large enough to prevent those norms from being broken," said a scientist involved in the study, which was published in the journal *Nature*.

A key tool used by complexity theorists is the study of the physics behind phase transitions—when water turns to steam, or ice turns to water, or an everyday market downturn accelerates into a crash. It was these phase transitions that fascinated Didier Sornette—beginning with his analysis of the sudden eruption of Ariane rocket pressure tanks—and led to his concept of Dragon Kings. Such transitions are sudden and disruptive. When mapped onto social phenomena, the phase transition can help explain how something stable suddenly becomes unstable and chaotic, such as a breakout of ethnic violence.

Such a transition, theoretically, could happen on a civilizational scale. In 2008, *New Scientist* magazine ran a pair of alarming articles: "Will a Pandemic Bring Down Civilization?" and "Why the Demise of Civilization May Be Inevitable." Bar-Yam was a key source. "What if the very nature of civilization means that ours, like all the others, is destined to collapse sooner or later?" the latter article asked. "A few researchers have been making such claims for years. Disturbingly, recent insights from fields such as complexity theory suggest that they are right. It appears that once a society develops beyond a certain level of complexity it becomes increasingly fragile. Eventually, it reaches a point at which even a relatively minor disturbance can bring everything crashing down."

Citing the work of Joseph Tainter, an anthropology professor at Utah State University and author of the seminal 1988 book *The Col-*

lapse of Complex Societies, the article described how civilizations throughout history, in their struggle to solve challenges ranging from food and water scarcity to barbarian invasions, evolve into ever more complex structures with intricate gradations of hierarchies. Societies have to continually solve new problems to survive and grow. That means accelerating levels of complexity. "Success generates a larger population, more kinds of specialists, more resources to manage, more information to juggle—and, ultimately, less bang for your buck. Eventually, says Tainter, the point is reached when all the energy and resources available to a society are required just to maintain its existing level of complexity."

It was the same phenomenon that led Sornette (who cited Tainter's work) to forecast a looming societal collapse—and Bar-Yam wholly agreed. "Complexity leads to higher vulnerability," he told the *New Scientist*. "This is not widely understood." Breakdowns in a highly complex system can spread due to the interlocking networks, like the global supply chain, which act like a vast complex ecosystem with myriad choke points. A car dealer in Rapid City can't sell cars because Ford can't get the computer chips it needs because a factory in Taiwan got flooded. A single container ship foundering in the Suez Canal disrupts supply chains worldwide. "The networks that connect us can amplify any shocks. A breakdown anywhere increasingly means a breakdown everywhere," Bar-Yam observed.

Corporations solely motivated by profit can make matters worse by optimizing their operations to the fullest extent possible. Just-in-time delivery can be very profitable, as long as supply chains work as planned. When they don't, the whole chain can fracture as slowdowns at choke points ramify through the system. Imagine an entire global economy based on optimized supply chains (and food chains), all backed and managed by computer-driven financial markets increasingly susceptible to extreme events. Communities linked by satellites, social networks, fleets of planes.

This was the world that existed in 2020 when Covid-19 hit. As businesses and whole economies ground to a halt, a chain reaction of slowdowns and work stoppages caused international supply chains to seize up—and as they did, humanity was also forced to confront the devastating effects of global warming, including floods, heat waves, wildfires, and superstorms.

Bar-Yam foresaw such a world in 2008. "Civilization is very vulnerable," he warned.

> > < <

In late 2010, Bar-Yam had noticed a troubling spike in food prices in the Middle East. Examining historical correlations between high food prices and social unrest, he found that whenever the United Nations' FAO food index climbed above 210, the risk of outbreaks of violence shot up. It was troubling, because food prices had been steadily rising, with periods of extreme volatility, for the past decade. NECSI researchers found two primary triggers for higher global food costs, and they both resided in U.S. policy. One was the 1999 deregulation of commodity markets that unleashed speculation by traders. The second was the use of American corn to make ethanol, which saw a huge increase under the George W. Bush administration.

The spike in food prices combined with signs of mounting social unrest and political instability led Bar-Yam to predict extreme turmoil in the Middle East and Northern Africa. In December, he reported his expectations to the U.S. government. Days later, Mohamed Bouazizi, a twenty-six-year-old fruit and vegetable vendor in Tunisia harassed by local police, lit himself on fire and died, sparking waves of protest that quickly spread to other countries in what became known as the Arab Spring. Bar-Yam's uncannily accurate forecast put him in the international spotlight along with the emerging science of complex systems.

"Times of change can be drastic—revolutions topple dictators, extreme weather kills tens of thousands, and market crashes plunge people into poverty—but for scientists studying complex systems they are fertile ground," a March 2011 Reuters article proclaimed.

"According to Yaneer Bar-Yam . . . this kind of science is a vital tool for protecting societies from such dangers as pandemics, natural disasters, terrorism, climate change, resource exhaustion and economic crises."

The goal, according to Bar-Yam, wasn't just predicting outcomes and weighing odds like a bettor in a casino. Rather, it was to figure out how things work, and what's gone wrong, in order to fix problems before they blow up in our collective face. It was, in a way, a proactive form of insurance. "Prediction tells you that something is going to happen, and that can be helpful so you can run away from it if you need to," he told Reuters. "But much better is understanding *why* it happens—that can enable us to take action that may prevent things."

> > < <

After the Global Financial Crisis, Bar-Yam began studying the complex system that is the stock market. He claimed to have helped discover a phenomenon that skeptics such as Taleb maintained was impossible—a system to predict market crashes, just like Didier Sornette's LPPLS model could detect Dragon Kings. In April 2011, Bar-Yam and a team of NECSI researchers produced a paper that identified internal market mechanisms that they claimed foretold a crash. When a bunch of stocks start moving up or down together—a trend the researchers called *mimicry*—that's a sign that the market is poised for panic, according to the study, which analyzed market crashes going back to 1985. "We have demonstrated mathematically that there is significant advance warning to provide a clear indicator of an impending crash," Bar-Yam boasted.

In January 2014, Bar-Yam spoke at the World Health Organization in Geneva about the impact of long-range transportation on the evolution of pathogens. He presented a video showing how Ebola could spread across the globe like wildfire due to increased transportation between continents. What starts as a tiny, seemingly harmless blob in Central Africa metastasizes with blobs quickly popping up in Europe, Cuba, the U.S., then spreading across South America, Russia, Asia, Australia, before covering the majority of the planet (except the oceans, Antarctica, and a lot of northern Canada). The rise of global mixing was making the world highly unstable and unpredictable. "The general expectation is that prior experience is a predictor of future events," he later wrote, describing the research, "but in this case it doesn't work."

A few months later, the world's largest outbreak of Ebola erupted in West Africa. Cases were nearly doubling weekly. Public health officials began contact-tracing to contain the disease. But it was ineffective, later analysis of the situation by NECSI showed. For one thing, most people didn't know at first that they had Ebola, which initially can feel like a regular viral infection. Also, because many people in urban centers of West Africa share cabs, it was often impossible to know who sick people had been in contact with. Finally, as the disease spread exponentially, the ideal number of contact tracers rose to a number that was logistically impossible. Some of those tracking the Ebola outbreak feared that 10 million people might die in Africa alone.

Bar-Yam and his colleagues at NECSI began crafting an alternative response as it became clear that contact-tracing wasn't working. They focused on intervening at the community level, restricting travel in discrete areas where infections popped up, and actively seeking out infected people through door-to-door canvassing. Such an approach would squeeze the virus until it could no longer spread at all, or so they hoped. In collaboration with the U.S. Army Corps of Engineers, they cobbled together a plan. Bar-Yam was in contact with key officials at the United Nations, the Centers for Disease Control, and the National Security Council at the White House. But he was growing worried that the response wasn't happening quickly enough as the fatal disease continued to spread.

Increasingly alarmed, he reached out to people on the ground in Liberia, where the Ebola outbreak was at its worst. It was October. To his relief, he learned that some communities had already begun implementing his approach. Teams were going door to door with infrared thermometers to screen for fever. "The results were dramatic," Bar-Yam wrote in a subsequent analysis. "The epidemic that was exponentially growing fell exponentially."

The same approach was later deployed in Sierra Leone, with the same favorable result. By the following year, Ebola had been wiped out in Liberia, and it was soon largely contained on the continent. "If this had been the earliest response to the outbreak, many more lives would have been saved and unimaginable suffering, as well as the economic and social disruption, would have been prevented," Bar-Yam observed.

Unnerved by the Ebola outbreak, and building on his 2006 research into the impact of transportation on the spread of viruses, Bar-Yam penned an alarming report called *Transition to Extinction: Pandemics in a Connected World*. He observed that, historically, highly deadly pathogens first spread quickly but then burn out as they kill all their hosts.

But like a wildfire consuming a forest, modern transportation, with its "get to any place in a day and a half" connectivity, serves up more hosts. In fact, it serves up virtually *everyone*. As the pathogen relentlessly spreads, humanity eventually arrives at the hinge moment that the title of Bar-Yam's report calls: the "transition to extinction."

That is, the extinction of the human race.

> > < <

After the 2014 NECSI conference in Cambridge, Bar-Yam got to work on Taleb and Read's precautionary principle paper, which at the time was a fairly sparse draft with multiple section headings such as "WHY RUIN IS SERIOUS BUSINESS" and "WHAT WE MEAN BY THICK TAILS" and about five pages of text. He delegated some of the work of filling it out to an assistant. She was baffled and went to a colleague, a young, new researcher at NECSI named Joe Norman, and asked for help.

"I don't know what to do with this," she said.

Norman took a look at the draft and got excited. It was a fascinating topic. *This is a good argument*, he thought. As a bonus, it had Taleb's name on it. Norman was an admirer of Taleb's work, especially *Antifragile*. After first reading the book, he bought twenty copies and handed them out to friends.

"Let me take a shot," he said.

Norman had literally been born into a world of complex systems. His father, Douglas, was a complex-systems engineer, which involved applying the often esoteric concepts of the field to the real-world challenge of building stuff. His work included military contracts, such as designing and building air control bases in Afghanistan and Iraq. At times, he collaborated with Bar-Yam at NECSI.

The younger Norman grew up with books about complexity science littered about the house. Following in his father's footsteps, he studied mechanical engineering at the University of Central Florida but later switched to philosophy and biology. He grew enamored of the school of enactivism, spelled out by the Chilean biologists Humberto Maturana and Francisco Varela in their 1992 tome *The Tree of Knowledge: The Biological Roots of Human Understanding*, which (to dramatically oversimplify) delves into the dynamic relationship between the human brain and the world.

After graduating from Central Florida in 2009, Norman earned a Ph.D. in the heady field of complex systems and brain sciences at Florida Atlantic University. His first job out of college, in 2014, was at NECSI. The first paper he coauthored there was "The Precautionary Principle." It went through multiple drafts circulated between Taleb, Read, Norman, and Bar-Yam.

They finally completed the paper in the fall. On October 17, 2014, at 12:30 p.m., Taleb hit a button on his computer and published "The Precautionary Principle (with Application to the Genetic Modification of Organisms)" on Cornell University's arXiv.org.

With the push of that button, Taleb had taken a leap into one of the hottest public firestorms of his life.

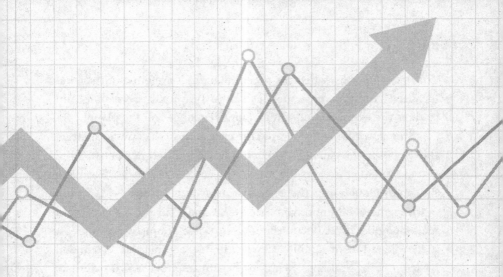

CHAPTER 18

RUIN IS FOREVER

Abstract—The precautionary principle (PP) states that if an action or policy has a suspected risk of causing severe harm to the public domain (affecting general health or the environment globally), the action should not be taken in the absence of scientific near-certainty about its safety. Under these conditions, the burden of proof about absence of harm falls on those proposing an action, not those opposing it.

Thus begins "The Precautionary Principle."

A long-standing complaint about the principle has been: It's too vague. When are risks so high that the principle needs to be invoked? To solve the conundrum, Taleb deployed his long history studying extreme events and devising trading strategies to protect against Black Swans. "We believe that the PP should be invoked only in extreme situations: when the potential harm is systemic (rather than localized) and the consequences can involve total irreversible ruin, such as the extinction of human beings or all life on the planet."

Strong words. But as is often the case with such complex matters, the devil is in the data. How to determine the difference between the risk of systemic, irreversible ruin and local harm? The answer had a direct correlation with the trading strategy at Universa.

Imagine one hundred gamblers entering a casino. Each gambler makes one bet of $1,000 at the roulette wheel. Some win, some lose it all. The failure of gambler 59 won't impact gambler 60. When they walk out of the building, their average gain amounts to $10—perhaps a bad day for the casino.

Now imagine one gambler who walks into a casino planning to make one hundred consecutive bets at the roulette wheel. He puts all his money on red, and keeps doing so. Will he make it to a hundred bets? Definitely not, assuming he loses even once (a pretty fair assumption!). If he loses his entire stake on bet 59, he won't make it to 60. He's done, one ruined gambler.

That's a ruin problem—specifically, gambler's ruin. Rather than an average of the sum of a series of disconnected bets from a group, ruin problems apply to an individual's trajectory *across time*. It's what blows up banks and hedge funds that don't manage their risk properly. They might get a lucky streak and beat the dealer ten times in a row, but on the eleventh bet they can lose it all. Taleb and his coauthors describe this as the difference between "localized non-spreading impacts" and "propagating impacts resulting in irreversible and widespread damage."

It's the risk Universa never takes. By suffering only small hits—cutting losses by loving to lose à la Everett Klipp—Spitznagel can't blow up like a devil-may-care hedge fund or investment bank packed to the gills with leverage (average investors who simply put their money into stock-and-bond mutual funds aren't playing a ruin game, because the market never loses 100 percent, but they can suffer large drawdowns in market crashes that can hurt their long-term wealth). Spitznagel can bleed, but he can't hemorrhage to death in a day.

Someone playing the ruin game, over and over, will eventually blow up, statistics show. Consider, for example, another ruin game—Russian roulette. "By the ruin theorems, if you incur a tiny probability of ruin as a 'one-off' risk, survive it, then do it again (another 'one-off' deal), you will eventually go bust," Taleb and his coauthors observed.

The precautionary principle seeks to protect humanity from ruinous losses by refusing to take risks that can result in a global systemic crisis—"an irreversible termination of life at some scale, which could be planetwide."

B. Ruin is forever

When the impact of harm extends to all future times, i.e. forever, then the harm is infinite. When the harm is infinite, the product of any non-zero probability and the harm is also infinite, and it cannot be balanced against any potential gains, which are necessarily finite.

When facing a ruin problem, don't weigh odds or calculate a cost-benefit analysis. Nothing is worth the risk, because ultimate destruction (ruin) is a mathematical certainty if the game is played forever. You might get lucky and make it through a few rounds of Russian roulette—or the first round might be your last. "Because the 'cost' of ruin is effectively infinite, cost-benefit analysis . . . is no longer a useful paradigm," the paper states. "In this case, we must do everything we can to avoid the catastrophe."

And since we're dealing with a very complex system—*all of nature and humanity*—models designed to evaluate risk are inherently limited. It's virtually impossible to prove "lack of harm."

This leaves humanity in a troubling spot. You can't use evidence, since that would entail taking the risk to see what happens—a bad idea when all humanity is on the line—and you can't even model out likely scenarios, because the system is too mind-bendingly complex. The answer, according to Taleb & Co., is to figure out if the risk in question is *globally systemic*. "The essential question is whether or not global harm is possible or not," they wrote.

Are there links in the chain, interdependencies, that can bring about what the authors call *cascades*, causing the harm to spread across borders?

"Consider the global financial crash of 2008," they wrote. "As financial firms became increasingly interdependent during the latter part of the 20th century, small fluctuations during periods of calm masked the vulnerability of the system to cascading failures. Instead of a local shock in an independent area of the system, we experienced a global shock with cascading effects."

That crisis was just one example of the greater risk of fat-tailed events due to increased communication capabilities, transportation, and economic interdependence. "The danger we are facing today is that we as a civilization are globally connected, and the fat tail of the distribution of shocks extends globally, to our peril," they wrote. "As connectivity increases, the risk of extinction increases dramatically and nonlinearly."

7. FRAGILITY

. . . The PP applies only to the largest scale impacts due to the inherent fragility of systems that maintain their structure. As the scale of impacts increases the harm increases non-linearly up to the point of destruction.

Complex systems are prone to collapse because of deep interconnections within the structure that tie one part to another. Pull one thread of the spiderweb and the whole web can fall apart. The impact is nonlinear since a small input can crash the whole edifice just as Luke Skywalker's tiny proton torpedoes blew up the Death Star in the blink of an eye.

Scale matters, as Taleb had noted in his Longplayer letter to Stewart Brand. Throwing a fifty-pound stone at a person's head can cause massive harm. Throwing ten thousand pebbles that, added up, weigh fifty pounds, causes zero harm.

Uncertainty about impacts and the reliability of models increases the risk of ruin and calls for more precaution. "More skepticism about models implies more uncertainty about the tails, which necessitates more precaution about newly implemented techniques, or larger size of exposures," Taleb and his coauthors wrote. "Nature might not be smart, but its longer track record means smaller uncertainty in following its logic."

> > < <

The section of "The Precautionary Principle" that invited a coordinated attack on the authors—none took more heat than Taleb due to his highly public profile—was its call for an outright ban on GMOs. "Genetically Modified Organisms (GMOs) and their risk are currently the subject of debate," they wrote. "Here we argue that they fall squarely under the PP because their risk is systemic."

Taleb and his coauthors believed the three decades of research behind GMOs were insufficient to conclude that these wide-ranging genetic experiments on nature were harmless. And that's a problem, because (they argued) GMOs pose the risk of a tail event—the risk of ruin. If a genetically modified form of rice somehow began to interbreed in the wild with natural rice—or if the new DNA was introduced into some other organism, like bacteria—the outcome is unknowable. And even if those risks were small, their existence required the application of the precautionary principle. The GMO cheerleaders, they said, need to prove beyond a shadow of a doubt there is nearly zero existential risk—a very tough challenge indeed.

Taking on the pro-GMO crowd had its risks. GMO critics are often tarred as anti-science conspiracy nuts, lumped in with the anti-vaccination crowd or climate-change deniers—a deep irony for Read, who'd spent years battling climate-change deniers. Read argued there was nothing "anti-science" about being against the mass implementation of a novel engineering method on the crops that fed much of the planet, nothing anti-science about asking logical, philosophical, ethical, political, and statistical questions about the proposed rollout, for profit, of a technology that could carry big hidden risks. Taleb & Co. wanted to change the debate. Not *science* versus *anti-science*, but *recklessness* versus *precaution*.

GMOs can "spread uncontrollably" and so can't be localized—they can cross international barriers, like a virus, and expand non-linearly through the Earth's ecosystems, they argued in the paper. Their impact can't be tested because nature is too complex and replete with randomness, chaos. In a nutshell: Introducing new genetically modified species is a dangerous roll of the dice.

GMOs are not the same as selective farming or interbreeding of different types of a certain crop, like corn that is native to Bolivia with corn native to Iowa, they argued. Selective breeding is slow and takes place over generations. It is generally localized, allowing for mistakes that die out before spreading. "There is no comparison between tinkering with the selective breeding of genetic components of organisms that have previously undergone extensive histories of selection and the top-down engineering of taking a gene from a fish and putting it into a tomato," they wrote. "We should exert the precautionary principle here . . . because we do not want to discover errors after considerable and irreversible environmental and health damage."

As for the common argument among GMO supporters that banning them would increase the risk of famine, the paper noted that widespread hunger is often due to poor economic and agricultural policies. The risk of catastrophe, even if fleeting, isn't worth it if there are other ways to solve the problem, such as improving transportation of foodstuffs from areas of abundance to regions of scarcity. Some one-third of all the food produced in the world goes to waste, according to supply-chain tracker Wiliot. Salvaging a fraction of that wasted food would go a long way toward solving the world's hunger problem.

"Given the limited oversight that is taking place on GMO introductions in the U.S., and the global impact of those introductions, we are precisely in the regime of the ruin problem," the paper argued.

Another problem: the massive buildup of chemical herbicides and pesticides in the environment, since one form of GMO had as its purpose making a plant resistant to chemicals, such as the herbicide Roundup—which encouraged the mass dispersal of such chemicals across the world. The resultant widespread use of herbicides such as Roundup amounted to a vast experiment on the global environment. Tested in small amounts, the risk was likely minimal. Tested on a global level, the risk compounded to something potentially systemic—a giant boulder thrown at mother nature rather than a bunch of pebbles.

One risk—which Monsanto had downplayed—was the evolution of weeds that Roundup couldn't kill and were more harmful to crops than previous strains, like a deadly virus that develops resistance to vaccines. It happened. In the mid-2010s, a fast-growing superweed called Palmer amaranth became resistant to Roundup. By the early 2020s, it had spread to more than two dozen states in America, confounding farmers who'd grown entirely reliant on the one-size-fits-all Roundup strategy. The weed could reduce soybean and peanut yields by 68 percent, corn yields by 91 percent. "Weed resistance to herbicides, especially multiple-herbicide resistance, poses a serious threat to global food production," a January 2021 study of the weed warned.

Other problems with Roundup emerged. In 2020, German pharmaceutical giant Bayer, which had purchased Monsanto in 2018, agreed to pay $10 billion to settle thousands of claims that Roundup caused cancer. Despite the settlement, Bayer maintained the herbicide was safe.

Such problems weren't confined to Roundup. Experimental man-made chemicals were everywhere, in everything. Plastics were found on the top of Mount Everest, and in the farthest depths of the world's oceans. By 2022, the planet was approaching—or may have even surpassed—a tipping point of chemical pollution. A sweeping new study by fourteen scientists at the Stockholm Resilience Centre and elsewhere found there had been a fiftyfold increase in the production of chemicals since 1950—an amount the study projected would triple again by 2050. That out-of-control megaproduction was pushing the global ecosystem over a "planetary boundary" beyond which ecosystems couldn't recover, the study warned. "The rise of the chemical burden in the environment is diffuse and insidious," Ian Boyd, a biologist at the University of St Andrews in Scotland, told the *Guardian*, commenting on the new study. "We are relatively blind to what is going on as a result. In this situation, where we have a low level of scientific certainty about effects, there is a need for a much more precautionary approach to new chemicals and to the amount being emitted to the environment."

>   >   <   <

With its publication online, "The Precautionary Principle" quickly began circulating among GMO experts. They were not amused. The authors were lumped in with anti-vaccination conspiracy theorists— or worse. A middle-school teacher named Stephan Neidenbach, founder of a website called We Love GMOs and Vaccines, compared Taleb with Hitler. New York University, which still employed Taleb as a professor, received hundreds of letters complaining about the paper. Some lobbied for his termination. He'd had plenty of controversies in his career, but he'd never seen such vitriol.

He got into multiple Twitter fights with what he called GMO "shills" or "propagandists," unleashing his propensity for unhinged name-calling. Opponents were *idiots, prostitutes, villains, animals*. It was the side of Taleb that bothered some of his friends the most. He saw Twitter as an intellectual gladiatorial battleground and engaged "enemies" like a wild-eyed prophet denouncing heresies and doling out ruthless sentences. Victims ranged from random nobodies to Nobel Prize winners. He'd taken to heart advice from a friend, Rory Sutherland—the outspoken vice chairman of ad agency Ogilvy UK who liked to quip that a flower is a weed with an advertising budget—who told Taleb that he advised CEOs to be rude and use foul language, since it made them seem more sincere and honest and signaled their freedom from constraining norms. The pugilistic diatribes and grade-school insults harmed Taleb's reputation with friend and foe alike. There's also little question he didn't care a whit.

It wasn't a new trait. People who'd known Taleb for decades said he'd always had a sharp side, a disposition he'd honed as a trader in New York and Chicago, where cursing like a drunken sailor was a prerequisite. Many forgave the insults as the price paid for Taleb's ability to cut to the chase, sometimes profanely. "Nassim Taleb is a vulgar bombastic windbag," economist and blogger Noah Smith once wrote. "And I like him a lot." And perhaps it took someone with a rough edge—a *very* rough edge, sometimes—to effectively denounce the vast majority of Wall Street as a band of grifting charlatans. "If he were more polite, he wouldn't have gotten the attention he did," his friend and frequent critic Aaron Brown told me. "If you say it politely, people brush it off. You have to say everyone is an idiot, is a charlatan, to get people to hear what you're saying—that there's a problem."

Still, despite the warnings of Taleb and others regarding GMOs and other forms of genetic manipulation, the genetically modified genie was out of the bottle. GMOs were everywhere. Some 90 percent of corn, soybeans, and sugar beets on the market in the U.S. were GMOs. With global warming altering climates around the world, well-meaning scientists were hard at work designing crops that could withstand higher temperatures, more arid environments, and other dystopian side effects of the changing climate. The Promethean, Stewart Brand–espoused "we are as gods" view of the world was ascendant.

> > < <

In 2015, Taleb, Read, Bar-Yam, and Norman wrote a short paper applying the precautionary principle to another global risk—that of runaway global warming. The climate-change policy debate too often revolved around the accuracy of models, they wrote. Believers in the models argue for specific actions to ward off the coming damage. Doubters point to their uncertainty and say there's not enough evidence to take dramatic action.

The authors posed an intriguing question. What if we had no reliable models at all? "Without any precise models, we can still reason that polluting or altering our environment significantly could put us in uncharted territory, with no statistical track-record and potentially large consequences."

"We have only one planet," they wrote. "This fact radically constrains the kinds of risks that are appropriate to take at a large scale. Even a risk with a very low probability becomes unacceptable when it affects all of us—there is no reversing mistakes of that magnitude. . . . Push a complex system too far and it will not come back."

The upshot: Reduce CO_2 emissions, "regardless of what climate models tell us."

> > < <

Taleb revisited the precautionary principle in 2018 with the publication of *Skin in the Game*, the fifth book in what he'd begun calling his Incerto collection, a study of how to live and act in a world ruled by extreme uncertainty—*Fooled by Randomness*, *The Black Swan*, *Antifragile*, and a book of aphorisms, *The Bed of Procrustes*. Like all of Taleb's books, *Skin in the Game* was wide-ranging, visiting subjects all the way from complexity theory to behavioral psychology to comparative differences between various political systems (democracy v. autocracy). Primarily, it's a book about virtue as defined by skin in the game—or the lack of it. Bankers who don't suffer when their firms blow up have no skin in the game (Taleb's "Bob Rubin trade"). In contrast, hedge fund managers who can lose a substantial portion of their own wealth in a blowup *do* have skin in the game and are therefore a lot more motivated to keep from blowing up (though many still do).

For investors, Taleb's most salient observations came in the final chapter, "The Logic of Risk Taking," where he compared two different ways of analyzing risk—"ensemble probability" and "time probability." Recall the two ways of thinking about gambling that helped define a ruin problem. In one, a hundred gamblers bet $1,000 on roulette. Some win, some lose it all. If gambler 59 goes bust, that has no impact on gambler 60, and the average profit of the group might be $10 per bet. That's "ensemble probability."

Next, a single gambler makes one hundred bets on the roulette wheel, putting all his money on red. Such a gambler will never make it to a hundred. That is the "time probability" way of looking at risk, which is path-dependent in time. It is, Taleb argued, the correct way to think about risk—especially when there's a chance of ruin. And while it might seem obvious that "time probability" is how the real world works, it's not how much of modern finance weighs market odds. Modern finance theory favors taking the average of all the bettors and using that as a proxy for the risk individual gamblers take. According to this view, the odds of surviving a round of Russian roulette are 83 percent—not so bad. And a risk practically no one would take, even if offered $1 million.

Taking an average of a collective series of bets hides the risk of disaster—of gamblers' ruin. As Taleb wrote in *Skin in the Game*, "never cross a river if it is *on average* four feet deep." By thinking of risk in this way, "more than two decades ago, practitioners such as Mark Spitznagel and myself built our entire business careers around it. . . . While I retired to do some flaneuring, Mark continued relentlessly (and successfully) at his Universa."

These scenarios of interconnected, self-reinforcing extreme risk are precisely where the precautionary principle applies. In the "time probability" realm, each roll of the dice or spin of the wheel is connected to the other. They can't be separated into independent units that are averaged out. In much the same way, systemic risk occurs when there are correlations and connections between people facing risks. One person dying in a bathtub won't increase the risk that his neighbor will die in a bathtub. One person dying of an infectious disease *does* increase the risk that his neighbor will get sick and die. When such risks become systemic, posing potential ruin to society as a whole, extreme precaution is required.

> > < <

Taleb wasn't the only expert in systemic risk applying lessons learned on Wall Street to the increased threats facing the world. In the 2010s,

Bob Litterman, who once managed one of the largest stock portfolios in the world for New York investment giant Goldman Sachs, turned his decades of risk management skills to one of the worst threats of all: global warming.

Unlike Taleb, who shunned models and argued that it was the uncertainty in forecasts for climate change that required extreme precaution, Litterman would go on to construct a model that prescribed the same precautionary approach practiced by chaos kings: When the risk is existential, you've got to panic early.

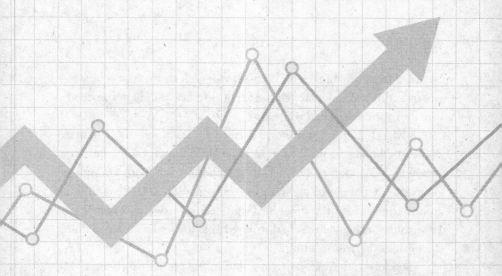

CHAPTER 19

IT'S WAY PAST TIME

Heavy rain splashed the windshield of Bob Litterman's Tesla as he maneuvered through light traffic on the New Jersey Turnpike. It was December 6, 2014, a Saturday. Litterman and his wife, Mary, were looking forward to a fun evening in New York City. Dinner and drinks with friends. A Broadway show. He set the Tesla's cruise control to seventy-two miles an hour. As the turnoff for the Garden State Parkway drew near, Mary screamed.

"Oh my God! Bob, watch out!"

He saw a large truck in the distance. Something about it was somehow . . . off. It was *bouncing*. It was *on fire*. It was coming directly toward them at high speed.

Focus. This could be tricky, Litterman told himself. He slammed the brakes, narrowly avoiding the tanker—and certain death. The 18-wheeler was a literal bomb full of nine thousand gallons of gasoline. It exploded right where Litterman's Tesla would have been had he failed to hit the brakes hard. His brush with death would be a lesson in real-world risk management that he'd later apply to the deadly threat of runaway global warming.

In March 2020, Litterman, a former top executive and risk manager at Goldman Sachs Group in New York, took a train from New Jersey to Washington, D.C., to testify before a Senate committee about the cost of global warming and how to address it. Like millions around the world at the time, he'd watched the rising cases of Covid-19 with mounting alarm. He'd stopped shaking hands, instead doing the perfunctory elbow bump.

The more Litterman thought about it, the more disturbed he was by the similarities between the pandemic and the climate crisis, a cause he'd taken up since retiring from a twenty-three-year career at Goldman. Covid-19 was spiraling out of control. The world had failed to stamp out the embers. Now it was on the cusp of becoming a raging megafire. The same was true for global warming, he felt. Uncertainty, as well as the fossil fuel industry's serial lies and denials, had paralyzed the world. Literal flames were frying its forests.

I met Litterman in Washington, D.C., hours after his Senate testimony. It would be my last face-to-face meeting for months—as well as his—as lockdowns gripped the country in the wake of the Covid-19 pandemic. Litterman told me he worried the Covid-19 virus would soon become a global pandemic, and he was right.

"It's a perfect example of when you have a risk-management problem—it's urgent, you don't know how much time you have," he said. "With coronavirus, we wasted so many weeks." The same was true for the climate. "We've got to slam on the brakes," he said, referring to carbon emissions—and his experience with the flaming tanker.

In other words, panic early.

Though with global warming, *early* is a fraught and relative term. Many climate experts would say *early* was the year 2000. Or 1990. "It's way past time," Litterman said.

The former risk manager was literally putting his money where his mouth was. A $2 billion New York hedge fund he'd joined after leaving Goldman a decade before, called Kepos Capital, was launching a strategy that bet on a rapid transition from fossil fuels to clean energy—a literal bet on the effects of climate chaos. Kepos Capital would short a bunch of energy stocks—oil drillers, coal miners— and bet on clean-energy stocks and other assets that would benefit from the transition (though since China, with its legions of coal-fired power plants and rampant industrial pollution, was a key component in the renewable technology supply chain, "clean energy" was a relative term). It was a gamble that the climate crisis would continue to intensify until the average investor turned his or her back on the polluting industries that had created it. While the rally in oil prices in 2022 after Russia invaded Ukraine marked a short-term reversal for the strategy, Litterman had little doubt that the long-term trajectory for the fossil fuel sector was implacably downward. And the sky was the limit for clean energy.

Earlier in the day when we met, the gray-haired sixty-eight-year-old Wall Street veteran had addressed the Senate Democrats' Special Committee on the Climate Crisis, which included Rhode Island Senator Sheldon Whitehouse. Elegantly dressed in a gray suit, blue shirt, and tie, Litterman projected an image that was the polar opposite of a wild-eyed hair-on-fire tree hugger screaming about evil oil companies. Still, his words conveyed a worried intensity.

"We are not pricing climate risk, not creating appropriate incentives to reduce emissions: a tragic and potentially catastrophic mistake," he told the senators. "Incentives are currently directing capital in directions that *increase* emissions, causing a growing accumulation of greenhouse gases in the atmosphere, which in turn is creating a rapid increase in the risk of permanent damage to the planet and the well-being of all future generations."

He then raised a point that seemed to spring straight from the precautionary principle. "The first principle of risk management is that you have to think about worst-case scenarios," he said.

With global warming, the *worst case* is unbounded, beyond models. It's a ruin problem. And when you don't know your risks, you can't price them appropriately. They're unknown unknowns. Cost-benefits are out the door. That's what happened in the financial crisis, Litterman told the senators. The systemic risk building up in mortgages wasn't priced accordingly, and it blew up. Today, society isn't pricing the risk of global warming appropriately. In fact, it's subsidizing the poisoning of the atmosphere by handing out billions of dollars of tax incentives to fossil fuel companies.

"Time is of the essence," Litterman said.

When you run out of time, you face disaster. The clock is ticking. "We do not know how much time we have before the planet's climatic system is pushed past a catastrophic tipping point, beyond which the consequences would become nonlinear and irreversible."

After Litterman spoke, Frédéric Samama, head of responsible investment for Amundi Group, Europe's largest asset manager with $1.8 trillion in assets, addressed the committee.

"Today, my testimony will focus on *The Green Swan*, a book I recently published with authors from the Banque de France, the Bank for International Settlements, and Columbia University," he began. "Central banks now recognize that climate change threatens financial stability. Either we do nothing, and then we put humanity at risk, or we adjust how we manage our systems."

The knee-knocking challenge: The magnitude of the task ahead is so massive that the financial stability of the global economy is at risk.

"This is why the book's authors developed the concept of Green Swans, inspired by the famous Black Swans of Nassim Nicholas Taleb," Samama said. "A Green Swan is a highly certain event with multiple nonlinear and interacting causes that threatens life on Earth. Climate change is an example of a Green Swan."

There was that inconvenient word again: *nonlinear*.

"Climate change carries a variety of nonlinear and interacting risks: physical, regulatory, and societal. It is very challenging to make such a complex model," the fund manager said. Climate change could lead to extreme short-term losses—and even the extinction of a large part of humanity. Extreme weather events, he said, have multiplied by four over the past forty years. And more heat waves, droughts, typhoons, pandemics, and rising sea levels are on the way, he warned.

Hearing the testimony that day, one might imagine the Senators were being subjected to tongue-lashings by Greta Thunberg—or Rupert Read—not a retired grandfatherly Goldman Sachs quant and an executive at Europe's largest money manager. The financial world, indeed, was waking up to the climate debacle. Big money—as well as the fate of humanity—was on the line.

Was it too late?

Litterman told me, *maybe so*. The Earth may already be past the crucial tipping points, the melting permafrosts and their methane bombs. The shrinking glaciers. The rising tides and superstorms. Global warming, he well knew, can lead to a sequence of events that spark self-reinforcing feedback loops that trigger unimaginable catastrophes. Ominously, he thought the people with the power to do something to turn the supertanker around were members of one of the most dysfunctional deliberative bodies of modern times. The very people he was addressing that day in March 2020: the United States Congress.

> > < <

Bob Litterman had always been something of a mental chameleon, moving from one field to another with relative ease in his academic career. He started off studying physics as an undergraduate at Stanford University. But it was the height of the Vietnam War, and he wasn't sure the abstract world of theoretical physics was the best place to be at the time. He switched to human biology, then a new program at Stanford. It was wildly interdisciplinary, incorporating biology, psychology, anthropology, and history. A lesson he picked up in the program that he never forgot was that understanding human behavior involved understanding *incentives*. It was a key lesson for the next field he'd study: economics.

He was also working for the *Stanford Daily*, the school newspaper, and became a stringer for *Time* magazine. He interned at the *San Jose Mercury*, and his first job after graduating in 1973 was as a reporter for the *San Diego Union*. But a fascination with the growing field of computer programming lured him back to academia, and he enrolled in the economics program at the University of California, San Diego, which gave him access to the school's computers. It was there that he met his future wife, Mary, who decided soon after to move back to her home in Minnesota. He followed, enrolling in the University of Minnesota's economics department. It was dominated by professors who worshipped at the altar of the Chicago School of Economics and all that entailed—the free and open markets of Milton Friedman and George Stigler, the efficient markets of Eugene Fama.

While working at the university's computer center, he answered students' questions about programming and supported the university's statistical software packages. His computer skills caught the attention of two young professors in the department: Tom Sargent and Chris Sims, both of whom went on to become Nobel Prize winners. Litterman spent time studying an obscure topic suggested by Sims called vector autoregressions, which use past economic variables to forecast current or future variables—such as looking at interest rate and employment levels to figure out future economic growth. These autoregression-derived forecasts formed the basis of Litterman's dissertation and would become the bedrock of his future career as what's known as an *econometrician*—a fancy word for someone who uses complicated math and computer programs to make predictions.

His first forecast attempt ended in failure. With too many free parameters to estimate, the results were all over the place and clearly didn't match what was going on in the real world. At Sims's suggestion, he tried a statistical method that combined information from two different sources—the variables under examination, such as interest rates, and a separate probability distribution based on prior historical events, such as annual economic growth rates. The historical data helped anchor the projections in the real world and kept them from spinning out of control. The results were then adjusted up or down, based on a formula, as new information came in.

Litterman found that this approach worked much better—in fact, the best forecasts were generated by giving more weight to the historical data, not the relationships embedded in the noisy variables.

His work landed him a job at the Minneapolis Federal Reserve, where he refined his forecasting skills. After a brief stint teaching at MIT (where he learned an important lesson about himself—he hated teaching), he focused on helping to launch a firm that sold statistical software for economic forecasting. The software was called RATS, short for Regression Analysis of Time Series. He then returned to the Minneapolis Fed, where his work on autoregressions became a key part of the bank's toolbox for taking the economy's temperature.

Another important lesson: Litterman saw that it was very difficult to project the economy's temperature based on its past temperatures. A big reason for the uncertainty, he found, was the randomness of Fed policy. A key role of the Fed is to apply shocks to the system from time to time, to jolt it out of a bad economic path. Inflation is too hot—crank up interest rates. The economy is too sluggish—ratchet rates down. The exact timing of such interventions is typically unforeseen by economic actors like banks and corporations, and the fallout from them can be chaotic. So while the models were able to make precise forecasts based on past events, the chaotic shocks often made those precise forecasts practically worthless.

In 1986, Litterman was contacted by Goldman Sachs. The firm had been dabbling in quantitative trading strategies. Its most prominent hire was the economist Fischer Black, co-creator of the Black-Scholes option pricing model and a staunch, practically religious believer in the efficient market hypothesis. In 1986, Litterman sat down for an interview with Black.

"So Bob, you're an econometrician," he said. "What makes you think an econometrician has any value to add on Wall Street?"

Litterman was baffled. Why wouldn't an econometrician have value on Wall Street? Coming from Black, in a job interview, it was nothing less than a challenge. "I suppose there might be parameters to estimate" was the best Litterman could come up with. Black didn't think it was possible to make money making forecasts about the economy. It was random—coin flip after coin flip. Econometricians sought to find correlations among economic factors (like interest rates and gasoline prices) that could predict future outcomes. Black, in a 1982 paper called "The Trouble with Econometric Models," had said that was a fool's errand—it confused correlation with causation. (Black, after seeing Goldman Sachs's money-making machine up close, soon realized that while markets might look efficient from a professor's podium, giant investment banks are able to squeeze oodles of dollars out of ubiquitous market inefficiencies.)

Despite Black's qualms, Goldman hired Litterman, who joined the bank's fixed-income department. Soon after, he was asked to help Japanese clients (at the time very wealthy clients indeed) put together global fixed-income portfolios. He went to Black for help.

"Well, you know, my attitude is to start out simple, and if it doesn't work, then you can always do something more complicated," Black said. He suggested using a standard risk-return model based on Harry Markowitz's Modern Portfolio Theory method that encouraged the multi-basket diversification approach (the very approach derided by Spitznagel and Taleb).

It didn't work, at least at first. Through a series of tweaks and new methods based in part on his work on vector autoregressions, Litterman ultimately designed a model that spit out optimal asset allocations depending on investors' risk appetites. It became known as the Black-Litterman model, which went on to become one of the most influential money management tools in the world.

In 1994, Litterman was elevated to head of risk management for the entire firm. But he was more interested in trading using the model he'd developed with Black. A year before taking on the firm's risk management assignment, he'd asked Goldman's managing partner—and future New Jersey governor—Jon Corzine for a spot in the portfolio-management department. "Nah Bob," Corzine said. "We have much more important things in line for you."

Around that time, Goldman hired a budding superstar and protégé of Eugene Fama at the University of Chicago, Cliff Asness. In 1995, Asness launched a trading outfit called Global Alpha, which quickly became a cash cow for the firm and its partners, with returns of 93 percent in 1996 and 35 percent in 1997. Litterman was amazed at Asness's success and pleased to learn that he was using both the Black-Litterman model and the computer program Litterman had helped launch after his brief MIT teaching stint—RATS. Asness left Goldman in 1997 to start AQR in Greenwich.

Soon after, Litterman got his wish taking a shot at trading. He began designing quantitative strategies for Goldman Sachs Asset Management, the bank's institutional money management operation. By the mid-2000s, his team, called the Quantitative Resources Group, or QRG, had become effectively the world's largest hedge fund, with some $150 billion in assets.

That $150 billion met a wrecking ball in 2008. The Global Financial Crisis devastated hedge funds (except for outliers such as Universa). Gary Cohn, Goldman's co–chief operating officer and a future Trump appointee, took control, trying to limit the firm's losses. Litterman by then was in the process of retiring. He provided advice but was no longer in day-to-day management.

During this period, Goldman's head of operations, Larry Linden, invited him to lunch.

"Are you worried about the environment?" he asked out of the blue.

"Larry, I'm still kind of busy," Litterman responded.

But the seed was planted. Linden later left Goldman and became chairman of the World Wildlife Fund. Litterman left Goldman in 2010, and quickly got back in touch with Linden, who brought him onto WWF's board. He also joined Kepos Capital, which a former colleague at Goldman had launched that same year.

Among Litterman's first self-appointed tasks: tackling the daunting economics of global warming. Along the way, he became something of an ever-present Zelig in climate-change circles. He accepted a position as co-chair of the Climate Leadership Council alongside Kathryn Murdoch (left-learning daughter-in-law of Rupert Murdoch). He joined the boards of Ceres (which pushes companies to disclose emissions and other environmental risks), Climate Central, Resources for the Future, the Woodwell Climate Research Center, the Stanford Woods Institute for the Environment, and the Stanford Natural Capital Project. He also chaired the board of a Washington D.C. center-right think tank, the Niskanen Center, which advocates for a tax on carbon emissions.

As Litterman was boning up on the nuts and bolts of climate-change economics, he realized the field had a big problem. No one had figured out how to price the risks posed by global warming. Those who'd tried had done an amazingly bad job of it, he believed.

I know how to price risk, Litterman thought.

The towering figure in the field of climate economics was a soft-spoken Yale professor named William Nordhaus, who for his life's work won the Nobel Prize in economics in 2018 alongside NYU economist Paul Romer. Litterman had briefly gotten to know Nordhaus back in his early days as a bright-eyed macroeconomist for the Minnesota Fed.

Nordhaus was drawn to the problem of global warming in the mid-1970s when he was on sabbatical in Vienna. He shared an office with a climatologist who told him about the emerging issue, which was then a matter of conjecture only among a small group of experts (and scientists at Exxon). For the next fifteen years, Nordhaus worked on a model to integrate climate science and economics.

The result was the Dynamic Integrated Climate-Economy (DICE) model. It examined a range of interrelated factors, such as population, economic growth (or decline), the price of oil, and the various impacts of global warming. It was a very complex challenge, in part because of how connected and dynamic the factors were. Feedback loops abound. A high rate of warming—and the economic damage it can cause—can perversely slow warming because emissions decline amid slower economic growth. Low emissions can limit the damage, boosting growth and causing emissions to ramp up.

The goal of it all: putting a price on carbon. A core problem a carbon price was meant to fix was that emissions are what economists call an externality—the cost isn't borne by those using the resource. By belching carbon into the atmosphere at virtually no cost, our modern fossil-fuel-powered civilization is effectively stripping economic opportunities from future generations, since someday the buildup will either have to be removed or it may wreak vast unbearable economic havoc. Putting a price on carbon today pulls that cost back into the present. That can limit how much carbon is consumed and give people an incentive to find alternatives. In this way, carbon is associated with a social cost. Calculations can be made regarding how much global warming will cost humanity—and how much it will cost to stop it or slow it down.

Nordhaus eventually came up with his price range for the social cost of carbon: about $30 to $40 a ton, a price that gradually rises over time, squeezing carbon out of the economic cycle.

Nordhaus's analysis bothered Litterman. The Yale professor was thinking about risk like an economist, an academic—not like a risk manager on Wall Street with real money on the line. He was using a complicated formula to put a price today on the value of the expected damage to the economy in the distant future under highly uncertain circumstances. *That's crazy*, Litterman thought. What you need to price risk is the full distribution of potential outcomes, including especially *catastrophic outcomes*. Insurers, who can diversify risk across many independent events, worry only about the expected loss. The risk is diversified away—transferred to other parties. But when there's no one able to provide insurance, for example against nuclear war, then you absolutely must worry about—and add a risk premium to—the worst-case scenarios, the ruin problems. Accounting for that risk premium is the essence of risk pricing on Wall Street, according to Litterman. (Taleb, of course, believed such risks—Black Swans—were impossible to price.)

In the case of climate risk, you need to slam on the brakes—now.

Litterman began working on his own method to set a carbon price. In 2019, alongside Columbia Business School professor Kent Daniel and climate economist Gernot Wagner, he introduced the so-called EZ-Climate model. In contrast to Nordhaus, it called for an extremely high price on carbon—more than $100 a ton.

"Bad news is costly," they wrote. "Bad news late, when it is more difficult to counteract with more active policy, is worse. It is precisely the inability to know upfront when good or bad news arrives that accounts for the insurance value of early mitigation."

> > < <

After flying to California following his Senate testimony in 2020 and as the pandemic dragged on month after month, making transcontinental flights a very bad idea indeed—Litterman and his wife decided they were staying in the Sunshine State for good. They sold their home in Short Hills. It was an exceedingly odd feeling. When they'd walked out of the place for their trip, they assumed they'd be home the following week. Now they'd never see it again.

Litterman had plenty to keep him busy. He'd been named chairman of a high-level Commodity Futures Trading Commission group to investigate and report on the risk of global warming to the financial sector. Companies involved in the project included Morgan Stanley, Bloomberg, Dairy Farmers of America, Citigroup, the British oil giant BP, the Environmental Defense Fund, Vanguard, ConocoPhillips, CalPERS, and J.P. Morgan.

The study, released in September 2020, presented alarming findings about the dangers lurking in the steadily rising global temperatures:

- *Climate change poses a major risk to the stability of the U.S. financial system and to its ability to sustain the American economy.*
- *A major concern for regulators is what we don't know.*
- *At the same time, the financial community should not simply be reactive—it should provide solutions.*

"As this report is being finalized, the United States is in the midst of a worldwide pandemic, with deaths already exceeding 180,000 from COVID-19, and an associated economic collapse," Litterman wrote in the foreword to the 196-page report. He noted the similarities between the pandemic and global warming, including the fact that delaying addressing both problems "can be devastating."

The report, released in the midst of the 2020 presidential election, ongoing fear about the pandemic, and nationwide protests over the murder of George Floyd, attracted almost no attention. Litterman wasn't surprised. But he hoped it would serve as a blueprint for future approaches to solving the problem.

He also believed the fossil fuel giants on the CFTC committee were sincere when they said they wanted to help. Many were publicly calling for a carbon tax, although none condoned a tax remotely close to the $100 a ton recommended by the EZ model. "I think they've changed," Litterman told me. "I actually do think they're sincere. They see it coming, they want to be involved."

Senator Whitehouse, who'd chaired the Senate hearing to which Litterman had offered testimony in March, had his doubts. Even though the fossil fuel companies *say* they support pricing emissions, their lobbying organizations oppose it behind the scenes, the senator told Litterman.

At least part of the truth was revealed in June 2021 when Greenpeace UK released a secret recording of an ExxonMobil lobbyist named Keith McCoy bragging about how the oil giant's support for a carbon tax was "a great talking point"—but it would never happen. "Nobody is going to propose a tax on all Americans," McCoy said. "And the cynical side of me says, yeah, we kind of know that."

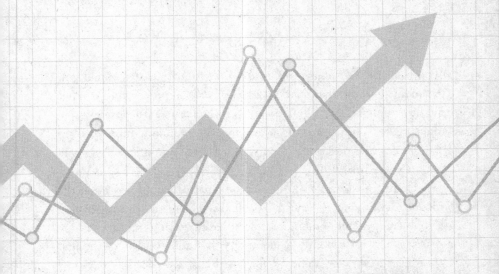

CHAPTER 20

THE GAMBLE

On January 27, 2021, the Bulletin of Atomic Scientists said its Doomsday Clock stood at one hundred seconds to midnight—unmoved since the previous year. Two big things had changed in those twelve months. Covid-19 was killing people around the world. And Donald Trump was no longer president of the United States. The second apparently offset the first to some extent—at least, the scientists nodded in that direction.

Covid-19 didn't pose an existential threat to humanity, the scientists said. It was highly deadly, but not lethal enough to kill billions. The problem it illuminated was that humanity—or at least *most* of it, since some countries, such as New Zealand, Australia, and South Korea, had fared relatively well—had seriously bungled its response, leading to the death of millions. The pandemic was a "historic wake-up call," Rachel Bronson, president of the Bulletin of Atomic Scientists, said in its annual Doomsday Clock statement.

The disastrous response to Covid-19 illustrated "that national governments and international organizations are unprepared to manage nuclear weapons and climate change, which currently pose existential threats to humanity, or other dangers—including more virulent pandemics and next-generation warfare—that could threaten civilization in the near future."

There was a measure, faint to be sure, of brightness amid the gloom. Renewable energy "has been resilient in the turbulent pandemic energy environment," Bronson wrote, noting that in the U.S. coal was now providing less electricity than renewables for the first time ever. "Globally, demand for fossil-based power has declined while demand for renewable power has risen."

Few were as unsurprised by the accelerating shift as Bob Litterman. Indeed, he'd bet millions on it.

In April 2021, Litterman once again faced ranks of lawmakers in the U.S. Senate. The venue this time was the Senate Budget Committee, chaired by Vermont senator Bernie Sanders. Litterman was testifying beside Nobel Prize–winning Columbia University economics professor Joseph Stiglitz and author David Wallace-Wells, whose 2019 book *The Uninhabitable Earth* spelled out in hair-raising fashion the extreme risks posed by a changing climate.

"In my view, we are living through a pivotal moment not only in the history of our country, not only in the history of the global community, but in the history of humanity," Senator Sanders said in his opening statement.

Senator Lindsey Graham, the ranking member of the committee, conceded that global warming was a thing to worry about. "I've come to conclude that climate change is real," he said. "And that human emissions create a greenhouse gas effect that traps heat. And that you see a rise in the oceans and acidity in the oceans. . . . So count me in on the idea that the science is real." Graham seemed enthralled by a world in which oil giants such as Iran and Russia had to go searching for another source of income. "Imagine a world where fossil fuels were not so readily available to rogue regimes," he said. "Imagine a world where the Iranian ayatollah couldn't rely on oil as almost 90 percent of his income. The Russians. I find it kind of interesting that the foreign policy consequences of moving to a clean energy business footprint would change the geopolitics of the world dramatically."

Wallace-Wells explained to the senators why the world needed to act immediately to start reducing carbon emissions—and the missed opportunity of failing to act earlier. "If the world had begun decarbonization in the year 2000, carbon emissions would only have had to fall by a couple of percentage points a year to safely avoid two degrees of warming," he said. "Now the number is almost 10 percent. Wait a decade and it will grow to 25 percent or more."

After Wallace-Wells, Litterman talked about the new tool he'd developed to examine, measure, and price climate risk.

"We used the same methods that asset managers use to set prices to estimate a price on carbon that would incorporate risk," he said. "This improves over previous models, like that created by the Nobel-winning economist William Nordhaus. Nordhaus's work showed us that acting to reduce emissions leads to substantial net benefits, but in his model that reduction could happen slowly and allow for large temperature increases. When we include risk in these models, including a small probability of a worst-case or 'catastrophic' scenario, the findings motivate an ambitious and rapid response."

Factor in risk and the value of avoiding catastrophes, the value of reducing emissions *increases,* he explained. It's cheaper to act now than to wait and see how bad things get, *then* act. The more you delay, the more expensive taking action gets. "This is the pricing version of braking hard," Litterman said. Delaying for a decade would cost the global economy $10 trillion a year—$100 trillion for a whole decade, according to his calculations. Further delays would cause costs to skyrocket.

Privately, Litterman thought the best approach would be an immediate carbon tax somewhere in the range of $80 to $100 per ton, as his EZ-Climate model calculated. But he was realistic. It would never pass Congress, especially the current hyper-partisan Congress.

Instead, he endorsed an initial tax of $40 per ton, starting in 2023, that would rise over time (and then fall as the benefits of reduced emissions kick in). The tax would provide a financial incentive for heavy consumers of fossil fuels—think electric utilities, big industrial operations like steelmakers and chemical plants, and automakers—to cut back on their exposure to oil and gas and switch to clean-energy sources such as wind and solar. Individuals might buy an electric vehicle rather than a car powered by a gas-guzzling internal combustion engine. It would also provide a flashing-red Buy signal to Wall Street for clean energy, channeling industrial-size rivers of cash to the sector, as well as a Sell signal for fossil fuel providers and consumers.

Income from the tax would be redistributed to the population, a move, Litterman said, that would benefit lower-income households since they're low carbon consumers, while taxing society's wealthiest carbon emitters.

Litterman's optimism about whether Congress would act was waning by late 2021. And his glum assessment of what had come out of the 26th Conference of the Parties, or COP26, to the United Nations Framework Convention on Climate Change—in which the world's leaders met in Glasgow, Scotland, to talk about global warming—also boded ill for the planet. Aside from some niche technical advances in tracking emissions, not much seemed to have been accomplished.

"Everyone I knew who was involved in the process had low expectations," he told me. The goal of the Paris Accords of 2015, keeping global temperature increases at or below 1.5 degrees Celsius, was in the rearview mirror, he believed.

One pocket of personal success that he could point to was Kepos Capital, which had bet strategically on a rapid transition to decarbonization. By mid-2022, his Kepos bet was up nearly 22 percent since its launch, despite a big rally in oil driven by the Russian invasion of Ukraine and a recent downturn in clean-tech stocks. A lot of the gains for Kepos were driven by Tesla, which Didier Sornette believed was in a massive Dragon King bubble, having surged above $1 trillion in market value. Ever a believer in efficient markets, Litterman was convinced Tesla's price was an accurate reflection of investors' expectations of its future profits.

If Congress would only impose a carbon tax, his strategy would do even better. But he was skeptical.

Increasingly, Litterman had started to wonder if humanity's only way out of a devastating climate crisis might be a drastic step known as solar geoengineering. Fly fleets of planes into the sky and dump billions of tons of sulphur dioxide into the atmosphere. As the particulates spread around and, through contact with moisture, turned into sulphuric acid, they would reflect sunlight back into space, in turn cooling the Earth. Scientists advocating for geoengineering point to the 1991 eruption of Mount Pinatubo in the Philippines, which ejected 20 million tons of sulphur dioxide and ash particles into the atmosphere. That alone cooled the entire planet by nearly one degree Fahrenheit the following two years.

There are other forms of geoengineering. In 1997, nuclear scientist Edward Teller, inventor of the hydrogen bomb, suggested putting giant mirrors in space. Other particulates such as calcium carbonate or even powdered diamond dust could be injected into the sky.

Most climate scientists shudder at the thought of purposefully replicating the violent eruption of a volcano over and over again *for decades*. Once humanity embarks on that type of geoengineering project, there's a risk the deployment can never stop—because the particles typically fall out of the atmosphere in a few years. If the project *were* halted, there'd be the possibility of sudden shock heating of the planet, causing untold chaos, damage, and death—an effect *New Yorker* journalist Elizabeth Kolbert described as like "opening a globe-sized oven door" in her 2021 book, *Under a White Sky*.

Another argument against geoengineering is that it creates a stark moral hazard. If it works, there's the chance that the costly worldwide effort to reduce carbon emissions will lose support. Is it any surprise that former ExxonMobil CEO (and Trump's first secretary of state) Rex Tillerson thinks geoengineering is a great idea?

There are also the unknown side effects, such as acid rain. What would the impact be on crops? Rainfall? Would some parts of the world suffer more? Almost certainly. Some models estimate geoengineering could eliminate or shorten the Asian monsoon season, on which two billion people depend for their food. The precautionary principle would seem to warn strongly against even considering geoengineering. It's global, systemic, and could have exponential societal and environmental ramifications and unknown ecological tipping points.

Still, a number of climate scientists have been reaching the harrowing conclusion, after years of warning about the danger of global warming, that we might have no other choice. Gernot Wagner, one of the coauthors of Litterman's EZ-Climate model, has been pushing for a reassessment of geoengineering. In his 2021 book *Geoengineering: The Gamble*, he wrote that when he first heard about it two decades ago, he thought it was nuts. "Two decades later—after having worked on this topic at Environmental Defense Fund, helping launch Harvard's Solar Geoengineering Research Program, and doing quite a bit of research and writing on the topic myself—I still think it is a rather healthy attitude to have toward the topic."

It's a gamble. The problem, he conceded, is that failing to take drastic action to address the world's rapidly changing climate is a different kind of gamble—arguably a larger one.

In the end, geoengineering is a terrible solution, and Wagner perhaps gives it too much credit by entertaining the pros and cons. Global warming is what's known as a *wicked problem*, a term coined in 1973 by design theorists Horst Rittel and Melvin Webber in a paper called "Dilemmas in a General Theory of Planning." Wicked problems are exceedingly complex and unique, with no precedents. Solutions are fiendishly hard to implement and, by and large, untestable. Because the solutions are irreversible, they can't be studied through trial and error. One component of the wicked problem posed by global warming is that a rapid reduction in the consumption of fossil fuels before alternative sources of renewable energy are available at a large scale poses the risk of immeasurable economic damage. People will die, growth sacrificed. Today, a billion people have no electricity, and the three billion who don't have access to clean cooking fuels choose to burn coal, charcoal, crop waste, or cow dung indoors. That indoor pollution causes extreme health outcomes—"the greatest environmental health risk in the world today," according to the World Health Organization, killing some four million people a year.

Additionally, as Lindsey Graham alluded to in his statement at the Senate Budget Committee hearing, many nations depend on fossil fuel production to generate revenue. Carbon Tracker, a London think tank, estimated that forty of these petrostates could face a nearly 50 percent drop in revenue because of climate policy and technological advances that strangle demand for fossil fuels—a shortfall of $9 trillion. Policymakers have virtually no solution to get hundreds of millions of people across this canyon-wide economic chasm—aside from vague recommendations that petrostates "diversify" their economies. Many of these countries, located in the arid Middle East and Africa, are among the most vulnerable to climate disasters such as heat waves.

But millions will die if humanity doesn't solve the climate problem—which is also a ruin problem.

And so, with geoengineering, the question boils down to one kind of existential risk versus another. "There are risks associated with geoengineering," Litterman told me. "But there are risks associated with warming the planet. We'll figure it out. It's stupid, because we didn't have to do it."

Perhaps it's too late, he said. Perhaps we have no choice but to roll the dice—the risk is exploding, fast.

Rupert Read, for his part, argues that geoengineering is a bad bet made in bad faith. In his view, it's a way to avoid facing up to the reality of pending climate catastrophes.

The only good thing about geoengineering, he believes, is that it highlights the terrible place humanity has found itself in. In gambling terminology, geoengineering might be a form of doubling down. Humanity destabilized the environment by pumping too much carbon dioxide into it, causing runaway global warming. So let's destabilize it again—and cross our fingers. As any gambler knows, doubling down is very risky. Do it too many times and the outcome is certain—ruin.

Avoid the dice—if that's even an option anymore.

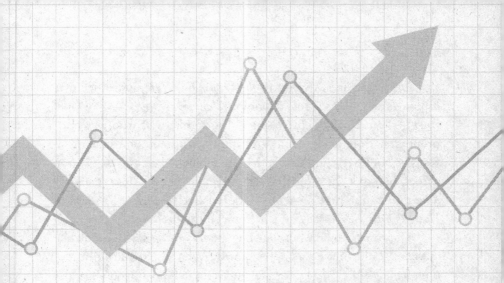

CHAPTER 21

THE TIPPING POINT AND BEYOND

In October 2021, Rupert Read stood to face a panel of magistrates in a London courtroom. He knew they'd find him guilty as charged. The previous year, he and two other activists had approached a building in Westminster that housed the Global Warming Policy Foundation, a policy group that UK newspaper the *Independent* said was Great Britain's "most prominent source of climate-change denial." Benny Peiser, Read's debate adversary at the 2013 Hay-on-Wye festival, ran the group.

The activists spray-painted "Lies Lies Lies" on the foundation's entrance. Then Read picked up a can of red paint and poured it down the steps.

Read and his activist cohort that day were part of a group called Writers Rebel, formed to support the goals of Extinction Rebellion. It included prominent authors such as Zadie Smith (author of *White Teeth*, *On Beauty*, and other novels), Irvine Welsh (*Train-*

spotting), Margaret Atwood (*The Handmaid's Tale* and other dystopian yarns), and George Monbiot (*Heat: How to Stop the Planet Burning*), an English environmentalist and activist who was once pronounced clinically dead after contracting cerebral malaria in Kenya. They'd gathered together and blocked access to Tufton Street, home of the Global Warming Policy Foundation. Academy Award–winning English actor Mark Rylance (*Bridge of Spies*, *Wolf Hall*, *The BFG*, *Don't Look Up*) emceed the protest.

"There are people whose business it is to make science look like opinion," Zadie Smith said to the crowd. "Who aim to transform genuine feelings of climate grief and guilt into defended ignorance and positive denial."

"Climate change due to human activity is not a theory, it is not an opinion, it is a fact," Atwood said in a video message. "Denial of this fact in the interests of big money will lead to our extinction as a species."

Then Read, the Australian author Jessica Townsend, and XR activist Clare Farrell approached 55 Tufton Street, the foundation's address, and committed their act of protest and alleged vandalism. They were promptly arrested and charged with criminal damage to the building. Among their fellow activists, they became known as the Tufton Three.

Facing his judges in court a year later, Read said the prosecution's argument—that their action wasn't done in the face of an imminent threat—was ridiculous. "Our defense of necessity is that the Global Warming Policy Foundation represents an ongoing and ongoingly imminent threat to life," he said. "Every day that climate action is delayed by climate delay and climate denial multiplies the threat that climate breakdown hangs over us all, over our very lives, over the future itself."

He said he knew he'd be found guilty. He *was* guilty in the technical sense that he'd visibly poured that paint down the steps.

"But I'm asking you now: What else would you have me do? Where else should I make my stand, if not as I did? And: If not now, then when? Would you have us wait till the Thames barrier is over-topped? Till the Palace of Westminster is flooded out?"

Read and his cohort were found guilty—and fined court costs of only 100 pounds and a compensation cost of another 100 pounds.

> > < <

They called it Lucifer. In August 2021, a deadly heat wave swept through southern Italy, torching Sicily and setting an all-time heat record for the European continent of 120 degrees Fahrenheit. Deadly forest fires gripped the Mediterranean. In Algeria, fires killed sixty-five people, including more than two dozen soldiers deployed to battle the blaze. As nearly six hundred wildfires scorched forests across Greece, Prime Minister Kyriakos Mitsotakis said his country was facing a "natural disaster of unprecedented proportions." Fires ravaged more than one-third of the Greek island of Evia. "These last days have been some of the most difficult for our country in decades," Mitsotakis said. "The climate crisis is affecting the whole planet."

Mitsotakis's alarm wasn't news to Rupert Read and Jem Bendell, a grim, no-nonsense professor of sustainability at the University of Cumbria. A few months before Lucifer struck Greece, the pair had published *Deep Adaptation: Navigating the Realities of Climate Chaos*. Adaptation in the context of global warming typically referred to efforts to avoid or prepare for the coming disasters spawned by extremes of the climate crisis—erecting flood walls, making build-ings resilient to high winds and storms, and raising structures above forecasted water levels. Adaptation was, in that sense, a tool often paired with another tool, mitigation—the long-fought battle to reduce the heat-trapping emissions that cause global warming. While every effort to cut emissions needed to be made, humanity, in Read and Bendell's view, needed to prepare for, and adapt to, the inevitable changes in the climate that were already baked into a heating atmo-sphere.

Deep Adaptation recommended transformative social changes such as moving large populations away from coastlines, "rewilding" urban landscapes, and shifting to local, community-based farming. The title was based on a controversial 2018 paper by Bendell that argued that accelerating global warming had made civilizational collapse a fast-coming certainty. Bendell gave humanity a decade. (He later backed away from claiming collapse was a literal certainty and conceded it was his strong opinion.) "It is time we consider the implications of its being too late to avert a global environmental catastrophe in the lifetimes of people alive today," he wrote. "We may be about to play Russian roulette with the entire human race, with two bullets loaded."

The paper went viral. *Vice* magazine called it "The Climate Change Paper So Depressing It's Sending People to Therapy." Penn State climate scientist Michael Mann said it was a "perfect storm of misguidedness and wrongheadedness." Other criticisms echoed attacks lobbed at Read for telling young people they might not survive the climate crisis—the worry was that Bendell's pessimism threatened to create a paralyzing sense of hopelessness that would keep people from taking actions to make things better.

Read agreed with this criticism to an extent. "I see Jem's stance on this front as making things too easy for people, when you say collapse is inevitable," he told me. "Some people breathe a sigh of relief. There's something a bit too psychologically simple about it. It evades the full complexity of the situation." Even so, he agreed to produce the book with Bendell—to make clear that, while they had disagreements, some level of mass societal harm was nearly certain, in their view. Deep adaptation, Read felt, was the ultimate insurance policy against the worst effects of the climate crisis on humanity.

It was a balancing act between hope and terror. Certainly, Bendell couldn't predict near-term civilizational collapse brought on by global warming with anything close to the requirements of mathematical rigor. Perhaps his intent was more rhetorical, an attempt to awaken people to the disaster barreling their way—to say, like the scientists telling the world about a planet-killing comet in *Don't Look Up*, "Look up!"

But there was another side to the story.

> > < <

Lamont Leatherman leaned over an egg-shaped boulder deep in the woods of North Carolina's Piedmont region, a rolling, hilly plateau on the flat coastal plain that expands westward from the Atlantic to the ancient Appalachian Mountains, and traced his hand along a silver streak running through the caramel-brown rock.

"You can see it there," the fifty-five-year-old geologist told me. "There's the lithium."

It was January 2021. Leatherman and the startup mining outfit he worked for, Piedmont Lithium, were at the vanguard of an effort to build an American supply of the ingredients that make up rechargeable lithium-ion batteries, the most popular power source for electric vehicles, smartphones, and tablets. Months before, Piedmont had inked a deal to supply lithium to Tesla once its mine was up and running.

Leatherman, who'd spent most of his career chasing gold and other hot commodities in Canada and who currently lived on a blueberry farm on Vancouver Island in British Columbia, hailed from Carolina's Piedmont. The region was home to the world's first lithium mine, which in the 1950s produced parts for America's early arsenal of nuclear weapons. Lanky, with the grizzled visage of a man who'd spent much of his life outdoors, Leatherman was well aware that the land was rich with lithium—the brown, silver-streaked rocks speckled the yard of the home in which he'd grown up—and by the early 2020s it was one of the hottest commodities in the world.

"We're going to build a big business here," Keith Phillips, Piedmont's CEO, told me. Piedmont had a market valuation of more than $1 billion by the summer of 2022. The hope was that once the mine was fully up and running, American rechargeable battery manufacturers would have a close-to-home sourcing option and would be less reliant on the big lithium players in China and elsewhere.

It was the beginning of a green gold rush in the U.S. and elsewhere, a story I covered for the *Wall Street Journal*. I spoke with dozens of people involved in the monumental shift, ranging from executives at some of the world's biggest companies to hedge fund managers to mining CEOs to boots-on-the-ground geologists such as Lamont Leatherman.

Months after stomping through the Carolina woods with Leatherman, I was a passenger on a boat owned by giant Mid-Atlantic utility Dominion Energy. Departing from a port in Virginia Beach, our destination was two massive offshore wind turbines deep in the waters of the Atlantic, one of only two offshore wind facilities in the U.S.

Dominion planned to build 180 more turbines on the site, making it the largest offshore wind farm in the U.S. "We've reached the tipping point and beyond" in the transition to clean-energy power, James Chapman, then-chief financial officer of Dominion, told me. The company was planning to spend $26 billion or more on clean energy by 2026, including billions on offshore wind.

Piedmont and Dominion and hundreds of other companies making efforts to accelerate the transition away from fossil fuels to clean energy—almost entirely from self-interested motives—posed a challenge to the doomsday scenarios spread by skeptics such as Bendell. Pessimists about humanity's ability to curb greenhouse emissions often ignored, or even criticized, a growing force in the world that represented perhaps the best possible hope that the planet might stave off the worst effects of the climate crisis: clean-energy technologies that were soaking up rivers—oceans—of Wall Street cash.

A tough-minded logic based on years of disappointment justified the skepticism, to be sure. Fossil fuels had greased the gears of the global economy for centuries, going back to the coal mines that powered the earliest days of the Industrial Revolution in Great Britain in the eighteenth century. The global economy remained fiendishly addicted to burning the stuff to generate power. Industrial farming was another prolific source of carbon emissions. But perhaps, some wild-eyed optimists thought, if capitalism got us into this mess, it could help get us out (with the assistance of strenuous government policy and spending). If the world truly was going to shift away from oil and gas—arguably the biggest business in the world—into alternative sources of energy as a way to help solve the climate chaos, that transition promised to be one of the most spectacular money-making opportunities in generations. Achieving a net-zero global economy—"net-zero" meaning any and all carbon emissions are balanced out by some form of carbon removal, such as a tree farm—by 2050 could prove to be the "largest reallocation of capital in history," according to McKinsey & Company, with an increase in spending of $1 to $3.5 trillion more *per year* than today.

There were encouraging signs the optimists might be onto something. By 2020, both solar energy and wind power were cheaper sources of electricity than all other alternatives, the result of decades of innovations (many of which came from Communist China). Electric vehicles, long the playthings of the wealthy, were getting more and more affordable. The cost of the rechargeable batteries that power EVs, which account for roughly 40 percent of the cars' cost, had tumbled 90 percent since 2010. Solar panels had seen a similar rate of cost decline.

A 2022 study by a group of Oxford scientists projected that dramatic decreases in costs would likely continue *for decades* based on an obscure metric called Wright's law. Named after Theodore Wright, a World War I flying ace and an airplane manufacturer in the 1930s, the basic idea is that the cost of certain technologies (say, airplanes) drops 10 to 15 percent every time their production doubles. If the Oxford projection was true, that meant global energy production by 2050 would be far cheaper—and far less damaging to the planet—than it currently is. It would, in fact, result in net savings of trillions, the scientists claimed.

"These are profound economic shifts," Reed Hundt, chairman of the Federal Communications Commission during the Clinton administration and a founder of the Coalition for Green Capital, told me. "The direction set by the market is to go to the cheapest possible fuels—which are wind and sun."

Spurring the transition were the Biden administration's plans to funnel hundreds of billions of federal spending and incentives into clean energy and other technologies designed to reduce America's carbon footprint. And, of course, Wall Street was keen to ride Biden's coattails. Cash allocated to assets focused on the environment and socially responsible goals were expected to hit $34 trillion by 2026, up from $18 trillion in 2021, according to PricewaterhouseCoopers. Electric utilities such as Dominion were shifting tens of billions into clean-energy sources like wind and solar, and shuttering coal-fired power plants. And automakers were spending billions on new factories to build EVs and batteries.

The green-technology revolution began attracting interest from the biggest investors on the planet. The two biggest U.S. banks—J.P. Morgan Chase and Bank of America—in 2021 pledged $4 trillion in climate-directed financing over the next decade. Around the same time, Bridgewater Associates, the world's largest hedge fund, launched a venture focused on sustainable investing strategies. "Every day we hear from a different client who we didn't think would be into" green investments, Karen Karniol-Tambour, co–chief investment officer of the venture, told me. "Now they are saying, 'It's part of my mandate.'"

A harbinger of the shift came in early 2020 when Larry Fink, CEO of BlackRock, the world's largest investment manager, wrote that climate change "has become a defining factor in companies' long-term prospects. . . . I believe we are on the edge of a fundamental reshaping of finance." How will the climate crisis impact the market for municipal bonds as cities raise cash for infrastructure projects? How does global warming impact mortgages? How could rising food prices in a changing climate impact inflation? What about emerging markets, among the most vulnerable to the worst effects of the climate crisis?

Fink posed these questions and more. As a result: "In the near future—and sooner than most anticipate—there will be a significant reallocation of capital." (Skeptics doubted, though, whether Fink would follow through if it turned out a greener portfolio also meant lower returns.)

And what of the carbon-removal industry? It remains tiny, but is growing quickly, a trend that will only accelerate, especially with the August 2022 passage of President Biden's Inflation Reduction Act (which had little to do with reducing inflation). The act provided huge incentives to the carbon-capture industry, including a $180-a-ton tax credit for removing CO_2 from the air.

Big money—the biggest money—sensed opportunity. "All the cool kids are doing carbon capture," the *Wall Street Journal* observed in February 2021, with ExxonMobil being the latest to embrace the trend with the formation of a new business unit to commercialize its carbon-capture technology. In the past few years, Chevron, Occidental Petroleum, and BHP, the world's biggest mining outfit, had become investors in a company called Carbon Engineering, founded by an applied physicist at Harvard, David Keith, who'd long had the backing of Bill Gates. In 2022, Occidental said it planned to fund the development of seventy Carbon Engineering facilities by 2035. The giant European plane maker Airbus, Shopify, and ThermoFisher were signing deals with Carbon Engineering to pay for carbon capture.

Despite the hubbub, the carbon-capture math remained head-poundingly daunting. Some 35 *billion* tons of carbon dioxide are pumped into the atmosphere *every year* from fossil fuels and industry. Each of those seventy Carbon Engineering plants is expected to pull a mere 1 *million* tons a year. And yet for the world to meet the Paris Accords' emission-reduction targets, some form of carbon removal is necessary, according to nearly every scenario sketched out by the Intergovernmental Panel on Climate Change, or IPCC, the United Nations body responsible for studying the science of global warming and its future risks.

Some experts estimate that at least $50 *trillion*—maybe double that, according to other experts—in clean-energy investments (wind, solar, batteries, carbon removal, etc.) would be required by 2050 to meet the goals of the Paris Accords. There is, clearly, still a long, *long* way to go. According to a 2021 report by Princeton researchers, the most cost-effective net-zero footprint for wind farms in the U.S.

would encompass an area equal to Illinois, Indiana, Ohio, Kentucky, and Tennessee *put together*; solar farms would take up Connecticut, Rhode Island, and Massachusetts.

The scale of the initiative beggars the imagination, and it needs to be accomplished at lightning speed. Still, as Wall Street's fat cats began to see gold in green energy, the sector was experiencing an unprecedented, lasting transformation. Clean energy would be one of the best bets of 2021 and 2022—and perhaps the decade, heralding a landmark revolution in power generation and consumption that promised to reshape the global economy. A McKinsey technology report in 2022 found that clean-energy technology had raked in $257 billion in investments the previous year, more than any other technology, including AI, 5G and 6G, and the metaverse. All thanks to scientists and geologists like Lamont Leatherman—and the bonanza-chasing Wall Street financiers backing them.

Rupert Read, unsurprisingly, was skeptical—with good reason. In his speech warning of the civilizational collapse, he said pinning our hopes on a total reordering of the world's energy system was foolhardy. "The kind of transformation we're talking about is a lot bigger, for example, than a large scale conversion to renewable energy," he said. "We're also talking about radically reducing the amount of transportation of goods and people around the world, radically relocalizing, radically changing our farming practices and the entire nature of our agriculture, radically reducing the amount of meat that we use in countries like this. It would be a total transformation the likes of which we have never known."

Read sincerely hoped it all would happen. But the scale of the transition was the most sweeping social and economic change in history, surpassing the agrarian and industrial revolutions that began in the seventeenth and eighteenth centuries—and which took centuries. The clean-energy revolution needed to happen in *decades*. "It will be a very risky bet to bet everything upon that kind of completely unprecedented transformation," Read said. He also didn't believe for a microsecond that oil giants such as Exxon and Occidental were acting in good faith by throwing wads of cash at carbon capture. It was, he believed, a deeply cynical attempt to fan hopes in the experimental technology, providing near-term social and political cover as they kept pumping vast quantities of fossil fuels from the earth.

The money and the technology couldn't come fast enough. Time was running out as the climate crisis grew more destructive and deadly year after year. An August 2022 study published in the science journal *Nature* showed that the Arctic was warming four times faster than the rest of the world—a gut-rumbling phenomenon called Arctic amplification—accelerating the risk of melting glaciers and rising seawaters. A UCLA study released around the same time found that Southern California faced the mounting risk of a megaflood, worsened by global warming, that could cause $1 trillion in damages and displace up to 10 million people. As the megadrought in America's Southwest intensified, drying up rivers and scorching crops, government officials were forced to cut back on distribution of water from the Colorado River to keep levels in Lake Mead above the point where the Hoover Dam would no longer be capable of producing electricity—an ominous level known as a *dead pool.*

Like many other weather patterns in our warming world, what was taking place in the Colorado River Basin was unprecedented. "This entire river system is experiencing something that's never happened before," Wade Crowfoot, California's natural resources secretary, told the Associated Press.

Making things worse: a pillar of the world order—American democracy—was lurching toward chaos.

CHAPTER 22

FLYING BLIND

"West front of the Capitol! We've been flanked and we've lost the line!" Robert Glover, a Metropolitan Police officer who specialized in crowd control, cried out in panic on a radio transmission as insurrectionists stormed the west wing of the U.S. Capitol. It was 2:13 p.m. on January 6, 2021. A mob of Donald Trump supporters had breached the building, smashing windows and pouring into the seat of American democracy to reverse the election of Joe Biden. Rioters marched through the halls of the Capitol chanting "Hang Mike Pence," looking to vent their wrath against the vice president. Soon after, at 2:24, Donald Trump posted a tweet that said Pence "didn't have the courage to do what should have been done to protect our country and our Constitution."

In the days and weeks that followed, right-wing media shifted the narrative of a violent mob attacking Congress on live TV to one of peaceful protestors rallying to protect democracy. The truth was that

American democracy was at its highest peril since the Civil War. In the aftermath of the attack, political risk analyst and author Ian Bremmer said the greatest threat facing the world was political polarization in the U.S. "The United States is the most powerful, politically divided, and economically unequal of the world's industrial democracies," he wrote.

"The democratic emergency is already here," Richard Hasen, a political science professor at University of California–Irvine, told *Atlantic* journalist Barton Gellman. "We face a serious risk that American democracy as we know it will come to an end in 2024."

Democracy wasn't just at risk in the United States. Freedom House's global index of worldwide democracy fell for the sixteenth straight year in 2021. "The global order is nearing a tipping point, and if democracy's defenders do not work together to help guarantee freedom for all people, the authoritarian model will prevail," the watchdog group wrote in its Freedom in the World 2022 report, "The Global Expansion of Authoritarian Rule."

The level of democracy in the world had reached the lowest level since 1989, the year the USSR collapsed, with a corresponding rise in dictatorships, according to an August 2022 study by Varieties of Democracy, which tracked democratization trends. "Democracy survives in the United States, but it remains under threat," the organization warned.

To their peril, investors were entirely complacent (the Dow rose 438 points on January 6). A January 2022 study by the Brookings Institution found that the threat to democracy in America posed a systemic risk to capital markets. Authoritarianism, it turned out, generally wasn't good for business. "Because the free market and democracy are interdependent, a systemic risk to one is, by definition, a systemic risk to the other," Brookings said.

If not a Black Swan, the risk to American democracy was at the very least a potential Gray Swan—or Sornetteian Dragon King— darkly hovering in the skies.

> > < <

A month after a mob stormed the Capitol, on a Tuesday, an official at the Electric Reliability Council of Texas, the state's electric grid regulator, noted at a board meeting that "pretty frigid temperatures" would hit the state in the coming week. The conversation about the storm lasted less than a minute. The following Monday, San Antonio woke up to a half foot of snow. Temperatures plunged to nine degrees Fahrenheit.

Rolling power outages swept across the state. A monster polar blast had lurched out of Canada into the U.S., hitting Ohio, Oklahoma, Mississippi, Louisiana, Texas, and more than a dozen other states. But it was in the Lone Star State that the Black Swan landed with a vengeance. The state's electric grid, unprepared for prolonged freezing temperatures, collapsed, leaving nearly 10 million Texans without electricity, some for weeks. Hundreds froze to death in their homes. On the evening of February 14, the grid came within five minutes of a statewide shutdown that might have lasted weeks, or even months.

The storm was a vivid reminder of how a world of shifting, chaotic weather patterns threatens critical infrastructure designed for one kind of climate now facing an extreme kind. A similar event occurred in August 2022, when the water-treatment system serving Jackson, Mississippi, was overwhelmed by floods, leaving 150,000 residents without access to clean water for weeks. It wasn't a short-term trend that would reverse course—it was the new normal. Climate Central, a nonprofit research group, found that in the decade ending in 2019, hurricanes, wildfires, heat storms, and other extreme weather events caused two-thirds more power outages in the U.S. than in the previous decade.

Fire followed Texas's deep freeze. In June 2021, a trend-shattering heat dome settled over the Pacific Northwest, pushing temperatures in Portland, Oregon, to a record-high 115 degrees. The extreme heat turned grasslands and forests into ripe kindling. A blaze southeast of Mount Rainier triggered by lightning strikes in August was dubbed a megafire by September after burning more than one hundred thousand acres. Smoke from fires all over the region and in Canada swirled across the continent, clouding skies over New York City and triggering health alerts in Toronto and Philadelphia.

As the heat intensified, a Seattle weather forecaster noted: "As there is no previous occurrence of the event we're experiencing in the local climatological record, it's somewhat disconcerting to have no analogy to work with."

On the morning of August 27, a U.S. Naval Academy helicopter dipped an instrument into the Gulf of Mexico to measure the water's temperature as Hurricane Ida barreled toward Louisiana. The instrument detected highly elevated temperatures close to the surface—a bad sign. Later that day, Pat Harr, a science fellow at extreme-weather tracker Jupiter Intelligence, sent an email to clients. "The developing Hurricane Ida is poised to move over some extremely high ocean heat content regions in the Gulf of Mexico and likely undergo periods of rapid intensification to CAT 3–5 levels," Harr wrote. "The current track places Ida on the coast of LA as a major hurricane Sunday night just west of the Mississippi Delta region."

It was a surprising, and surprisingly accurate, forecast. At the time, Ida was just a relatively weak Category 1 hurricane. Two days later, the sixteenth anniversary of Hurricane Katrina, the storm had reached Category 4 with sustained winds of 150 miles per hour as it crashed into Port Fourchon, matching records for the most powerful storm to ever hit the state. Remnants of Ida dumped torrential downpours over New Jersey and New York, shutting down New York City's subway system and killing more than a dozen people trapped in their basements.

Ida's rapid intensification, fueled by the unusually hot Gulf waters, scrambled preparation plans. Climate experts began to worry they'd have to scrap old models used to project hurricane paths and strength. "The entire accelerated time sequence of rapid cyclonical development effectively neutralizes a good bit of the emergency management pre-event response, and that greatly increases human and asset exposure," Jesse Keenan, a leading expert on property exposure to extreme weather events, told me. "Any technological advantage that we have gained in climate-services intelligence is being neutralized by the increased speed of the rate of change. At some point, we run the risk of totally flying blind."

> > < <

Cyberattacks. Climate catastrophes. Terrorism. Pandemics. Deadly power outages. Rogue AI. A future of extremes. This is Marcus Schmalbach's world, his bread and butter—and his business. The young German insurance executive was the CEO and founder of Ryskex, a new kind of insurance company that focused solely on systemic disasters. The hurricane that takes out a company's supply chain. The deadly crash that grounds an airline's fleet. The cyberattack that destroys a company's reputation. The virus that decimates a workforce.

Using artificial intelligence and blockchain, Schmalbach had created an entirely new, tradeable asset class: systemic risk. With Ryskex, hedge funds and banks could buy and sell systemic risk like a bushel of corn. Fortune 500 companies could use it to protect themselves against calamitous shocks.

In the late 2010s, it remained a fledgling effort. At the start, much like Mark Spitznagel in the early days of Universa, Schmalbach had few takers for his highly unique and strange offering. Then Covid-19 happened. Systemic risk was suddenly tangible, something you read about every day in the morning paper (or during your morning coffee doom-scrolling on Twitter). By late 2021, Schmalbach's operation, which had offices in Berlin and New York, had arranged for half a dozen deals. Among his clients were a pair of automakers who took out protection against climate-change events and a large European airline that purchased insurance against a major business disruption—like a pandemic.

It wasn't normal insurance. The contracts were arranged via blockchain, the Internet ledger that could efficiently track financial transactions. Unlike traditional insurance, which could take months or years to pay out, this was so-called parametric insurance. With parametric insurance, a payout happens automatically when a certain trigger point is reached. Say Company X buys Ryskex insurance against a devastating flood that causes its shares to go down 20 percent. The flood happens, the shares fall, and bingo, the payment is made via the blockchain. The risk-takers—those providing the insurance—were typically hedge funds eager to get the steady premiums, much like the firms that sold far-out-of-the-money put options that paid off in a crash to Universa.

It was hard to know if the concept would take off. Schmalbach believed systemic risk represented a $1 trillion asset class—maybe more. What was interesting about Ryskex was that it was trying to do something most in the insurance industry believed to be impossible: put a price on systemic risk—a dollar figure on Black Swans.

> > < <

Schmalbach had been drawn to the insurance world at an early age due to one of the industry's idiosyncratic features. Each year there are two big conferences put on by the reinsurance industry in Europe (reinsurance being policies that insurers buy to protect themselves if called upon to make unexpectedly huge payouts). One was in Monte Carlo. The other was in Baden-Baden, a quaint spa town in southwestern Germany's Northern Black Forest where Schmalbach grew up. Every year, a flood of well-dressed businessmen with fancy watches, fast cars, and fat wallets would suddenly materialize. Schmalbach wanted in.

After studying insurance in college, he joined the German financial giant Allianz as a trainee, then later landed at Munich Re, another German giant. While there, he began working on his Ph.D. and teaching classes on insurance and finance.

After class one day in 2015, a student walked up to Schmalbach. "I think there's something going on with blockchain," he said. "It's getting important. I think it could destroy your whole industry."

Schmalbach had long been interested in finding alternatives to the old-school form of insurance, which he believed had become inefficient, hampered by a long, legalistic, and highly complex money supply chain. Prodded by his student, he immersed himself in blockchain and quickly realized it could provide an alternative method of delivering insurance. Blockchain offers something called "smart contracts," which is software that can automatically execute a transaction when certain conditions are met. That made it an ideal tool for parametric insurance, Schmalbach's specialty. If an airline wants to insure against the risk of a Category 5 hurricane hitting its operation, the contract is immediately triggered and the payment made if, in fact, a Cat 5 storm happens and harms the carrier's business by some tangible metric, such as an airport closure for more than one week.

Schmalbach thought back to a book he'd read in 2008 when he was working on his Ph.D.: *The Black Swan*. What are the odds that a devastating event—a Black Swan—could bankrupt a massive company like Tesla or Apple? What are the existential risks for Fortune 500 companies? What kind of events can have a deep, irreversible impact on a company's balance sheet?

It might be impossible to imagine Tesla or Apple suddenly going bankrupt. In 2008, it was also impossible to imagine Bear Stearns or Lehman Brothers or AIG going bust. "There are systemic risks," Schmalbach told me. "Cyber, pandemics, climate change. So we defined that and developed risk as an asset class."

Looking across the insurance industry for a comparable approach to onetime devastating risks, he knew of only one company that provided such policies: Lloyd's of London, the storied centuries-old British insurer. In Elizabethan times, Lloyd's Coffee House, owned by Edward Lloyd and situated near the Thames, was a favorite meetinghouse for sailors and shipowners. The latter, which included numerous owners of slave ships, became interested in an increasingly popular product for shippers: marine insurance. It grew from there.

Schmalbach asked acquaintances at Lloyd's how they assessed and priced systemic risk. He quickly came to the conclusion that they didn't have a rigorous model. It was seat-of-the-pants dartboard tossing, he thought, more akin to gambling than risk management.

He decided Ryskex would have to do the job itself. He hired an analytics firm with expertise in artificial intelligence, which began feeding reams of data into their models to compile a global risk index that Ryskex could stylize for individual companies. The model scraped data from the Internet looking for patterns and correlations with extreme events, and scanned newspapers such as the *New York Times* and *Wall Street Journal*. The model wasn't focused on *predicting* extreme events, like Sornette's LPPLS model, rather it was designed to assess probabilities based on myriad factors to help clients better understand their risk exposure in the event of a disaster. If violence rose sharply in the U.S., historically that had a negative impact on Europeans traveling to America, which can hit an airline's profitability. Fewer cars are sold after a terrorist attack. This is what happens to your supply chain if there's another wave of Covid-19, etc.

Using his AI machine, Schmalbach created the VUCA World Risk Index. VUCA is short for volatility, uncertainty, complexity, and ambiguity. Introduced in the late 1980s by the U.S. Army War College amid the fog-inducing end of the Cold War, VUCA has been adopted by multiple industries (and hordes of business-management consultants) as a model to help executives deal with crises and disasters. Schmalbach's algorithm took the metric and automated it to measure risks such as pandemics, cybercrime, global warming, and terrorism. The index, in theory, could show companies their vulnerability and how to use the model to limit their own risks.

So far, it was just an idea on a blackboard. Schmalbach had a unique idea—and no customers. He had to go out into the market and drum up interest. Most companies he spoke to weren't interested. He realized that he was selling it wrong—as insurance. Instead, he told them that it was *risk financing*. You're exposed to this specific risk, he explained. If you pay X amount, you're taking that risk off the books—just as Universa investors paid to remove the risk of a crash from the equation (or at least reduce it). The pitch seemed to work with a few companies.

Then he started talking to a corner of Wall Street he thought might be interested in financing that risk—investment banks. He spoke with executives at J.P. Morgan, Goldman Sachs, Morgan Stanley, and more. Their uniform response: Why would we do that? It seemed far too risky.

Schmalbach began discussing his scheme with John Thomson, a longtime insurance industry veteran and assistant dean of the University of Hartford's Barney School of Business. Thomson thought it was brilliant, but he also recognized the challenges Schmalbach faced. His biggest mistake, Thomson told him, had been setting up the company in Vermont, which had a business-friendly climate for certain kinds of insurance outfits—but no money.

"I'd look at this differently if I were you," Thomson told Schmalbach. "You need to be close to a world financial capital. Burlington, Vermont, is not that. I think you need to get as close to the Tristate of New York, New Jersey, and Connecticut as possible. The financial capital of the world. That's a better place."

"The guys in Vermont said they want to work with me," Schmalbach said, referring to the state's insurance regulator.

"I'm sure they told you that," Thomson replied. "It doesn't matter."

Thomson was saying that Schmalbach had an interesting idea, and no money.

Go where the money is.

In the fall of 2020, Schmalbach got a call from Andrew Mais, the insurance commissioner for the state of Connecticut. Mais had heard about Schmalbach's pitch from Thomson and was intrigued. He felt the insurance industry had failed in fundamental ways during the pandemic, leaving many businesses exposed to unforeseen risks. It was also failing to protect businesses and households from the increasingly devastating impacts of extreme weather.

Mais told Schmalbach he could help him access those fonts of cash Thomson had told him about.

He was talking about Taleb and Spitznagel's old stomping ground—the land of hedge funds. Greenwich, Connecticut.

Schmalbach quickly got to work knocking on hedge fund doors around Greenwich. Many were skeptical. The products could be extremely risky because the blockchain mechanism made the payout nearly automatic—typically within forty-eight hours—rather than the months or years it can take a normal insurer to pay on a claim. That meant the hedge fund offering to provide the insurance needed to be ready to fulfill a claim at the drop of a hat. It was also tied to massive, in some ways unquantifiable risk.

But some were intrigued. The deals had interesting, complex aspects that draw highly quantitative hedge funds like bees to honey. By the end of 2021, Schmalbach had inked six deals worth about $3 billion (that is, the products covered $3 billion worth of risk).

By 2022, Schmalbach, acting again on Thomson's advice, opened an office in Hartford, Connecticut, handily close to the state insurance regulators and a forty-five-minute drive from Greenwich. On the plus side, it appeared there was no shortage of companies seeking systemic protection from disasters ranging from cyberattacks to wildfires to flooding.

Climate-related risks were the biggest concerns, executives told Schmalbach. Companies in California, Texas, Florida, and elsewhere were increasingly worried about the impact of hurricanes, flash floods, and wildfires on their facilities and supply chains.

Another worry: the hidden risk of carbon emissions deep in a firm's supply chain as regulators increasingly pressed companies to disclose those emissions in corporate filings. A luxury German automaker told Schmalbach it had grown concerned that its extended supply chain could be generating far more carbon dioxide emissions than it disclosed. If it emerged that it was submitting inaccurate reports of its emissions, the company could face billions in fines. It wasn't the direct supplier of parts it was worried about, or the supplier to the supplier. It was the supplier to the supplier to the supplier to the supplier and even several more steps down the chain. If, say, a company in Thailand that supplied an ingredient that ended up in the paint on its cars was a major emitter of greenhouse gases, the automaker feared it could face punishing fines for having failed to disclose it—even if it didn't even know about the emissions.

But when Schmalbach brought to hedge funds a financial product designed to protect the German automaker, the funds wanted a premium far higher than it was prepared to shell out. Intangible systemic risk, it turned out, could be very hard to put a dollar figure on.

Another mounting climate-related risk companies were facing was the proliferation of uncontrollable wildfires in the West, home to billions of dollars' worth of massive data-storage centers owned by tech giants such as Microsoft, Google, Apple, and Amazon. If a fire caused a power outage that in turn took down one or more of these companies' data centers, resulting in an extended outage of services for all the clients of that company, the financial impact could be devastating both reputationally and financially. It was a low-probability event—with a severe, catastrophic impact.

The solution: Ryskex and its lineup of hedge funds willing to take on that risk.

Who knew if Ryskex would take off? In 2022, as a major land war broke out in Europe and talk of nuclear war reemerged as a serious threat, systemic risk was on everyone's mind. Climate change, the never-ending pandemic, the always looming threat of cyberattacks—the world seemed to be endlessly poised on the brink of some new disaster. And Ryskex seemed to have a solution for those looking for protection from the looming chaos.

It wasn't completely crazy to think it might work out for Schmalbach. History provides plenty of examples of niche instruments becoming core financial products on Wall Street. In the 1970s, few traders had heard of options, much less how to price them. In the 1990s, another product with insurance-like properties—the credit default swap—was little more than a theoretical construct sketched out on whiteboards by Wall Street's growing legions of quants. By

2008, swaps valued in the trillions of dollars, euros, and yen had spread through the innards of the global financial system like a contagious virus.

And then they blew up, causing a collapse from which the system barely recovered.

> > < <

In the early 2020s, Schmalbach wasn't the only person in the insurance world tinkering with systemic risk, long a verboten topic in the industry. The mathematical backbone of insurance is the Law of Large Numbers—the steady-state realm of the predictable, the safe, fat belly of the bell curve. What's the risk of death of a longtime smoker aged seventy-five? What's the rate of injury in copper mining in Arizona? How often do sixteen-year-old male drivers crash a car? The insurance industry can calculate such figures in a flash, down to the nth decimal point.

But things were changing. Flood insurance, fire insurance, catastrophic-event insurance were all being turned upside down because the past was no longer a faithful predictor of the future. Systemic risk was suddenly a hot topic. Insurance bosses were seeing Taleb's dreaded Black Swans around every corner. Aon PLC, a British-American insurance behemoth, said it was focusing not on Black Swans—but on Gray Swans, those extreme, rare events that were in some measure predictable, like Sornette's Dragon Kings.

"We are witnessing a fundamental reordering of client priorities on a global scale," Aon CEO Greg Case said in April 2021 when introducing the new research project, *Respecting the Gray Swan*. "It is also why—now more than ever—reputational crises remain one of the major risk concerns for any organization anywhere in the world. Clearly, how leaders respond to these long-tail or 'Gray Swan' risks are a key indicator of the overall strength of their leadership and their business."

In 2020, Lloyd's of London—perhaps prompted by discussions with Schmalbach—introduced the idea of a government-backed Black

Swan reinsurance scheme that would provide businesses protection from systemic shocks: cyberattacks, solar storms, pandemics (after two years it still remained little more than a thought experiment). In February 2021, Lloyd's launched Futureset, a project to reconsider the insurance industry's role in a world that was getting increasingly risky and chaotic. The project included a series of webcast conversations it called the Systemic Risk Masterclass that gathered together the world's top thinkers and leaders in insurance.

In the series' opening keynote, Lloyd's CEO John Neal said systemic risk was a challenge the industry needed to tackle—and yet it was fiendishly problematic.

"What is systemic risk or indeed a systemic catastrophic event?" he asked. "Systemic risks, or Black Swan events, are the most difficult to quantify, understand, and protect against. As they unfold as a systemic catastrophic event, they can be global in impact, more often than not hitting multiple industries, countries, and billions of people simultaneously with potentially devastating consequences." One example of such an event: the Covid-19 pandemic. Future pandemics "could be more severe, could have more damaging consequences," Neal said.

Neal listed examples of other looming systemic risks. An extreme geomagnetic solar storm that could shut down critical electricity, GPS, and transportation infrastructure around the world for days or months. Accelerating global warming that acts as a risk multiplier amplifying wildfires, flooding, and other natural disasters. Animal disease. Food or critical resource failures, driving a global supply-chain shock. Widespread electricity failure. Widespread telecommunication failure. Widespread cyberattack.

"While these scenarios often seem extreme, in our highly interconnected society they may be much more likely than people think," Neal warned.

CHAPTER 23

THE GREAT DILEMMA OF RISK

Nassim Taleb lay sprawled in his bed on the top floor of a house in Beirut breathing through an oxygen mask. It was early 2021. He'd caught Covid-19, and it was a bad case. He'd traveled to Beirut to help his elderly mother, who was sick in the hospital. He wasn't sure how he'd contracted the virus. His best guess was that he'd gotten it while conversing with medical students at the hospital. Over fifteen days, he didn't see a single person. A Sri Lankan nurse who communicated with him on Google Translate delivered his meals via an elevator. He spent the entire time combing through papers about Covid-19. He was scared.

He eventually recovered, though weakness and shortness of breath lingered. He wondered at times if he suffered from so-called long Covid, in which debilitating ailments continued to plague victims, possibly for years. Taleb had the bad luck to catch the disease just before vaccines were widely available, heightening the potential for long-term symptoms. For much of 2021, he felt exhausted, need-ing naps in the morning and afternoon. He started taking ten-mile walks every day to get back into good health.

Joe Norman, one of Taleb's collaborators on "The Precautionary Principle," had meanwhile started worrying *vaccines* were the prob-lem. They were experimental, and were being tested on a vast pop-ulation of billions. He was especially agitated by vaccine mandates, which he claimed represented a systemic risk to the human race.

"Broad-scoped mandates ensure that the impact will be large-scale," he wrote on his Substack page. "Large enough to impact the system as such, and therefore large enough to present the possibility of harm to the system as such. Moreover, it is irreversible."

His concerns about the harmful impact of vaccines weren't very specific, boiling down to "we don't know." Norman thought it a bad idea to tamper at large scale with something whose repercussions were anyone's guess.

Taleb found Norman's analysis highly aggravating, a mis-application of the precautionary principle. Vaccines weren't multipli-cative like viruses, Taleb pointed out on Twitter. If your neighbor got a vaccine, that didn't mean you were at the risk of getting a vaccine. However, if your neighbor didn't get a vaccine, that *heightened* the risk that you might catch the virus. "The antivax [proponents] are lunatics," he wrote on Twitter in December 2021. Taleb observed that the sample size of the vaccinated population was so large—roughly four billion when he posted the remark—that any potential for systemic harm would already have been discovered.

The widespread, often self-destructive reaction of people across America against efforts to contain the virus—mask mandates, test-ing requirements, and *free life-saving vaccines*—increasingly turned Taleb against the political philosophy long espoused by Spitznagel (and at times by himself): libertarianism. The virus, he saw, exposed inherent contradictions in the philosophy that espoused individual freedom as the supreme moral good in society. But when does one's individual freedom harm the freedom of others?

"'Libertarians' are . . . incoherent," Taleb tweeted in May 2020, "they deny stores the right to require masks & constrain their freedom yet ask for freedom . . . Nothing to do with libertarianism: rather a collection of marshmallowbrained psychopaths and misfits taking their hatred of humanity too far."

Taleb and Spitznagel's friendship, to be sure, remained solid. It was just one more disagreement among many over the years. Their bond went deeper than spats about political philosophy. It was wholly expressed in one place: Universa.

> > < <

Spitznagel had recently taken up a popular activity in Northern Michigan: deer hunting. Rather than use a long rifle, however, he chose to hunt with a custom-made German compound bow.

In October 2021, after a long day of deer stalking—unsuccessful, as usual—Spitznagel climbed down a rope ladder that hung from a hunting stand high in the canopy of the woods on Idyll Farms. He panned his headlamp through the thick brush as he scrambled out of the woods into a wide-open cherry orchard. It was eerily quiet. Then he heard a yipping howl, then more. In an instant, the high-pitched *yip yip yip*s were all around him, like war cries. Coyotes. He'd heard them many times before, deep in the woods high up in the hills of the farm. But he'd never confronted them. It seemed as if they'd been waiting to ambush the hedge fund trader as he left the cover of the woods. He could see them, their many eyes reflected back at him as he pointed his headlamp in every direction. A headline flashed through his mind, "Black Swan Trader Devoured by Coyotes." He started walking more briskly. Then he broke into a run, heading for his truck a few hundred yards away in the brush. The pack followed. He could hear them, their paws padding the ground, howling on all sides as he dashed across an open field. He made it to his truck and dived in. From then on, he always carried a pistol when he ventured into the woods at night.

Spitznagel's heart-pounding encounter with coyotes was a sharp contrast with his day job managing Universa. The year 2021 had been relatively quiet for the hedge fund. With stocks stuck in rally mode, and volatility subdued, the firm continued to follow the Black Swan protocol—buy cheap put options with explosive upside potential and wait for the next crash. Spitznagel, as always, had no idea when they'd pay off. It could be months, years. But the sky-high stock market, which plowed through record after record, was making investors nervous. It felt bubble-like. To get protection from a collapse, many came knocking on Universa's doors.

One sign of trouble for the market, and the Fed's efforts to keep monetary stimulus flowing full tilt, was the slow creep of inflation. A variety of factors—supply chain hang-ups, strong demand from American consumers, the rebound of the global economy from the devastation of 2020, spiking oil prices after Russia's attack on Ukraine—began to cause prices of goods ranging from beef to toys to cars to zoom higher. By the summer of 2022, inflation was hitting nose-bleed levels in America and the rest of the world.

To fight it, the Federal Reserve started cranking up interest rates. After more than thirteen years of extremely loose policy, the U.S. central bank was forced to tighten things up and squeeze inflation out of the economy.

2021 had also seen the publication of Spitznagel's second book, *Safe Haven: Investing for Financial Storms*. At a slender 208 pages, the book was a distillation of his investment strategy, largely free of the Austrian diversions found in *The Dao of Capital* (but with a healthy dose of the German philosopher Friedrich Nietzsche). It amounted to a frontal assault on Modern Portfolio Theory and the vast money-management industry that was captive to it. Taleb, in a foreword to the book, declared it Spitznagel's "monumental f*** you to the investment industry."

Put simply, Spitznagel's argument in *Safe Haven* is that investors can both lower risk and raise returns *at the same time*. In fact, higher returns can and should follow lower risk *as a direct conse-*

quence, when done right. That contradicted a key tenet of MPT: the trade-off between risk and return. To boost your chance of making bags of money, you need to bear the risk of losing a lot. A startup electric-vehicle maker has a lot more potential upside than your local electric utility. But it's a hell of a lot more risky. You could lose everything. Spitznagel called this conundrum the *great dilemma of risk*.

MPT-constructed portfolios adjust risk and return to provide the optimal payout—in theory. The method typically measures how volatile an investment is historically relative to a stable asset, such as Treasury bonds. It also measures an investment's performance relative to its past performance. The approach has gone through multiple iterations over the years. Litterman's Black-Litterman model is just one variation of the theme.

Universa is the counterfactual to the risk-reward calculation, Spitznagel said. "People think of risk mitigation as a liability, as a trade-off against wealth creation, because it usually is," he wrote in *Safe Haven*. "Universa is, if nothing else, a real-life case study and out-of-sample test that unequivocally proves the point that risk mitigation doesn't have to be viewed that way. Risk mitigation can and should be thought of as being additive to portfolios over time—with the right risk mitigation, that is."

Even better, he said, an effective risk-mitigation strategy allows you to take *more* risk. Recall the various portfolios Spitznagel wrote about in his investor letters and in *Barron's*. The hypothetical Universa portfolio had an allocation of 97 percent in stocks and 3 percent in put options with potentially explosive returns, compared with 75 percent or lower in stocks for other strategies. By protecting against the big losses with a bet that turns into a jackpot during crashes, you can put nearly all your chips into the market. A good defense lets your offense get more aggressive—you can throw more Hail Marys, swing for more home runs, shoot more three-pointers, drive faster, pedal to the metal.

Universa's approach was, in a way, a form of panicking early *all the time*. Spitznagel was permanently panicking for his investors—so they didn't have to.

The logic behind it all can be daunting, and in *Safe Haven* Spitznagel at times complicates his argument with overly sophisticated language. ("As investors, what we are really doing is trying to perform a mathematical optimization of this logarithmic objective function so we can maximize our geometric returns.")

Warren Buffett, perhaps, said it best and in the simplest terms. Rule No. 1 for investing: Don't lose money. Rule No. 2: Don't forget Rule No. 1.

While Universa itself lost small amounts on a regular basis, the strategy combined with a large stock position consistently gained money. Over thirteen years, Universa's Black Swan risk-mitigation strategy, on average, had outperformed the S&P 500 by more than 3 percentage points a year. And it did so by "having far less risk," Spitznagel claimed in *Safe Haven*.

Spitznagel's argument captivated Peter Coy, a financial writer for the *New York Times*. In a November 2021 review of *Safe Haven* called "The Risk-Return Trade-Off Is Phony," he wrote: "Conventional wisdom in investing says there's a trade-off between risk and return. To make a lot of money, you must take the chance of big losses. Play it safe and you'll most likely have to settle for meager returns. The investor Mark Spitznagel says that reducing risk actually increases returns, and he has evidence."

Spitznagel was on to something "the rest of the industry should heed," Coy wrote. "The basic idea is simple: Survival is essential. If a portfolio does well on average but by bad luck has a series of big losses, it may never be able to recover. So it's essential to protect against losing a lot of money in any one period. And don't count on the passage of time to rescue it: If a portfolio isn't well insured, the risk of blowing up and losing everything goes up over time, not down."

The idea of lowering risk to boost returns is "counterintuitive to anyone who studied Modern Portfolio Theory, a business school staple," Coy noted.

That's why Taleb said *Safe Haven* amounted to Spitznagel's "monumental f*** you to the investment industry." "Hedge fund managers hate my book," he told me. Because he was essentially arguing that nearly everything they do—diversifying, market timing, buying gold and bonds, leveraging up to juice returns—is wrong, mere theater. "The whole asset allocation industry is an empty narrative," he said.

Spitznagel does make an exception for value investors in the vein of Warren Buffett and Buffett's mentor, Benjamin Graham. Value investors search for unloved, beaten-down investments that for one reason or another have fallen out of favor. As such, they are priced below their true worth and provide the opportunity for substantial upside. They also are (usually) less risky than more popular stocks, because they've already taken a beating. It also means they don't have to become world-beaters to provide a solid return. "This is the cornerstone of our investment philosophy," Buffett once wrote in a letter to his partners. "Never count on making a good sale. Have the purchase price be so attractive that even a mediocre sale gives good results."

"The value approach is a kissing cousin to what I do," Spitznagel told me. "I'm buying stuff people think is garbage, and most of the time it is."

To be sure, it isn't easy. Value investing is by definition contrarian—it works by going against the crowd, and many investors find that very hard to do. What's more, sometimes stocks are beaten up for a reason—they are so-called value traps—afflicted by entrenched flaws such as poor management or an outdated business model. You wouldn't have wanted to invest in a horse-and-buggy business at the start of the twentieth century no matter how cheap it was. But the benefits of value investing are numerous. It not only provides the chance for substantial upside, it also protects investors from the Black Swan crashes that can level a more risky portfolio. Value stocks have already taken the hit, making them far less vulnerable to extreme downsides.

Taleb, for his part, has recommended what he calls a barbell approach. The idea: on one side of the barbell put roughly 80 percent of your wealth in super-safe assets like short-term Treasury bonds, and on the other side put the rest in a bunch of risky stuff like startup tech firms or biotechs or newly minted clean-energy stocks that have a chance of going stratospheric. With the latter allocation you get exposure to what he calls *positive* Black Swans. While most of the bets won't pay off, those that do—the Amazons, Apples, and Teslas of the investing universe—can potentially more than compensate for the losses.

Taleb's point is that mom-and-pop investors, in their own portfolios, should focus on preserving their assets, protecting them from Black Swans, rather than taking a gamble that stocks will keep going up over the long term.

Some academic research has lent credence to the strategy. "The [barbell] idea is partially rooted in the notion that because of behavioral biases, investors tend to avoid the extremes of any variable or asset characteristic like valuation, so the extremes of an asset class are often overpriced," George Mason University finance professor Derek Horstmeyer wrote in July 2022 in the *Wall Street Journal*. Horstmeyer's analysis of barbell strategies in both stocks and bonds showed that they tend to outperform the broader market during times of rising interest rates—periods when market crashes are more likely.

An intriguing new option for investors aiming to protect themselves from big drawdowns hit the market in September 2020 when a novel exchange-traded fund called Simplify US Equity PLUS Downside Convexity (ticker SPD) was launched. Formed by ex-Pimco ETF manager Paul Kim, the fund was, for retail investors, a potential mini-Universa. It put a big chunk of its assets into the market, with a sliver—roughly 3 percent—allocated to far-out-of-the-money put options that would surge in a market crash.

"It's a type of tail-risk strategy that a Universa would implement that's not available to Main Street," Kim told me. "We put it inside an ETF." Sounding much like Spitznagel describing his crash-bang strategy, Kim said the ETF "kicks in and protects you from the draw-downs, and you end up with much better geometric returns. You stay in the game and compound."

By early 2023, the Simplify Downside ETF had about a quarter billion dollars betting on it. The fund was the product of a shift in market regulation in 2020 that gave retail funds more latitude in the kinds of investments they could make—including in derivatives. Kim saw the shift as a massive opportunity to bring hedge fund–like strategies to the masses. Of course, Kim's fund and a host of other ETFs launched by his firm, Simplify Asset Management, were largely untested. While volatility had shot up in 2022, it wasn't enough to trigger the explosive payouts the ETF promised during crashes. It was also unclear whether Kim and his team could manage the costs of implementing the strategy—the tedious day-to-day bleeding—over the long fallow periods when the market kept ticking higher, the periods that tested the patience of even the most sophisticated investors.

Who knew what the future held? Perhaps such products would take off as more and more investors realized the benefits of protecting themselves from crashes. And perhaps, say a decade from now, amid the smoking ruins of yet another market collapse, investigators will finger the 2020 rule that gave retail funds greater access to risky derivatives as complicit in the blowup.

Unsurprisingly, Spitznagel was skeptical of the fancy new ETFs. Expenses alone would eat investors alive, he thought. "They'll just continue to cost people far, far more than they'll even hope to save them in a crash," he told me. For all investors, the key is to know what kinds of risk they're taking—and what they're missing out on. There's no magic formula, and every investor has his or her own unique ability to handle risk. A thirty-year-old accountant has an entirely different risk profile than a seventy-year-old retired steelworker. What investors should avoid at all costs is shifting cash in and out of the market based on a premonition, or even a well-informed forecast, that stocks will go up or down—a guaranteed churn-and-burn recipe for losing money.

Spitznagel has always admitted he's a terrible forecaster, having warned about a terrifying crash in the market for some two decades, year after year (getting it right a few times like the proverbial broken clock). That was one of the tricks behind Universa. Unlike predictors such as Didier Sornette, who believed he could detect Dragon Kings looming in the market's tea leaves, Spitznagel didn't need to forecast to be successful.

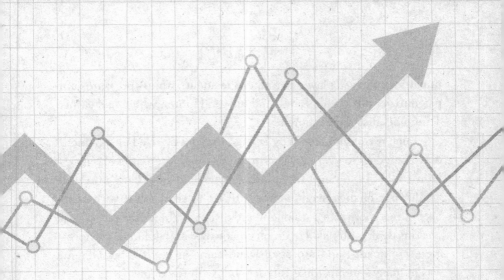

CHAPTER 24

DOORSTEP TO DOOM

As Nassim Taleb made his way through customs in the Kyiv airport, he mused on how different the process was in Ukraine versus Russia. In Ukraine, customs officials barely glanced at his passport before stamping it and waving him through. In Russia, officials scrutinized his passport as if it contained some inscrutable, diabolical secret. He was always tense when visiting Moscow, aware that a government official at any moment could demand to see his passport, with unknown consequences. In Ukraine, he could relax.

It was August 2021. Taleb had traveled to Kyiv at the invitation of Ukrainian first lady Olena Zelenska, who'd organized a summit celebrating three decades of Ukrainian independence in the thousand-year-old complex of the St. Sophia Cathedral. "She likes your books," a conference representative told Taleb. "Can you come?" While there, Taleb briefly met Ukrainian president Volodymyr Zelensky, who at the time was known outside Ukraine for the

unwitting role he'd played in former President Trump's pressure campaign to get dirt on Joe Biden and his son Hunter, which had earned
Trump his first impeachment.

Taleb was unimpressed by Zelensky, whom he sized up as a mediocre comedian in over his head in the realm of international politics.
How could this guy ever face down a stone-cold killer like Putin? (He
would soon change his mind about that.) Taleb also met with members of the Ukrainian parliament and discussed how various political
systems dealt with risk. He drank copiously with Ukrainian businessmen, politicians, and professors, and came away thinking Ukraine
was in many ways just like Russia—but with freedom.

Shortly before Taleb's visit to Ukraine, he'd made waves on Wall
Street with a paper that claimed the value of the popular cryptocurrency bitcoin was *zero*. Bitcoin couldn't be used as a currency, it wasn't
a short- or long-term store of value, it wasn't an inflation hedge, and it
wasn't a safe haven for one's investments, since it was highly correlated
to the market, Taleb claimed in his study, "Bitcoin, Currencies, and
Fragility." Because bitcoin had no inherent value, unlike gold and other
precious metals, it required constant maintenance by bitcoin miners—the computer whizzes that use complex formulas to create more
and more bitcoin—to prop up its value. Given the chance that miners
could at some point lose interest in bitcoin, in theory reducing its value
to zero, he argued that its present value *was zero*. What likely made
Taleb even more dismissive about the digital currency was that it had
fallen even more than the market in the crisis of March 2020, showing it was demonstrably worthless as a tail hedge against Black Swans.

After tumbling in the Covid-pandemic crash, bitcoin rallied in
2021, hitting an all-time high of $67,801 in November. But in 2022,
as the Fed began to crank rates higher, it and other cryptocurrencies
collapsed, wiping roughly $2 trillion from the broader crypto market.

As bitcoin plunged, one crypto billionaire was marshaling his
forces—and his billions—to salvage it. Sam Bankman-Fried, the
thirty-year-old titan of a sprawling crypto empire, started snapping up
struggling crypto exchanges from Canada to Japan. Seeking to boost

popular interest in crypto, the mercurial CEO of cryptocurrency exchange FTX Trading appeared in magazine ads alongside supermodel Gisele Bündchen and shelled out millions for a pro-crypto commercial featuring Larry David during the 2022 Super Bowl.

Bankman-Fried, who'd become known for his unruly shock of curly hair and aversion to business suits, was an adherent of an increasingly influential semi-apocalyptic worldview known as *longtermism*—a movement that shared elements of Taleb's precautionary principle. It was an outgrowth of a moral philosophy developed in the 2000s known as effective altruism, a quantitative philanthropic method designed to estimate probabilities about which causes were most important in terms of humanity's well-being. Will alleviating global poverty do more good than preparing for the next pandemic? Will preparing for a killer AI be more effective than spending money to send a human colony to Mars? By the early 2020s, more than $40 billion had been invested in the effective-altruism movement, and its members were advising top officials in the United Nations and the U.S. government. A central credo was that followers of EA, as it was known, would give away a large chunk of their earnings to worthy causes. That inspired people such as Bankman-Fried to pursue career paths that would produce the highest possible winnings, resulting in the highest possible giving, a model of philanthropy called "earning-to-give." Rather than a career in medicine or chemistry, EAs sought jobs on Wall Street and in Silicon Valley—or in crypto.

By the early 2020s, longtermism had become a powerful force among America's tech goliaths. Backers—the computer whizzes that use complex formulas to create more and more bitcoin—included Elon Musk, Bill Gates, and Jeff Bezos. It had its roots in the work of Swedish philosopher Nick Bostrom, founder of Oxford University's Future of Humanity Institute, which studies extreme risks to humanity (Musk had donated $1.5 million to the sibling organization of FHI called the Future of Life Institute). The core idea behind the belief system is that humanity's future, if it plays its cards right, is virtually unbounded and that the number of future humans—think over a period of millions or even billions of years—far outdistances the number of humans alive on Planet Earth today, or that have ever lived. (Bostrom included in his calculations humans living in computer simulations.) That being so, today's humans have a back-bending responsibility to those future trillions of unborn humans, or digital humans, who will live in the very long term—an endless, daz-zling future in which people meld with computers and populate the stars. Bostrom and others took the logic of this thought experiment to the extreme of the extreme—the long-term existence of the human race was all that mattered.

That led to some radical conclusions. Since saving the human race is the one and only priority, "making even the minutest prog-ress on avoiding existential risk can be seen as more worthwhile than saving millions of people alive today," observed a September 2022 *Washington Post* editorial called "The Trouble with 'Longtermism.'" Crunching the numbers, that meant near-term problems such as poverty and global health—and, some argued, global warming—don't have much of an impact on the future existence of humanity. The climate crisis? A speed bump on the road to humanity's future dom-ination of the galaxy.

What to *really* worry about? A super-virulent human-engineered pathogen (Bankman-Fried funded the Washington, D.C.–based political action group Guarding Against Pandemics, run by his brother, Gabe) . . . or a Frankenstein AI gone rogue, a topic Bostrom mused about in his 2016 bestseller, *Superintelligence: Paths, Dangers, Strategies*, whose cover quoted Bill Gates ("I highly recommend this book") and which Elon Musk promoted on Twitter ("We need to be super careful with AI. Potentially more dangerous than nukes.") . . . or a killer asteroid . . . or, yes, nukes.

Such concerns, on the surface, seemed to mirror the warnings about global ruin issued in "The Precautionary Principle." The differ-ence was that the precautionary approach was largely passive, a rec-ommendation *against* taking actions that could pose extreme danger to humanity (though there are examples of active precaution, such as

NASA's path-breaking DART program designed to protect the Earth from a planet-killing asteroid). Longtermism was far more prescriptive. Advocates were making multibillion-dollar bets on space exploration and colonization, the symbiosis between humans and AI (to hopefully outrace or defeat our future superintelligent AI overlords), and genetic engineering (of humans, animals, and foods). It was, in a way, the polar opposite of the precautionary principle, advocating extreme Hail Mary experimentation in order to secure humanity's boundless future.

Causes the Longtermists cared less about? Poverty, an issue that had initially launched the effective altruism movement; health care; causes of inequity; and wealth gaps between nations. The debates the Longtermists sparked inspired weird and dystopian notions of who deserved to live—or die. Nick Beckstead, a prominent Longtermist at Oxford University, wrote in his doctoral thesis that since wealthier countries "have substantially more innovation, and their workers are much more economically productive" it makes sense to him that "saving a life in a rich country is substantially more important than saving a life in a poor country." Bostrom floated the idea of putting a tracking device on every person in the world to make sure no one was cooking up a humanity-killing virus in their basement.

Peter Singer, the Princeton philosopher and ethicist whose work inspired many of the founders of effective altruism, saw longtermist thinking as a threat. "The dangers of treating extinction risks as humanity's overriding concern should be obvious," he wrote in an October 2021 article. "Viewing current problems through the lens of existential risk to our species can shrink those problems to almost nothing, while justifying almost anything that increases our odds of surviving long enough to spread beyond Earth."

Rupert Read thought longtermists, in a dark irony, could usher in the future apocalypse they were dead set on fending off. "The so-called 'agents of doom' carry around what my colleague Nassim Taleb calls 'silent risk': in trying to buttress their own power, and even in trying (I am sure, with the best intentions) to decrease the long-term existential risk to our species, they themselves pose a terrible risk to civilization, and perhaps to life on Earth," he wrote in July 2022. By downplaying current risks such as climate breakdown, for instance, because they don't see it as *existential*, and by betting the future of humanity on techno-utopian scientific breakthroughs, longtermists were taking a dangerous gamble that could seriously backfire, Read believed.

Taleb just thought they were bad at math. He'd met Nick Bostrom at a dinner in Oxford in 2008 and quickly chalked him up as a perhaps well-intentioned, head-in-the-clouds dreamer who lacked common sense. "These guys have gone haywire," he told me. "They're modeling, but what if the model is wrong? I doubt they're very good at probability. Before colonizing Mars, make sure the Earth works."

Bankman-Fried, for his part, went a long way toward making Taleb's case that cryptocurrencies are a cash-incinerating house of cards when his exchange, FTX, imploded in late 2022. Unnerved by rumors of a liquidity crunch at the exchange, its customers rushed to pull their cash out. Within days, FTX's funds spiraled from billions of dollars in the bank to essentially zero (or, in fact, *negative* billions of dollars). One day FTX was estimated to be worth $32 billion. The following day it was worth virtually nothing. It was a harsh lesson for young Bankman-Fried in the chaotic, often violent nature of financial markets dominated by Black Swans and Dragon Kings. And it later turned out, of course, that much of Bankman-Fried's woes appeared self-inflicted amid allegations that he had scampered off with the funds of FTX customers. (Bankman-Fried denied the allegations and plead not guilty at his arraignment in New York.) The long-term future for the effective altruist, by early 2023, would surely involve a non-trivial amount of time spent in oaken-paneled American court rooms, if not worse.

> > < <

Universa, meanwhile, continued to pull in new investors as the stock market, fueled by government stimulus and generous monetary policy, rocketed to all-time highs. In November 2021, the Dow Jones Industrial Average topped 36,000 for the first time. Investors were giddy in the rarified air of those delirious heights, but many were increasingly worried the party could come to an end at a moment's notice. It was hard to keep grinning when you feared Black Swans lurked in the shadows.

On January 20, 2022, the Bulletin of the Atomic Scientists set the Doomsday Clock at one hundred seconds to midnight—exactly where it had stood since ticking closer to Armageddon in January 2020 as the Covid-19 pandemic exploded across the planet. While the election of Joe Biden as U.S. president had eased tensions, it wasn't enough to reverse civilization's death dance with catastrophe, the atomic scientists said. Tense relations between the U.S., China, and Russia, North Korea's nuclear expansion, the frightful military standoff on the border of Ukraine, the expanding pursuit of biological weapons, the coronavirus pandemic and the threat of future pandemics, unchecked emissions of greenhouse gases that caused global warming, a plague of toxic disinformation on the Internet that had persuaded millions of Americans that the 2020 U.S. presidential election was fraudulent, among a host of other existential risks—all put the world on the edge of a cliff.

"The Clock remains the closest it has ever been to civilization-ending apocalypse because the world remains stuck in an extremely dangerous moment," the scientists wrote. "In 2019, we called it the new abnormal, and it has unfortunately persisted. . . . The doorstep to doom is no place to loiter."

A month later, on the morning of February 24, Russian President Vladimir Putin ordered thousands of Russian troops to invade Ukraine in what he said was a "special military operation" to "denazify" the country. Experts expected hostilities to be over in days, with Russia's elite, well-funded military quickly overrunning Ukraine's ragtag forces, capturing Kyiv, and replacing Zelensky's administration with a puppet government beholden to the Kremlin. Most expected Zelensky to flee the country with his family. That didn't happen, of course.

Instead, the TV comedian-turned-president stayed in the Ukrainian capital, reportedly telling U.S. officials who'd offered to help him escape, "The fight is here. I need ammunition, not a ride."

As Zelensky became a hero of the West, Taleb realized his initial impression of the Ukrainian president was one of the greatest personal misreads of his life. Zelensky was putting his skin in the game, literally. Taleb also began to reassess Putin, as did much of the rest of the world. Despite Russia's brutal wars in Chechnya and Syria and his penchant for assassinating his domestic opponents, Putin somehow had retained a level of respect among Western leaders and businessmen. Taleb had viewed his regime as a mild version of nationalism, a lesser evil, disagreeable but no threat to the global order. In *Skin in the Game*, he wrote somewhat approvingly of Putin, arguing that his position as an autocrat who doesn't face elections allows him to act "as a free citizen confronting slaves who need committees, approval, and who of course feel like they have to fit their decisions to an immediate rating."

"It turns out there's no mild version of nationalism," Taleb told me.

The war triggered economic and financial cascades that rippled worldwide. Oil prices surged, providing another kicker to inflationary pressures that had started with Covid and its stranglehold on global supply chains. Stocks nose-dived, hitting bear-market territory in weeks. "The market is in a state of shock," Brian O'Reilly, head of market strategy at Mediolanum International Funds, told Morningstar in March. Nickel prices doubled in a day amid jitters that the war would disrupt access to the metal—Russia was one of its biggest producers. Grain prices shot up as supplies from Ukraine, one of the world's largest wheat producers, were blockaded in Black Sea ports. Spiking food prices caused by the war created the worst global food crisis since at least 2008, the International Monetary Fund said, posing mounting risks of widespread social unrest—a risk Yaneer Bar-Yam had studied for years.

The oil price spike reversed a years-long decline in the fossil fuel sector as investors eyed record profits thanks to Putin's war. At the same time, the wind appeared to come out of the clean-energy sails as the Biden administration struggled to pass a spending bill to address the climate crisis. West Virginia's Democratic senator, Joe Manchin, whose fortune was tied to coal, continued to block the bill, citing concerns about inflation.

Taleb and Spitznagel had been predicting a spike in inflation for more than a decade (Taleb in 2010 was predicting hyperinflation and told investors to short the U.S. Treasury market). But for years, inflation remained contained despite all the stimulus provided by the Federal Reserve. Then, in 2022, due to a myriad of factors, prices shot up. In response, Fed chairman Jerome Powell began to ratchet interest rates higher to put the brakes on America's hot-rod economy.

That spelled trouble for fixed-income assets such as bonds, whose prices move inversely to interest rates. The simultaneous decline in bonds and stocks—the 20 percent decline in the S&P 500 was the worst midyear performance for the index in more than half a century—was a disaster for the beloved 60/40 portfolio so many investors had long relied on. The standard 60/40 portfolio fell by one-fifth in the first half of the year, the weakest six-month start to a year for the strategy since 1976. It continued to falter for the rest of the year, putting 60/40 portfolios on track for their worst year since 1937.

Spitznagel, ever the skeptic, worried there'd be an epic bond crash if the Fed continued to crank up rates. He told Bloomberg the global financial system was in "the greatest credit bubble of human history," spurred by more than a decade of rock-bottom interest rates and other forms of economic steroids. "If this credit bubble ever pops, it's going to be the most catastrophic market failure that anyone has ever read about—but let's hope that doesn't happen," he said.

Spitznagel doubled down on his diagnosis of bomb-market doom in a January 2023 letter to investors that triggered alarm bells across Wall Street. "[W]e are living in a mega-tinderbox-timebomb," he wrote. "It is objectively the greatest tinderbox in financial history—greater than in the late 1920s and likely with similar market consequences."

"A Great Depression style wipeout is quite the call," the *Wall Street Journal* observed.

> > < <

Back in Zurich, Didier Sornette was preparing for a major life change. At sixty-five years old, after fifteen years as chair of entrepreneurial risks at ETH Zurich, he was retiring. In April, to commemorate his departure, he gave a farewell lecture to students and staff called "Dynamical Risk Management and Dragon Kings: Prediction and Response to a Wild World." He rolled out his favorite hits—his lifelong focus on extremes, his love of risk-taking and hot-rod motorcycles, his successful market forecasts, his contempt for Taleb's Black Swan concept, which he said was "wrong and dangerous" because it let people—especially bankers and politicians—off the hook when it came to their complicity in disasters. Dragon Kings, he said, are predictable—if you know what to look for. Sornette believed he did.

He discussed recent advances he and a team of former students had made in earthquake prediction. Together, they'd launched a website called RichterX, which was based on the so-called Epidemic Type Aftershock Sequence Model or ETAS. According to ETAS, earthquakes trigger other earthquakes, which can trigger more and more earthquakes, causing a cascade that behaves like an epidemic—or a chaotic market crash. The site scanned the globe and made predictions in real time about the likelihood of earthquakes. Users could click on practically any site in the world and get a prediction. For example, click on a spot in Indonesia, and you might get the following: "The probability of at least one earthquake with magnitude M5+ within 100 km in the next 7 days is 10.2%."

A unique feature of the site: Users could create an account, deposit money, and bet against the predictions made by the RichterX team. "The system allows any one of you who have a better prediction to bet against us," Sornette told the audience. "If you win, you get rewards. Money!" The site could then learn from successful bets.

Sornette showed how dynamics found in earthquakes also could be detected in financial markets and blowups, factors tracked by the Financial Crisis Observatory he'd launched in 2008. Most crashes aren't caused by outside or "exogenous" events like bad news, such as a negative earnings season, he explained. Rather, they're caused by "endogenous" events that take place *inside* the market, strategies reacting to strategies, cascades causing cascades—earthquakes triggering earthquakes. Similar phenomena could be found in book sales, species extinctions, social unrest, and more.

He wrapped up his speech with a nod toward a looming problem he said gave him the greatest concern in the world today— the clean-energy transition away from fossil fuels. Sornette said he believed much of the talk behind efforts to decarbonize the global economy was an "aspirational infantile fantasy" that didn't take into account the fact that the project was an energy *replacement*, rather than an addition of new energy sources. It was a monumental effort on a scale of World War II, taking place at a time when vast regions of the world were clamoring for *more* energy.

"India is coming, Africa is coming," Sornette warned.

What's required is the creation of a "social bubble" of risk-taking on new energy innovation, which Sornette said needed to include nuclear power. These "useful bubbles" were akin to the Apollo space program that brought men to the Moon and kicked off a host of other technologies (for instance, the Black & Decker Dustbuster vacuum). Sornette wasn't optimistic. After shocks such as the Global Financial Crisis and the Covid-19 pandemic, risk-taking had become an endangered species.

"We are a zero risk society," he said. "We are a sick society, which is death."

> > < <

With the onset of summer 2022, the inevitable climate disasters descended like sinister clockwork. A punishing heat wave battered Europe, sending temperatures in London above one hundred degrees. Extreme heat across large parts of China, where more than 260 weather stations set records, sent residents to the cool of underground fallout shelters. Another heat dome descended on Seattle, pushing temperatures above ninety degrees for a record six straight days. South Asia saw months of temperatures north of one hundred degrees *nearly every day*. In France, water had to be poured on pavement during the Tour de France to keep the asphalt from melting. Land in Europe suffered fire damage double the average between 2006 and 2021. Flooding in Pakistan, triggered in part by melting glaciers, left one third of the country under water, killing hundreds and displacing more than 30 million people.

"This is insanity, this is collective suicide," UN secretary-general António Guterres said in a press conference from Islamabad. "End the war with nature, invest in renewable energy now. As the crisis gathers pace, it's clear that most countries are nowhere near prepared."

"This summer is just a horrorscape," Kim Cobb, a climate scientist at Brown University, told the *Washington Post*.

Things didn't improve in the fall—they got worse. In late September, Hurricane Ian, a deadly Category 4 megastorm, slammed into the west coast of Florida like a buzz saw made of water and air. "We're in the destructive phase," Bill Karins, NBC News meteorologist, said as the storm, one of the most powerful in U.S. history, made landfall. "I just can't believe Mother Nature would do something like this," declared a resident of Fort Myers Beach, which suffered a direct hit from the storm. "My God."

There were some rare positive developments on the climate front that might have even encouraged die-hard pessimists such as Rupert Read—or Didier Sornette. In August, West Virginia's Joe Manchin reversed his position on Biden's climate bill and gave it the thumbs-up. Congress promptly passed a nearly $400 billion package to boost investments in electric vehicles and renewable energy sources such as wind and solar. Climate gurus said the bill would go a long way toward helping the U.S. reach its target of cutting greenhouse emissions in half from 2005 levels by the end of the decade. Investors in the green power sector such as Bob Litterman celebrated as clean-energy stocks took off.

Not included in the bill, to Litterman's chagrin—a carbon tax.

>   >   <   <

At 7:14 p.m. Eastern time, September 26, 2022, a tiny NASA spacecraft traveling 15,000 miles an hour slammed into a 530-foot-wide asteroid moonlet named Dimorphos, slightly altering its trajectory, in a successful demonstration of the space agency's DART mission, short for Double Asteroid Redirection Test. The so-called Planetary Defense mission confirmed that NASA had the capability to guide a spacecraft millions of miles from Earth to collide with an asteroid in order to deflect it, a technique known as kinetic impact. DART's success "demonstrates a viable mitigation technique for protecting the planet from an Earth-bound asteroid or comet, if one were discovered," NASA said. While NASA's Planetary Defense mission might seem like a cliché cooked up by Hollywood's summer blockbuster brain trust, it was a deadly serious project headed by deadly serious scientists. While exceedingly rare, a collision between Earth and a large asteroid posed an existential threat to humanity. Taking steps to protect against such a dire event, as unlikely as it might be, made all the sense in the world.

NASA was effectively adopting the precautionary principle.

>   >   <   <

Back at Universa, the spike in volatility in 2022 was the firm's natural habitat—its calm seas comfort zone. In June, when the market had plunged 20 percent for the year, the firm's quantitative system signaled that it was time to take profits on their positions. Another moneymaking opportunity came in the fall as stocks tumbled into a bear market while the Fed and other central banks around the world kept ratcheting interest rates higher amid persistent signs of inflation.

Spitznagel, ensconced at Idyll Farms, frequently spoke with the firm's traders over Zoom as they managed their trades. Because of the bond-bubble powder keg Spitznagel had warned about, he told them he was highly skeptical that the Fed would aggressively remove the monetary-policy punch bowl. Which meant the stock market would likely rebound—and the party would keep going.

"They are bluffing," he told his team, referring to the Fed. If the economy began to contract, or if inflation metrics eased, the Fed chairman Jerome Powell would reverse himself in a flash, he believed. Historically, the central bank had rarely tightened policy in a slowing economy. Pushing rates higher as a potential recession loomed "would require a Fed chair who is suicidal," Spitznagel told me, and would result in an economic collapse worse than 2008.

As he was quick to concede, he could be wrong. And as he also conceded, if he *was* wrong, that would be good for Universa and its investors—and terrible for just about everyone else. Jitters about the Fed, inflation, and all the other looming risks had investors still clamoring for a piece of the fund. By late 2022, Universa was providing crash protection for some $20 billion in assets, the highest in its fifteen-year history, making it the 24th largest hedge fund in the world, according to *Insitutional Investor*. With a mere 21 employees at Universa, that averaged out to nearly $1 billion per employee.

Toward the year's end, as temperatures in the far wilds of Northern Michigan plunged to the subzeros, Spitznagel stood and peered over the edge of his hunting stand into the thick forest surrounding him and aimed his compound bow, scanning for motion. He was thirty feet high in the stand stalking a monster buck he'd been tracking on the farm's array of cameras. He'd been hunting it for years. So far, the buck had lain low. Spitznagel had been waiting there in silence since dawn, after sleeping the previous night in the woods. Stalking deer, he sometimes thought, was a bit like preparing for chaos at Universa. You wait for that one shot, maybe a very long time, and you only get that one shot. Hesitate for a second and your prey has fled into the bush.

The hours built up, it was getting late, and he was cold. He decided to pack up his bow for the day and head back home in Northport, always on the watch for coyotes.

He didn't mind. He knew he'd get his shot one of these days.

> > < <

On January 24, 2023, the Bulletin of the Atomic Scientists moved the hands of the Doomsday Clock forward to 90 seconds to midnight, the closest to global catastrophe in its history. The primary reason: Putin's war in Ukraine. "Russia's thinly veiled threats to use nuclear weapons remind the world that escalation of the conflict—by accident, intention, or miscalculation—is a terrible risk," the scientists warned.

At the same time, climate scientists were warning that the Thwaites Glacier in Antarctica, which had the charming nickname the "doomsday glacier," was ticking towards collapse. Researchers with the British Antarctic Survey reported in the journal *Nature* that warm water was tunnelling into the glacier's cracks and crevices a half mile below its surface. The scientists, who'd deployed an underwater robot called Icefin and drilled boreholes 2,000 feet into the glacier, detected evidence that while the pace of melting underneath the ice shelf might be somewhat slower than expected, cracks inside the glacier were melting much faster than previously thought.

The Florida-sized glacier was critical because it acted something like a dam of solid ice holding back the much larger glacier on land in Western Antarctica. Shatter the dam, and all that other ice could begin to slip-slide into the sea, causing catastrophic sea-level rise across the world.

When could that happen? The scientists had no idea.

ACKNOWLEDGMENTS

First and foremost, thanks to my wife, Eleanor, who came up with an idea to write a book about doom forecasters more than a decade ago and who discovered that obscure French Dragon Hunter, Didier Sornette. Thanks to Rick Horgan, of course, patient and endlessly demanding editor now for all three of my books. Lisa DiMona, my agent at Writers House, who suffered through endless waves of shaky book ideas before finally, in the dark days of early 2020, we landed on the idea that would become *Chaos Kings*. This book would not have been possible without the cooperation of Mark Spitznagel, Nassim Taleb, and Brandon Yarckin. Thanks to Rupert Read, always encouraging and responsive, and Yaneer Bar-Yam, who patiently fielded my questions about complexity theory with insightful advice and guidance. Robert Litterman, an extremely busy man, never found himself too busy to respond to calls or emails. Also thanks to Didier Sornette, another endlessly busy person, who kindly dedicated precious hours to phone calls about his fascinating journey hunting Dragon Kings. Thanks to Bill Ackman. Aaron Brown was extremely helpful on several fronts, providing deft insights into many of the book's themes as well as the complex personality of his friend, Taleb. Thanks to Ken Brown, my editor at the *Wall Street Journal*, who backed me through the at times thorny process of getting leave from the paper to write a book.

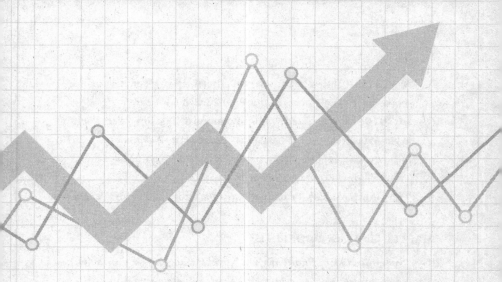

NOTES

PROLOGUE

This account is based on an interview with Bill Ackman as well as several articles published about his trade, including Liz Hoffman, "Bill Ackman Scored on Pandemic Shutdown and Bounceback," *Wall Street Journal*, January 31, 2022, https://www.wsj.com/articles/bill-ackman-scored-on-pandemic-shutdown-and-bounceback-11643634004.

Some details of Ackman's trade were taken from Emil N. Siriwardane, Luis M. Viceira, Dean Xu, and Lucas Baker, "Pershing Square's Pandemic Trade," Harvard Business School, July 2021, https://www.hbs.edu/faculty/Pages/item.aspx?num=60603.

PART I: SWANS AND DRAGONS

Details of Mark Spitznagel's and Nassim Taleb's careers in finance are based on dozens of interviews with both men as well as people who knew and worked with them. Some details were taken from their published books.

CHAPTER 1: BOOM!

15   ***"The 2008 financial crisis was a car crash"*** Justin Baer, "The Day Coronavirus Nearly Broke the Financial Markets," *Wall Street Journal*,

May 20, 2020, https://www.wsj.com/articles/the-day-coronavirus-nearly -broke-the-financial-markets-11589982288?mod=e2tw.

16   *In 2010, he predicted in the* **Economist** "Nassim Taleb Looks at What Will Break and What Won't," *Economist*, November 22, 2010, https://www.economist.com/news/2010/11/22/nassim-taleb-looks-at -what-will-break-and-what-wont.

16   **"The Precautionary Principle"** https://arxiv.org/pdf/1410.5787.pdf.

CHAPTER 2: RUIN PROBLEMS

20   *"Systemic Risk of Pandemic via Novel Pathogens—Coronavirus: A Note"* https://necsi.edu/systemic-risk-of-pandemic-via-novel-pathogens -coronavirus-a-note.

CHAPTER 3: WORSE LIES AHEAD

31   *"There is a specter haunting globalization and modern life"* Miguel Centano, Peter Callahan, Paul Larcey, and Thayer Patterson, "Globaliza-tion as Adaptive Complexity: Learning from Failure," in Adam Izdebski, John Haldon, and Piotr Filipkowski (eds.), *Perspectives on Public Policy in Societal-Environmental Crises,* (Springer, 2022).

34   *Heading into the 2020 election, the* **Atlantic** *described the environment* Larry Diamond and Edward B. Foley, "The Terrifying Inad-equacy of American Election Law," *Atlantic*, September 8, 2020, https:// www.theatlantic.com/ideas/archive/2020/09/terrifying-inadequacy -american-election-law/616072/.

34   *A Washington Post/University of Maryland poll in late 2021* https://www.washingtonpost.com/politics/2022/01/01/post-poll -january-6/.

34   *The study, "The Nonlinear Feedback Dynamics of Asymetric Political Polarization* https://www.pnas.org/doi/10.1073/pnas.2102149118.

34   *In response to a query by* **New York Times** *columnist Thomas Edsall* Thomas B. Edsall, "America Has Split, and It's Now in 'Very Dangerous Territory,'" *New York Times*, January 26, 2022, https://www. nytimes.com/2022/01/26/opinion/covid-biden-trump-polarization.html.

36   ***"Roughly 65 percent of Russia's territory is covered in perma-frost,"*** "How Is Climate Change Impacting Russia?," *Moscow Times*, November 2, 2021, https://www.themoscowtimes.com/2021/11/0 2/how-is-climate-change-impacting-russia-a75469.

36   ***It was just such problems*** The paper included another author, Raphael Douady of Stony Brook University, but his contribution was minimal according to Taleb, so I am not including him here.

CHAPTER 4: THE SIZZLER

45   ***The world's most active futures-trading pit*** Scott McMurray, "Riding High: Tom Baldwin's Trades in Chicago T-Bond Pit Can Move the Market," *Wall Street Journal*, February 4, 1991.

CHAPTER 5: THE WORLD ACCORDING TO NASSIM TALEB

58   ***"Here was a guy living in a mansion with a thousand books"*** Malcolm Gladwell, "Blowing Up," *New Yorker*, April 22, 2022, https://www.newyorker.com/magazine/2002/04/22/blowing-up.

59   ***"The World According to Nassim Taleb"*** https://merage.uci.edu /~jorion/oc/ntaleb.htm.

CHAPTER 6: THE TURKEY PROBLEM

68   ***Luckily for Sussman he'd abandoned the fund*** Ann Davis, Henny Sender, and Gregory Zuckerman, "What Went Wrong at Amaranth: Mistakes at the Hedge Fund," *Wall Street Journal*, September 20, 2006, https://www.wsj.com/articles/SB115871715733268470.

69   ***In 1999, $264 billion was sitting inside hedge funds worldwide*** https://www.statista.com/statistics/271771/assets-of-the-hedge-funds-worldwide/.

73   ***The maverick French mathematician and inventor of fractal geometry*** The Mandelbrot lecture is based on a similar lecture he gave at MIT around the same time. According to Taleb, it is the same lecture he delivered at Courant. https://www.youtube.com/watch?v=ock9Gk_aqw4.

78 ***Then the next speaker took the podium*** "Daniel Kahneman Changed the Way We Think About Thinking. But What Do Other Thinkers Think of Him?," *Guardian*, February 16, 2014, https://www.theguardian.com/science/2014/feb/16/daniel-kahneman-thinking-fast-and-slow-tributes.

79 ***Taleb had gotten a real-world look at a looming Black Swan*** Alex Berenson, "Fannie Mae's Loss Risk Is Larger, Computers Show," *New York Times*, August 7, 2003, https://www.nytimes.com/2003/08/07/business/fannie-mae-s-loss-risk-is-larger-computer-models-show.html.

CHAPTER 7: DRAGON HUNTER

This chapter and other sections focused on Didier Sornette are based largely on multiple interviews I conducted with Sornette as well as his 2003 book, *Why Stock Markets Crash: Critical Events in Complex Financial Systems* (Princeton University Press). A few details, such as the balloon-pin analogy, were taken from a chapter about Sornette in James Owen Weatherall, *The Physics of Wall Street* (Mariner Books, 2013).

85 ***"Stock Market Crashes, Precursors and Replicas"*** https://arxiv.org/abs/cond-mat/9510036.

CHAPTER 8: THAT WAY LIES MADNESS

103 ***Taleb also became a target*** Joseph Nocera, "A Skeptic Who Merits Skepticism," *New York Times*, October 5, 2005, https://www.nytimes.com/2005/10/01/business/a-skeptic-who-merits-skepticism.html.

104 ***"The problem, insists Mr. Taleb, is that most of the time"*** David A. Shaywitz, "Shattering the Bell Curve," *Wall Street Journal*, April 24, 2007, https://www.wsj.com/articles/SB117736979316179649.

105 ***Experts complained Taleb wasn't telling them anything new*** Gregg Easterbrook, "Possibly Maybe," *New York Times*, April 22, 2007, https://www.nytimes.com/2007/04/22/books/review/Easterbrook.t.html.

CHAPTER 9: A VERY DARK TUNNEL

111 *"There is a downward spiral of fear"* Vikas Bajas, "Panicky Sellers Darken Afternoon on Wall Street," *New York Times,* October 9, 2008, https://www.nytimes.com/2008/10/10/business/10markets.html.

111 *"We're in the middle of a very dark tunnel"* Phil Izzo, "Economists Expect Crisis to Deepen," *Wall Street Journal,* October 10, 2008, https://www.wsj.com/articles/SB122349368554816267.

112 *"I am very sad to be vindicated"* Bill Condie, "Secret of the Black Swan— How a Trader Forecast the Crash and Cashed In," *Evening Standard,* April 11, 2012, https://www.standard.co.uk/business/secret-of-the-black-swan-how-a-trader-forecast-the-crash-and-cashed-in-6867331.html.

114 *"The system is very unstable"* I attended this talk.

CHAPTER 10: DREAMS AND NIGHTMARES

120 *"Trading floor on fire about comments"* "Overheard," *Wall Street Journal,* February 14, 2009, https://www.wsj.com/articles/SB123457658749086809.

120 *"With interest rates at zero"* https://www.wsj.com/articles/SB100014 24052748704471504574443600711779692.

122 *That's why some economists, such as* **New York Times** *opinion writer* Paul Krugman, "The Big Inflation Scare," *New York Times,* May 28, 2009, https://www.nytimes.com/2009/05/29/opinion/29krugman.html.

122 *"Marking a 15-year period of stagnation"* https://www.pewre search.org/social-trends/2020/01/09/trends-in-income-and-wealth -inequality/.

123 *As Nassim Taleb's taxi turned down 1 Rocket Road* The account of Taleb's visit to the Edge Master Class was first told to me by Taleb: Direct quotes are taken from a video of the presentations on the Edge. org website, https://www.edge.org/events/the-edge-master-class-2008-a -short-course-on-synthetic-genomics.

124 *It was a "forum for big, intriguing and/or disturbing ideas* John Naughton, "John Brockman: The Man Who Runs the World's Smartest Website," **Guardian***,* January 7, 2012, https://www.theguardian.com/ technology/2012/jan/08/john-brockman-edge-interview-john-naughton.

CHAPTER 11: FLASH CRASH

129 ***"Healthy investments are those that produce goods"*** https://www.wsj.com/articles/SB10001424052748704340504575447950667158906.

130 ***"A growing number of money managers"*** Jane J. Kim, "Preparing for the Next 'Black Swan,'" *Wall Street Journal,* August 21, 2010, https://www.wsj.com/articles/SB1000142405274870379180457543956236141453200.

131 ***cotton "was and still is in a bubble without showing a clear change of regime."*** https://arxiv.org/ftp/arxiv/papers/0911/0911.0454.pdf.

134 ***In late July, Spitznagel took a Bloomberg reporter*** Seth Lubove and Miles Weiss, "Black Swans Boom as So Much Else Goes Bust," *Financial Review*, October 7, 2011, https://www.afr.com/markets/black-swans-boom-as-so-much-else-goes-bust-20111007-i46pg.

CHAPTER 12: THE DISORDER CLUSTER

140 ***One of the main draws: a debate between Taleb and Larry Summers*** The account of Taleb's debate with Larry Summers was told to me by Taleb and Brandon Yarckin. Quotes from the debate were taken from https://www.yahoo.com/entertainment/news/larry-summers-takes-fight-nassim-172010890.html and https://www.marketwatch.com/story/too-big-to-fail-battle-between-larry-summers-nassim-taleb-1400205931.

149 ***"There's a panic in the West"*** Video, 37:40, https://arxiv.org/ftp/arxiv/papers/0911/0911.0454.pdf.

CHAPTER 13: VOLMAGEDDON

153 ***"You might get lucky"*** Interview with Lagnado.

154 ***"It feels like I've been shelled all week by artillery"*** Corrie Driebusch and Riva Gold, "Wild Week for Stocks Ends in Gain—Final-Hour Bounce Caps Worst Week in Two Years for U.S. Equities, With Volatility Seen Ahead," *Wall Street Journal*, February 10, 2018.

156 ***Investing "does not require great intelligence"*** https://www.berkshire hathaway.com/letters/2017ltr.pdf.

159 ***"There [are] some really weird numbers on this page"*** https://www. calpers.ca.gov/docs/board-agendas/201908/invest/transcript-ic20190819 _a.pdf.

CHAPTER 14: THIS IS THE WORLD WE LIVE IN

162 ***In a March 2020 article about Feigl-Ding's Twitter post*** David Wallace-Wells, "Why Was It So Hard to Raise the Alarm on the Corona-virus?," *New York*, March 26, 2020, https://nymag.com/intelligencer/2020 /03/why-was-it-so-hard-to-raise-the-alarm-on-coronavirus.html.

162 ***"Now if f is nonlinear"*** Author interview with Taleb.

164 ***To find answers, he called Spitznagel*** William D. Cohan, "'No Longer Tethered to the Fundamentals': A Nassim Taleb Protégé on How to Pre-pare for the Coming Market Crash," *Vanity Fair*, February 12, 2020, https:// www.vanityfair.com/news/2020/02/nassim-taleb-protege-on-how -to-prepare-for-coming-market-crash.

165 ***"Your fund offers investors protection"*** https://www.youtube.com /watch?v=xiBjBkXBHLw.

166 ***"Any moment, we should absolutely expect to see a response"*** Author interview with Spitznagel.

167 ***"There is skepticism about whether central bank actions can mitigate"*** https://www.wsj.com/articles/wall-street-and-white-house-diverge-on-coronavirus-11583553510.

CHAPTER 15: LOTTERY TICKETS

171 ***"Ben, can you tell me how our left-tail investments are per-forming?"*** https://www.institutionalinvestor.com/article/b1l6npn5lqyd8g /Board-Member-Says-CalPERS-Kept-Quiet-About-Cutting-Tail-Hedge-Strategy.

175 ***"Universa's 12 years of results"*** https://www.institutionalinvestor .com/article/b1lft49hkwdjpv/CalPERS-CIO-Called-Out-By-Ex-Head-of -Tail-Risk-Program.

175   ***Knowing what we know, we would make the exact same decision***
      Cezary Podkul, "Calpers Unwound Hedges Just Before March's Epic Stock
      Selloff," *Wall Street Journal*, April 18, 2020, https://www.wsj.com/articles/cal
      pers-unwound-hedges-just-before-marchs-epic-stock-selloff-11587211200.

176   ***The*** **Wall Street Journal** ***called him a*** *"**hedge-fund star**"* https://www.wsj.
      com/articles/hedge-fund-star-behind-4-000-coronavirus-return-peers-into
      -crystal-ball-11586343603.

176   ***"Spitznagel's mathematical view of the world"*** https://www.forbes.
      com/sites/antoinegara/2020/04/13/how-a-goat-farmer-built-a-doomsday
      -machine-that-just-booked-a-4144-return/?sh=556697a3b1ba.

176   ***A fund managed by LongTail Alpha*** https://dealbreaker.com
      /2020/04/long-tail-universa-aqr-covid-19.

176   ***CalPERS was reportedly in the process of unwinding its Long-
      Tail position*** Julia Segal, "The Inside Story of CalPERS' Untimely
      Tail-Hedge Unwind," *Institutional Investor*, April 14, 2020, https://www
      .institutionalinvestor.com/article/b1l65mvpw5xpts/The-Inside-Story
      -of-CalPERS-Untimely-Tail-Hedge-Unwind.

176   ***Cliff Asness's AQR, meanwhile, like many hedge funds*** Thorn-
      ton McEnery, "Billionaire Cliff Asness' Hedge Fund AQR Hit with
      $43B COVID-19 Losses," *New York Post*, April 9, 2020, https://nypost.
      com/2020/04/09/billionaire-cliff-asness-hedge-fund-aqr-hit-with-43b
      -covid-19-losses/.

179   ***Bitcoin is*** *"**one of the largest speculative bubbles**"* https://papers
      .ssrn.com/sol3/papers.cfm?abstract_id=3599179.

CHAPTER 16: THIS CIVILIZATION IS FINISHED

This chapter is based largely on multiple interviews with Rupert Read
as well as video recordings of his speeches.

185   ***"Any plan or policy of yours"*** https://www.weforum.org/agenda
      /2020/01/greta-speech-our-house-is-still-on-fire-davos-2020/.

188   ***"Following Sweden's hottest summer ever"*** https://www.theguardian
      .com/science/2018/sep/01/swedish-15-year-old-cutting-class-to-fight-
      the-climate-crisis.

188 ***"There are no gray areas"*** https://www.youtube.com/watch?v=H8 prVarP-rQ.

192 ***"It became one of those little nuggets"*** https://longplayer.org/letter sto-nassim-nicholas-taleb/.

194 ***"I look at environmental issues"*** https://iai.tv/video/in-the-beginning -was-nature.

CHAPTER 17: TRANSITION TO EXTINCTION

This chapter is based largely on multiple interviews with Yaneer Bar-Yam as well as an extensive review of his research.

206 ***Bar-Yam and his colleagues at NECSI began crafting an alternative response*** https://necsi.edu/how-community-response-stopped -ebola.

CHAPTER 18: RUIN IS FOREVER

"The Precautionary Principle" can be found here: https://arxiv.org/ pdf/1410.5787.pdf.

215 ***"Weed resistance to herbicides"*** https://www.nytimes.com/2021 /08/18/magazine/superweeds-monsanto.html.

216 ***"The rise of the chemical burden"*** https://www.theguardian.com/ environment/2022/jan/18/chemical-pollution-has-passed-safe-limit-for -humanity-say-scientists.

217 ***"Nassim Taleb is a vulgar bombastic windbag"*** http://noahpinion blog.blogspot.com/2014/01/of-brains-and-balls-nassim-talebs-macro. html.

217 ***"Without any precise models, we can still reason"*** https://necsi .edu/climate-models-and-precautionary-measures.

CHAPTER 19: IT'S WAY PAST TIME

This chapter is based on multiple interviews with Robert Litterman, as well as an account of his career at the Minneapolis Federal Reserve. https:// www.minneapolisfed.org/article/2019/interview-with-robert-litterman.

224 ***"Today, my testimony will focus on* The Green Swan"** https://www. democrats.senate.gov/climate/hearings/climate-crisis-committee-to -hold-hearing-on-economic-risks-of-climate-change.

232 ***"Bad news is costly," they wrote*** https://www.pnas.org/content /116/42/20886.

CHAPTER 20: THE GAMBLE

236 ***In April 2021, Litterman once again faced ranks of lawmakers*** https://www.budget.senate.gov/imo/media/doc/Robert%20Litter man%20-%20Testimony%20-%20U.S.%20Senate%20Budget%20 Committee%20Hearing.pdf.

CHAPTER 21: THE TIPPING POINT AND BEYOND

244 ***"There are people whose business"*** https://www.theguardian.com /environment/2020/sep/02/ground-zero-of-lies-on-climate-artists-protest -at-london-thinktanks.

244 ***"Our defense of necessity"*** https://writersrebel.com/rupert-reads -court-statement/.

246 ***"It is time we consider the implications"*** https://lifeworth.com/deep adaptation.pdf.

246 ***The paper went viral*** https://www.vice.com/en/article/vbwpdb/the -climate-change-paper-so-depressing-its-sending-people-to-therapy.

246 **Vice *magazine called it*** https://www.bbc.com/news/stories-5185 7722.

249 ***"These are profound economic shifts"*** https://www.wsj.com/articles/ green-finance-goes-mainstream-lining-up-trillions-behind-global-energy -transition-11621656039.

249 ***A 2022 study by a group of Oxford scientists*** https://www.cell.com /joule/fulltext/S2542-4351(22)00410-X.

250 ***A harbinger of the shift*** https://www.blackrock.com/us/individual/larry -fink-ceo-letter.

251 ***"All the cool kids are doing carbon capture"*** Jinjoo Lee, "Exxon's Well-Timed Hop onto Carbon-Capture Bandwagon," *Wall Street Journal,*

February 8, 2021, https://www.wsj.com/articles/exxons-well-timed-hop
-onto-carbon-capture-bandwagon-11612785602.

251 *According to a 2021 report by Princeton researchers* Princeton
Professor Jesse Jenkins in a September 2022 interview on the *Ezra
Klein Show* podcast.

253 *An August 2022 study published in the science journal* **Nature**
Mika Rantanen et al., "The Arctic Has Warmed Nearly Four Times
Faster Than the Globe since 1979," *Nature*, August 11, 2022, https://
www.nature.com/articles/s43247-022-00498-3.

253 *A UCLA study released around the same time* Louis Sahagún, "Risk
of Catastrophic California 'Megaflood' Has Doubled Due to Global
Warming, Researchers Say," *Los Angeles Times*, August 12, 2022, https://
www.latimes.com/environment/story/2022-08-12/risk-of-catastrophic
-megaflood-has-doubled-for-california.

253 *"This entire river system is experiencing something"* Sam Metz and
Kathleen Ronayne, "Crisis Looms Without Big Cuts to Over-Tapped Colorado River," Associated Press, August 19, 2022, https://apnews.com/articl
e/las-vegas-arizona-lakes-colorado-91409f8e5f4e2270899d19b3e0
e41985.

CHAPTER 22: FLYING BLIND

256 *"The democratic emergency is already here"* Barton Gellman,
"Trump's Next Coup Has Already Begun," *Atlantic*, December 6, 2021,
https://www.theatlantic.com/magazine/archive/2022/01/january-6
-insurrection-trump-coup-2024-election/620843/.

256 *The level of democracy in the world had reached the lowest level*
https://v-dem.net/media/publications/dr_2022.pdf.

256 *A January 2022 study by the Brookings Institution* https://www
.brookings.edu/research/is-democracy-failing-and-putting-our-economic
-system-at-risk/.

256 *"As there is no previous occurrence of the event"* https://www.knkx.
org/2021-06-28/the-pacific-northwest-has-limited-a-c-making-the
-heat-wave-more-dangerous.

258   **On the morning of August 27, a U.S. Naval Academy helicopter**
Author interview with Jupiter Intelligence CEO Rich Sorkin.

260   **"I think there's something going on with blockchain"** Author
interview with Schmalbach.

260   **"We are witnessing a fundamental reordering"** https://www.aon
.com/reputation-risk-report-respecting-grey-swan/index.html.

CHAPTER 23: THE GREAT DILEMMA OF RISK

274   **Spitznagel's argument captivated Peter Coy** Peter Coy, "The
Risk-Return Trade-Off Is Phony," *New York Times*, November 15, 2021,
https://www.nytimes.com/2021/11/15/opinion/risk-investing-market
-hedge.html.

CHAPTER 24: DOORSTEP TO DOOM

280   **Bitcoin rallied in 2021, hitting an all-time high** Elaine Yu and
Caitlin Ostroff, "Bitcoin's Price Climbs Above $20,000 After Sharp
Crypto Selloff," *Wall Street Journal*, June 19, 2022, https://www.wsj
.com/articles/bitcoins-price-falls-below-20-000-11655542641.

280   **As bitcoin plunged, one crypto billionaire** Alexander Osipovich,
"The 30-Year-Old Spending $1 Billion to Save Crypto," *Wall Street
Journal*, August 23, 2022, https://www.wsj.com/articles/crypto-bitcoin
-ftx-bankman-fried-11661206532.

282   **Since saving the human race is the one and only priority** Chris-
tine Emba, "Why 'Longtermism' Isn't Ethically Sound," *Washington
Post*, September 5, 2022, https://www.washingtonpost.com/opinions
/2022/09/05/longtermism-philanthropy-altruism-risks/.

283   **Peter Singer, the Princeton philosopher and ethicist** https://www.
project-syndicate.org/commentary/ethical-implications-of-focusing
-on-extinction-risk-by-peter-singer-2021-10.

283   **"The so-called 'agents of doom'"** https://www.abc.net.au/religion
/rupert-read-the-dangers-of-longtermism/13977152.

286   **"The market is in a state of shock"** https://www.morningstar.com.au
/insights/stocks/219544/global-market-report-09-march.

287 **It continued to falter for the rest of the year** Akane Otani and Karen Langley, "The Classic 60-40 Investment Strategy Falls Apart," *Wall Street Journal*, November 13, 2022, https://www.wsj.com/articles /investment-retirement-stocks-bonds-market-11668015638.

287 **He told Bloomberg the global financial system** https://www .bloomberg.com/news/articles/2022-06-03/black-swan-investor-watching -for-greatest-credit-bubble-to-pop.

288 **In April, to commemorate his departure** https://oc-vp-distribution 03.ethz.ch/mh_default_org/oaipmh-mmp/8f881c6a-93c1-48e5-8119-f0d 6ed75ace6/933bfbad-a6c1-43c1-adf8-541139d05d3b/20220412 _HGF30_AV_Sornette.mp4.

290 **"This is insanity"** https://www.un.org/sg/en/content/sg/press-encounter /2022-09-09/secretary-general%E2%80%99s-remarks-press-conference -the-foreign-minister-of-pakistan-bilawal-bhutto-zardari.

290 **"This summer is just a horrorscape"** Editorial Board, "Foreboding New Studies Show the Climate Battle Is Not Over," *Washington Post*, August 14, 2022, https://www.washingtonpost.com/opinions/2022 /08/14/climate-change-studies-warming-antarctica/.

290 **"We're in the destructive phase"** https://twitter.com/msnbc/status /1575139361133404161.

290 **I just can't believe Mother Nature would do** Zachary T. Sampson, "Absolute Devastation: Hurricane Ian Decimates Fort Myers Beach," *Tampa Bay Times*, September 29, 2022, https://www.tampabay.com/ hurricane/2022/09/29/absolute-devastation-hurricane-ian-decimates -fort-myers-beach/.

291 **At 7:14 p.m. Eastern time, September 26, 2022** "NASA's DART Mission Hits Asteroid in First-Ever Planetary Defense Test," September 26, 2022, https://www.nasa.gov/press-release/nasa-s-dart-mission-hits -asteroid-in-first-ever-planetary-defense-test.

INDEX